Mirrors of Our Lives

Mirrors of Our Lives

Reflections of Women in Tanach

Rebbetzin Holly Pavlov

Edited by Sarah Granovetter

TARGUM/FELDHEIM

First published 2000
Copyright © 2000 by Holly Pavlov
ISBN 1-56871-161-1

All rights reserved

No part of this publication may be translated, reproduced, stored in a retrieval system, or transmitted in any form or by any means, electronic, mechanical, photocopying, recording, or otherwise, without prior permission in writing from both the copyright holder and the publisher.

Published by:
Targum Press, Inc.
22700 W. Eleven Mile Rd.
Southfield, MI 48034
E-mail: targum@elronet.co.il
Fax toll-free: 888-298-9992

In conjunction with:
She'arim, College of Jewish Studies for Women in Jerusalem
23 Agassi Street
Jerusalem, Israel 91350
Tel: 9722-651-4240; Fax: 972-2-651-8370
E-mail: shearim@shearim.com
www.shearim.com

Distributed by:
Feldheim Publishers
200 Airport Executive Park
Nanuet, NY 10954
www.feldheim.com

Printed in Israel

Dedication

This book is dedicated to the memory of our beloved mother and grandmother,

Femma Hoed-Delmonte

(Chava *bat* Shlomo veBetsy, *a"h*)

A woman of valor, whose faith and courage sustained her during two-and-a-half years of slave labor in the Bergen-Belsen concentration camp. Widowed and destitute, but reunited with her only child, who survived through the grace of God in the loving care of righteous gentiles, she found the strength to remarry and rebuild her life. She was imbued with a unique capacity to reach out to, appreciate, and accept the individual spirit in others. Those fortunate to know her were forever deeply touched by her kindness, warmth, and compassion. May her memory continue to be a source of joy and inspiration to all those desiring to enrich their lives.

Rabbi CHAIM P. SCHEINBERG
Rosh Hayeshiva "TORAH-ORE"
and Morah Hora'ah of Kiryat Mattersdorf

הרב חיים פינחס שיינברג
ראש ישיבת "תורה-אור"
ומורה הוראה דקרית מטרסדורף

סיון תש"ס
פעיה"ק ירושלים תובב"א

    In every generation, through the study of Torah, Jews have identified with and become connected to the *Avos* and *Imahos*, our great Patriarchs and Matriarchs, who are the very soul of the Jewish people. Mirrors of Our Lives: Reflections of Women in Tanach is a book that will give the English speaking public a deeper understanding of the foundation on which our nation is built.

    Rebbitzin Holly Pavlov has devoted her life to the field of educating women and in *Kiruv Levavos*, bringing Jews closer to Torah and mitzvos. The excellence of her teaching and the success of her *Kiruv* work at She'arim, College of Jewish Studies for Women can now be found in her superb book on the matriarchs. The guidance provided by these Torah ideas will not only elevate and strengthen the reader; they will give practical tools that can be utilized in everyday life.

    May *HaShem* bless her with renewed strength and continued success in teaching *Am Yisroel* and in bringing those who have wandered away closer to Torah.

הכו"ח לכבוד התורה ולומדי'

[signature]

חיים פנחס שיינברג

בס"ד

כ״ה אלול ה' תשנ"ט

Dear Friends, לאי״ט,

Rebbetzin Holly Pavlov, לאי״ט, has shown me the manuscript of her book, *Mirrors of Our Lives*. I was very impressed with the caliber of the Torah ideas it contains. They are deep and intellectually stimulating ideas and concepts that are brought down to the practical level to guide one's day-to-day living.

I highly recommend this book, and am sure that both men and women will find it a source of knowledge of Torah and inspiration.

With Torah blessings,

RABBI ZEV LEFF
Rav of Moshav Matityahu
Rosh Hayeshiva
Yeshiva Gedola Matisyahu
D.N. Modiin 71917 Israel
08-926-1138 Fax 08-926-5328

Table of Contents

Acknowledgments 11
Preface 15

Life Lessons 19
And God Remembered Sarah 21
To See Good Is to Feel Good 41
The Sound of Silence. 62

Creating a Relationship with God. 79
The Destiny of Rachel 81
Voices in Prayer 98
How Did Miriam Know to Bring a Tambourine?. . . . 120
What's in a Name? 140

Men and Women 161
Women: Bridging Heaven and Earth 163
Rivkah: Prophecy and Voice 184
Man of Exile, Woman of Return 204

Building the Future. 227
Leah and Rachel: Inside and Out. 229
In the Merit of the Righteous Women 248

Acknowledgments

Over the years, I have taught thousands of women in Jerusalem and around the world. I say "taught" and not "lectured" because a teacher not only imparts information, but also elicits reactions, listens, and responds to input. She is often forced by her students to defend her arguments. The student serves as the learning partner of the teacher, thus sharpening the minds of both. This book is the reflection of this interactive process of education. My students have asked me life's questions and together we searched the Torah for the answers.

I thank my dear colleagues for their unending support of She'arim. They are unstinting in their time and devotion to the institution and its students and supportive of all its educational endeavors. They have been a sounding board for the ideas in *Mirrors* and have offered their wisdom and knowledge freely. My gratitude goes to Gitty Appel, Rivi Brussel, Rabbi David Derovan, Barbara Friedman, Rachel Hershberg, Marci Jablinowitz, Rabbi Jeremy Kagan, Esti Klebanow, Shoshana Raff, Chaya Tavin, and Rabbi Moshe Weiden.

Technical and moral support by Miriam Shaul, Nina Fixler, Ayala Perecman, and Idy Schneck, the She'arim office staff, is always forthcoming and cheerful, not only with this project but with all of the administrative functioning of She'arim. I thank those students who transcribed the tapes of my lectures: Tamara Shira Jacobs, JoAnne Marron, Michelle Segal, and my dear friend, Jeanne Arenstein.

Gila Green spent hours helping me clarify what I hoped to accomplish in this book. Without her assistance, I would never have been able to begin this project.

Sarah Granovetter transformed the tapes of my classes into articles. It was a labor of love and she offered her friendship and encouragement as part of the deal.

My son Chananya served as my research assistant, checking out sources and adding greatly with his ideas, giving me both help and *nachas* simultaneously.

Leslie Gold, Laura Greene, Lauren Lapinsky, Arleeta Lerner, Janet Kaplan, Rivka Kravitz, Sharon Schuldiner, Esther Sha'anan, and Miriam Trout read the working draft at various stages of its development and offered invaluable insights and advice.

The staff of Targum Press has been wonderful to work with. Since this is my first publication, I have been especially blessed with the gentle and professional hand of my editor, Chaya Baila Kaganoff.

A special thanks to Joanna Wiseman and Yochana Stone who, lovingly and on a weekly basis, prepared Shabbos for my family, allowing me to write and rewrite to my heart's content.

The most deeply felt and therefore hardest to express acknowledgments always come last. My mother, Mrs. Nita Quint, and, *yb"l*, my father, Mr. Maurice Quint (*a"h*), gave me love and taught me discipline, encouraged my passion for learning, and were somehow always there when I needed them. I thank, as well, my father-in-law, Mr. Chananya Pavlov (*a"h*), and my in-laws, Rabbi Chaim Uri and Rebbetzin Faye Lipschitz, who have always been kind to me and supportive of all my endeavors. There is a warm place in my heart for my aunt, Mrs. Esther Babad, who has always been my biggest fan.

The deepest joy of my life comes from my wonderful children, Arona, Elan, Ariela, Chananya, Levi, Eliyahu, and Miriam, and my children-by-marriage, Reuven and Uri. They have provided me with insights into Torah and life, constant support, unending *nachas*, and grandchildren. Thanks do not suffice for the delight they bring me.

My greatest thanks go to my dear husband, Yosef. His wisdom has always guided me, his strength has always supported me, and his belief in me has always moved me. He is the driving force behind She'arim and behind this book.

Ultimately, all thanks go to *HaKodesh Baruch Hu*. Even if my mouth were as full of song as the waters in the sea, it would be impossible to thank Him enough for His kindness to me and my family.

Preface

When I was a child, I was impatient for the time when my questions about life's mysteries would be answered, and the paradoxes of the world would become clear. As I matured, it became apparent that I would never truly understand God's ways. Nevertheless, I discovered that sometimes the questions mattered more than the answers, because the search for truth reveals that the lessons in life are endless, and a person's potential is unlimited.

I also discovered that although it is not possible to understand everything, much of what we *need* to know can be grasped by looking to our matriarchs, whose experiences, personalities, and struggles reflect our own. Their voices continue to ring out with strength and wisdom, and their examples serve as channels through which Divine wisdom is revealed to us. The lives of the matriarchs, prophetesses, and righteous women thereby function as a mirror for our own. It is through this mirror that we can see reflections of our own hopes and dreams, our fears and frustrations. Through this mirror, we see ourselves as Jews and as women, as individuals and as part of the whole Jewish people. The stories of our ancestors provide a reference point from which we can understand life's tragedies and joys, and they provide guidance as to how we should approach relationships with one another and with our Creator.

But how can we tap into this wisdom? To hear the message of our righteous women most clearly, to absorb it and truly acquire it, we must delve into the intricacies of the Torah. Learning Torah requires us to interact with the text from which we learn. It is an active, vibrant process. We read the text carefully, and ask questions. One question leads to another, and the second to a third, and, soon, what began as a simple passage becomes quite complicated. While engaging in this process, a mass of seemingly unrelated or confusing information confounds us, and it seems that we will never "get it." However, with dedication, and with the help of our commentaries and the Oral Torah, our persistence is rewarded with a deep and clear understanding of the story's Divine message; everything fits together. Such learning is like a tapestry woven of different panels. Each panel has its own beauty and tells its own story, but when the panels are sewn together, one is able to see a truly magnificent work of art.

I have attempted to sew some panels together in this work. My desire is to give the reader a sense of the excitement of learning, and to heighten his or her awareness that the Torah is a living Torah and speaks to all of us today. Each essay combines the methodology of learning with the philosophy of Torah and its practical application to life. In order to involve the reader in the process of exegesis, I wrote each chapter as a lecture, so that the book conveys the voice of a teacher addressing her class.

The Torah cannot be grasped without proper tools. The tool that allows us to penetrate the deeper aspects of the philosophy of Judaism is found in the Midrash (nonlegal Oral Torah). When, due to the impending long exile, the great Sages made a decision to write down the Oral Torah, they required a venue that would preserve the elasticity of the Oral Torah and at the same time protect its integrity. The legal portions of the Oral Torah were recorded in the format known as Mishnah and Gemara, and are explicitly detailed.

The complexity of the philosophy of Oral Torah, however, required a different style. These concepts were intentionally concealed in subtle riddles, parables, and hints, so that their essence would not be accessible to those who would misuse and pervert them. All that could be attained by reading this work without a teacher would be the superficial and literal, and the hidden meanings of the text would be accessible only to the great scholars and their students. In order to accurately interpret the riddles and parables of the Midrash, one must be given the keys, which are available only though the oral learning tradition. It continues to be handed down from generation to generation, thus protecting the glory of God's Torah (see Ramchal, *Maamar al Aggados Chazal*).

I rely heavily on Midrash, then, in order to uncover the eternal philosophical truth hidden within the metaphor. The words of the Sages are "like golden apples in mesh casings of silver" (Mishlei 25:11) — from a distance one sees the valuable silver, but only when one peers through the external casings does one see the true value of the gold. Only in the depths of the Midrash will we discover its essential truth (the Vilna Gaon).

Although I had been teaching Midrash using classic expositors as my guides, my approach was deeply enhanced by learning from the teachings of HaRav Chaim Goldvicht (*zt"l*). A disciple of the Chazon Ish and the Brisker Rav, Rav Goldvicht founded and served as the *rosh yeshivah* of Keren beYavneh for over forty years. Toward the end of his life, he left his position and moved to Jerusalem. Although poor health did not permit him to teach a full schedule, his desire to teach was great, and he began to give weekly lectures in Midrash. By attending these classes I was given an opportunity to learn from a great Torah scholar. I am indebted to Rav Goldvicht, and I have referenced his direct verbal transmission where appropriate.

The wisdom of the Torah is multifaceted. It is possible to interpret a passage in many ways, each of which reflects a different ethical or ideological truth. One interpretation does not preclude another, for the inner truth is unlimited. Therefore, this work includes several chapters that look at the same events in radically different ways, extracting equally important life lessons each time.

The lectures compiled in this book were originally given at She'arim College of Jewish Studies for Women, a seminary for adult women which I founded in 1994. She'arim attracts women who have a hunger to learn, to grow spiritually and intellectually, and to share what they learn with others. They range from beginners searching for a connection to Torah to advanced students of Torah who wish to continue their growth through intense textual learning. The sophistication of these women requires an approach that challenges the adult mind while fostering personal growth and spirituality. Despite the variation of range and experience, all the women at She'arim have eagerly embraced the opportunity to identify with and learn from our mothers, the great women of valor.

As I taught these classes about the women in Tanach to my students, I found that the messages resonate clearly, so much so that, over the years, many women have asked me to put these teachings in writing for the benefit of others. The result is this book, which I hope will enable the modern woman to look closely into the mirrors of the Torah and see — herself.

Life Lessons

And God Remembered Sarah

We live in a world where we think that seeing is believing. In truth, however, human beings see only a partial, external reality, and the depth of our insight is limited. Only God can see the entire and unbiased truth, both externally and internally. In addition, God confines our understanding of reality, allowing us to see only that which He wants us to see. Most of us, however, believe in our judgments, unconscious of the fact that they are based on incomplete vision.

This becomes apparent on Rosh HaShanah, the Day of Remembrance. During the High Holidays, we approach God in humility and repentance, no longer so sure that we have seen everything 100 percent clearly and aware that we have made errors and mistakes over the past year.

On the first day of Rosh HaShanah, we read about the banishment of Yishmael from the home of Avraham and his subsequent *teshuvah* (repentance). On the second day, we read about our Patriarch Yitzchak bound at the altar. The purpose of these readings is to draw us closer to God at this critical time, so it is curious that the first day's reading is about an outcast from the

Jewish people, while we wait until the second day to read about our Patriarch Yitzchak. Why did the Rabbis choose the Yishmael reading for the Day of Remembrance?

What is the connection between a "bad boy" who is told to leave home and the Jewish people?

The Text

Three story lines appear in sequence in this reading: the birth of Yitzchak, the confrontation between Sarah and Avraham concerning sending away Yishmael, and the subsequent suffering of Yishmael in the desert. These stories are linked together in the same chapter, but what is their connection?

I. The Birth of Yitzchak

And God had remembered Sarah as He had said; and God did to her as He had spoken. And Sarah became pregnant and bore to Avraham a son in his old age, at the time that God had said.

Avraham called the name of his son that was born to him, whom Sarah had borne him, Yitzchak. And Avraham circumcised his son, Yitzchak, who was eight days old, as God had commanded him. Avraham was one hundred years old when Yitzchak, his son, was born to him.

Sarah said, "God has made a laughter for me and all who will hear will laugh at me." And she said, "Who would have said to Avraham that Sarah would nurse children, for I bore him a son in his old age?"

The child grew, and was weaned, and Avraham made a large feast on the day that the child Yitzchak was weaned.

(Bereishis 21:1–8)

II. A Marital Dispute

Sarah saw the son of Hagar, the Egyptian woman who had borne a son to Avraham, mocking. She said to Avraham, "Chase away this woman, this maidservant, and her son, because the child of this maidservant will not inherit with my son, with Yitzchak."

This thing was very bad in Avraham's eyes concerning his son. And so God said to Avraham, "It should not be bad in your eyes concerning the boy or concerning this maidservant. Everything that Sarah says, you should listen to her voice, because Yitzchak will be your inheritor. [But] I will also make the son of this handmaiden a nation because he is your seed."

(Ibid., 9–13)

III. Hagar and Yishmael Are Sent Away

Avraham got up early in the morning and he took bread and a flask of water. He gave the flask of water and the bread to Hagar, and he put it on her shoulders and also the child, and he sent her away.

She left and got lost in the desert of Be'er Sheva. When the water was finished from her flask, she threw the boy under one of the bushes in the desert. She went and sat herself down at the distance of a bow-shot away, because she said, "I do not wish to see the death of the child." She lifted up her voice and cried.

God heard the voice of the boy, and an angel of God called out to Hagar from heaven. The angel said to her, "What troubles you, Hagar? Don't be afraid because God has heard the voice of the lad where he is. Get up and lift up the boy and hold him in your hand because I will make him into a great nation."

God opened her eyes, and she saw a well of water. She

went and filled the flask of water, and she gave the lad to drink.

God was with the boy and he grew up. He lived in the desert and became an archer. He lived in the desert of Paran, and his mother found him a wife from Egypt.

(Ibid., 14–21)

The Grammar

And God had remembered Sarah as He had said.

(Ibid., 1)

The grammatical structure of this verse is striking. In Hebrew, the verse would normally read, "*vayifkod Hashem* — God remembered," but here it says, "*veHashem pakad* — and God had remembered." It seems a minute grammatical point, but nothing in the Torah is insignificant, not even grammar. So what is the difference? There is a distinction between simple past tense ("remembered") and past perfect ("had remembered"). "Had remembered" is distant past, something that happened a long time ago, as compared to "remembered" which implies the near past, something that happened recently. God's remembering of Sarah happened some time before we read about it.

If so, why is the remembrance mentioned now, instead of when it occurred? Rashi answers this question with a message about the nature of prayer. At the end of the previous chapter, Avraham prayed for the wellbeing of Avimelech. All the members of Avimelech's household had been struck with a plague, causing their wombs (and every other orifice) to close. Although Avraham himself had no children, the Torah doesn't record Avraham praying for children for himself. However, when the wombs in Avimelech's household were closed, Avraham prayed for that plague to end. And indeed, Avimelech's people were relieved.

Immediately afterwards, we are told that God had remembered Sarah. Rashi explains that when a person asks for mercy for his friend and he requires the same mercy himself, God will answer both the person who prays and that person's friend. We learn this from the connection of these three events: Avraham's prayer, the healing of Avimelech's family, and God's remembrance of Sarah. In Torah exegesis this is called *"semichus parashios,"* the connection of seemingly disparate texts.

In other words, Sarah had already been remembered, after Avraham had prayed but before Avimelech's household was relieved. The remembrance is mentioned here in order to teach us to pray for other people and to care for their pain as we do our own. The message is important enough to rearrange the chronological order of the text.

When, in fact, did Sarah conceive? Previously, God had sent three messengers to inform Avraham and Sarah that they would have a son. These messengers, angels, appeared on Pesach at the door of Avraham's tent:

> [The angel] said, "I will surely return to you [Avraham] at this time next year, and behold Sarah, your wife, will have a son."
> (Bereishis 18:10)

Indeed, one year later, the following Pesach, the child was born. God had sent messengers to Avraham and Sarah when they lived in the plains of Mamrei, some months before they sojourned in Gerar, the kingdom of Avimelech. God remembered Sarah and she conceived on Rosh HaShanah.

A close reading of the text provokes another question. Bereishis 21:1 states that God had remembered Sarah, and He did for her what He had promised to do. However, if the chapter had begun with the second verse, "And Sarah became pregnant and bore to Avraham a son in his old age, at the time that God had said," we would surely know that God had remembered Sarah. Is the first verse necessary?

The Torah is telling us that when God remembered Sarah, it was very personal, very specific. The first verse makes it clear that this pregnancy was a personal remembrance from God. This conception and birth is not recorded as an impersonal historical event; it is a remembrance, a miracle, a personal gift from God.

In addition, "God had [already] remembered" her — previously, a while ago, in the past. This conveys information that is not included in verse two, which tells us that "she conceived and she gave birth" in simple, straightforward language. Perhaps this implies that in between the time "God had remembered" and the time "she conceived," there was a brief period of time when Sarah had been remembered, but she hadn't realized that God had remembered her. The significance of this will become clear as we proceed.

Deposits

Sarah was given a special gift. We might ask, however, is not every pregnancy a special gift, especially one after so many years of infertility? In order to understand why the Torah implies that this particular pregnancy was special, we must interpret the Hebrew word for *remember*. Our text uses the word *pakad* for remember, not the more commonly used *zachar*. Why? The Midrash explains the significance of the usage of *pakad*.

> Hashem said: "I am the keeper of deposits [*pikadon*]. Amalek deposited [*pakad*] bundles of brambles in My care, and [I,] the Holy One, blessed be He, returned to him bundles of brambles, as it says, 'I remember what Amalek did to [the people of] Israel' (Shmuel I 15:2). Sarah deposited [*hifkidah*] mitzvos and good deeds in My care. [I,] the Holy One, blessed be He, returned to her mitzvos and good deeds, as it says, 'God had remembered [*pakad*] Sarah.' "
>
> (*Bereishis Rabbah* 53:18)

And God Remembered Sarah

The *midrash* explains that God is the Master of Deposits, the caretaker of deeds. He collects things and takes care of them. Two examples demonstrate this. The first one involves Amalek and bundles of brambles. What are these "bundles of brambles"?

> Amalek came and battled Israel in Refidim.
>
> (Shemos 17:8)

Amalek attacked *klal Yisrael* in the desert, after the nation left Egypt and after the splitting of the Sea of Reeds. God took this deed and, in a manner of speaking, deposited it. Hundreds of years later, in the time of King Shaul, God said, "I remember what Amalek did. It's in the bank. I'm going to give Amalek what they deserve." Thus, God sent King Shaul to destroy Amalek.

In the second example given by the *midrash*, God had on deposit Sarah's mitzvos and good deeds, an accumulation of the ninety years of her life. When the Torah tells us that "God had remembered Sarah," we can understand that at this point God made the decision to take that deposit "out of the bank" and return it to her. God was keeping those mitzvos and good deeds for Sarah, guarding them for her, and now He desired to return them.

When a person does a mitzvah, such as an act of kindness, this deed "belongs" to him. God is the Bank Manager and He puts the deed in the person's bank account. God guarantees that the act of kindness will be returned, but only when God deems it to be the right time. The difference between God's banking and human banking is that in a financial bank, a person can go and withdraw his holdings when he chooses. In God's bank, the choice of when and how the deposit is returned is up to Him.

This is why the Torah uses the word *pakad*, rather than *zachar*, in the opening verse of our chapter. *Zachar* is the much more commonly used word for remember. *Pakad*, on the other hand, connotes the repayment of deposits, righteous or evil deeds, at a time and in a way that God decides. Nothing slips God's "mind"; it's not as if, until now, He had forgotten about Sarah, and suddenly He remembered. The word *pakad* is used to tell us that God had been accumulating deposits for Sarah, and the time had come to activate the process of withdrawing Sarah's holdings and handing them back to her, in the form of the blessing of a child.

The Day of Judgment

God remembered Sarah on the Day of Remembrance with the conception of Yitzchak. Thus, the returning of her deposit occurred on Rosh HaShanah.

On Rosh HaShanah, God sits in His heavenly court and judges His people. We read this chapter on Rosh HaShanah to remind ourselves that the idea of deposit is connected to judgment. God's judgment is based on "you get what you gave," measure for measure. You deposit mitzvos, you get back mitzvos. You deposit transgressions, you get back transgressions. God the Bank Manager returns to us our deposits. However, despite the fact that we know God judges us on Rosh HaShanah, we aren't always aware of the connection between our deeds and what happens to us. Unlike the earthly bank account, where a person who deposits dollars gets back dollars, in God's bank, we deposit mitzvos and good deeds and get back...perhaps a baby.

Another difference between a financial bank and the Bank of God is timing. We can go to the bank to withdraw our deposit whenever we so desire; the timing is up to us. When God returns our deposit, however, the timing is not in our control; it is up to Him. We may not even be aware that the withdrawal is happening. We might find out retroactively. For example, there is generally a period of time when a woman is pregnant and she doesn't yet know she's pregnant. She will know in a little while, and she can then discover when she became pregnant, but at the time of conception she is unaware of God's plans for her. When deposits are returned to us, we may not know what's happened for a short time, or perhaps a longer time, or perhaps not at all. It's also possible that we will misunderstand what has happened.

Human Perception

Human perception is very limited and, therefore, we frequently make judgments based on false understandings. Another Torah reading demonstrates this point:

> So Sarai, Avram's wife, took Hagar the Egyptian, her maidservant...and gave her to Avram, her husband, as a wife. He came to Hagar and she conceived; and when she saw that she had conceived, her mistress was lowered in her esteem.
>
> (Bereishis 16:3–4)

Before Avraham's covenant with God (Bereishis 17:4–5), his name was Avram and Sarah's name was Sarai. Since they were unable to have a child, Sarai gave her Egyptian maidservant, Hagar, to Avram, hoping he would have a child through Hagar. The Torah informs us of three things: (1) she conceived, and then (2) she "saw that she had conceived," and then (3) she lost respect for Sarah. After the Torah tells us that Hagar had conceived, why does it need to tell us that she *saw that she conceived*? Are we to understand that she looked down at her stomach and thereby "saw" that she had conceived? If so, why is the effect of "seeing" the despising of her mistress?

Rashi explains that Hagar conceived from the first intimacy with Avraham and, as a result, her mistress was despised in her eyes. She thought,

> *This Sarai is not the same on the inside as she is on the outside.*

> She shows herself as if she's a righteous woman, but she's not a righteous woman because she couldn't conceive with Avram for years, and I conceived from the very first union.
>
> (*Rashi*, Bereishis 16:4)

In other words, Hagar concluded that Sarai was not what she seemed to be. She thought, *Sarai is very deceptive. If she were righteous she wouldn't suffer like this; she'd be able to have a baby, too.*

The Torah does not mean that Hagar "saw" in the visual sense. Hagar "saw" and made a judgment. In her perception, she became pregnant because she deserved to be pregnant, and her mistress was not pregnant because she didn't deserve it. Hagar assumed she knew what was going on. She was in error, however, because none of us can know what is going on inside another person. Hagar made her assumption because she believed that God's judgment is totally visible and clear in this world: "I can understand the way God functions in this world. I know that I deserve this or you don't deserve that. I see very clearly. God is just, everything He does is visible, and therefore I can make a judgment about what's going on."

Hagar erred because she believed that a human being is capable of understanding God's judgment. She failed to grasp the fact that human perception is faulty, that we see through a small lens.

The human vision of the world, man's understanding and perception, is not the reality. A human being cannot perceive reality because he can't see the whole picture — people are not given access to God's plans. In addition, although a human being can see certain external aspects of reality, he can't see the internal essence of something. A human being can understand an earthly bank account, but he can't understand God's accounting system.

The first part of the reading, the birth of Yitzchak, teaches us that our deeds are on deposit with God and He will repay us, measure for measure. God waits to redeem the deposit until the appropriate time, and we usually don't see the connection between our deposit and the "withdrawal." We don't see the deposit go in, and we don't see the deposit come out. We are not capable of making judgments about God's system of banking — Justice.

Sarah's Judgment

The second section of our reading concerns another judgment. This time, Sarah judges Yishmael.

> Sarah saw the son of Hagar, the Egyptian woman who had borne a son to Avraham, mocking. She said to Avraham, "Chase away this woman, this maidservant, and her son."
> ... This thing was very bad in Avraham's eyes concerning his son. And so God said to Avraham, "It should not be bad in your eyes.... Everything that Sarah says, you should listen to her voice, because Yitzchak will be your inheritor. [But] I will also make the son of this handmaiden a nation because he is your seed."
> (Bereishis 21:9–13)

Once again, the Torah uses "seeing" to mean perception. Sarah perceived, she saw, that this boy was making a jest of the holy principles of her family. She saw Yishmael doing something wrong. Based on this perception, she told Avraham, "Send away the child. I think Yishmael is a bad influence on Yitzchak. Send him away." But Yishmael was Avraham's son and he did not want to send him away. Sarah had called Yishmael "the child of this maidservant," while Avraham was holding onto his perception of Yishmael as his son. God interceded and told Avraham that his perception was wrong. He said, "Listen to the voice of Sarah. She has the right perception. She judges the situation correctly and you must listen to her."

God validated Sarah's decision on two points: (1) Yishmael was a negative influence on Yitzchak and he had to be sent away; and (2) Yishmael was not going to be Avraham's spiritual heir. In other words, God confirmed Sarah's words that Yishmael was "the son of this handmaiden"; He did not refer to him as Avraham's son. Only Yitzchak was to inherit the mantle of leadership of the Jewish people — Yishmael was Avraham's biological seed but not his spiritual son. God comforted Avraham, however, and told him not to feel bad because He would make Yishmael into a great nation.

At this point, an incongruity may occur to us. When Hagar "saw" and made a conclusion, her conclusion was wrong. When Sarah, on the other hand, "saw" and made a conclusion, her decision was so correct that God Himself validated her judgment. Why should this be so?

The difference is that when Hagar became pregnant, there was no decision to make. There was nothing to do. She became pregnant, period. There was no reason for her to draw any conclusions about Sarah's character or to believe that she now understood how God's "mind" works. She was not called upon to act and it was not necessary for her to gratuitously "see" anything.

Sarah, on the other hand, was raising a child, and she was raising this child in a very particular, special way. She was raising her son to be the spiritual heir of Judaism. Yitzchak was to have a crucial role in the formation of the Jewish people, and it was Sarah's obligation as a mother and as a matriarch to see that he was protected from negative influences. Unlike Hagar, Sarah did not make any judgments about anyone's internal character or motivation. She saw that Yishmael mocked. This was clearly a negative influence and it was her job to rectify the situation. Her decision was to separate her son from Yishmael in order to protect him. Sarah reached her decision after an examination of the information that she had, and God validated her decision.

No individual has enough information to make judgments about why God blesses or does not bless other people, and it's an error to attempt to assess a person's character from blessings like children, wealth, or health. On the other hand, we are not to become emotionally and mentally paralyzed, believing that since we don't know what God's plans are, we shouldn't interfere, make decisions, or act. We must be aware of what's going on in our lives, and we must take steps, when necessary and if possible, to correct anything that is wrong.

Would Sarah's decision have been different had she known that God would make Yishmael into a great nation in the future? No, because, again, we cannot base our judgments on the blessings or misfortunes God bestows on other people. We must process the information we have at hand, and make the wisest decisions possible.

Yishmael and Hagar in the Desert

In the third section of the reading, Yishmael and Hagar were sent away and journeyed into the desert. They lost their way and ran out of water under the hot desert sun. Hagar saw that her son was dying of thirst. She couldn't bear the pain of watching him suffer, so she threw him under a bush and distanced herself from him. Then she lifted up her voice and cried bitterly. The obvious question is, why did Hagar move away from her dying child? She obviously loved him, so how could she abandon him?

Hagar repeated the error she had made earlier. She thought she understood reality. According to her human reasoning, her child was going to die and there was nothing she could do about it. There was no way out, and she couldn't bear to watch it. Can we not feel ourselves in Hagar's place? She was like a mother sitting in her child's hospital room who is told the child will die. She can't bear to watch, so she leaves to grieve, saying, "Tell me when it's over." True, the Torah says we must be with a dying person until the end comes, but can we not empathize with Hagar's desire to walk away, to avoid watching the death of her child?

Meanwhile, what about Yishmael? Rejected by his father, he would have no share in the destiny of the house of Avraham. And now, when he was dying, he was abandoned by his mother. Feeling utterly rejected, utterly alone in the world, what did he do? The Torah tells us, "And God heard the voice of the boy." From this we understand that Yishmael was crying out to God. Yishmael prayed. Unlike Hagar, he did not give up on himself. Unlike Hagar, he did not give up on God. While her tears were the tears of hopelessness, his were the tears of prayer.

A Heavenly Dispute

While Yishmael and Hagar were suffering on earth, a debate was going on in Heaven. The angels were arguing with God. The Midrash tells us that they did not want God to save Yishmael:

> They looked into the future and denounced Yishmael, saying, "Master of the Universe! The nation that is going to come from Yishmael is destined to harm Your children through thirst."
> (*Rashi*, Bereishis 21:17, from *Bereishis Rabbah* 53:19)

After the first Temple was destroyed, the Jews were exiled to Babylonia, in chains, in tears. On the road, when they were anguished by thirst, they encountered the children of Yishmael and begged to buy water from them. The children of Yishmael refused to sell water.

On this basis, the angels demanded that God withhold water from Yishmael. "Let him die here and now and save Your children from grief from his seed," they said. "What kind of justice is this? Should God give water to a nation that will deny water to His children?"

Why didn't the angels add, "And, anyway, this Yishmael is a troublemaker! You saw what he did back in Avraham's house. He's a mocker, a scoffer. He doesn't deserve to be saved"? The angels didn't try this argument because they understood *teshuvah* (repentance). Although Yishmael had behaved badly in Avraham's home, at this moment, he was crying to God in pain and repentance, and *teshuvah* supersedes justice.

But what about the future? Yishmael was going to father descendants who lacked even basic human decency — why should God allow him to survive? Yishmael's descendants, knowing that their very existence was based on God saving their ancestor from thirst, nevertheless would withhold water from God's children. If a person is going to end up terrible, why should God let him live? "Let him die!" begged the angels.

God's Response

> An angel of God called out to Hagar from heaven. And the angel said to her, "What troubles you, Hagar? Don't be afraid because God has heard the voice of the lad where he is. Get up and lift up the boy and hold him in your hand because I will make him into a great nation."
>
> (Bereishis 21:17–18)

Rashi asks, why does the Torah emphasize that "God has heard the voice of the lad where he is"? Why not simply say, "God has heard the voice of the lad"? What do the words "where he is" add to our understanding?

"Where he is," explains Rashi, is not referring to a geographic location. Rather, it is referring to Yishmael's spiritual situation. God's answer to the angels was, "Where is he now? What is he doing now? Is he good or bad?" The angels were forced to answer that now Yishmael was praying and repenting, so he was righteous. God told them, "I am going to judge him according to his present actions" (*Rashi*, Bereishis 21:17, from *Bereishis Rabbah* 53:19). Yishmael's father had sent him away and his mother had distanced herself from him. He was alone in the world, abandoned by those closest to him, but he knew that he wasn't actually all alone. He knew that God could hear him, so he called out to God and begged God to save his life. At this point, "where he is now," God judged him.

We might wonder why God chose to judge Yishmael mercifully. Hadn't God agreed with Sarah that Yishmael was a bad influence on Yitzchak and that he should be sent away? It was true that at this moment, the lad was in pain; but what about the past and the future? God wasn't merciful regarding Yishmael when he was at Avraham's house; why was He merciful in the desert? And what about the *pikadon*, the bad deeds that Yishmael had on deposit?

We cannot say that God's merciful judgment of Yishmael makes sense according to human logic. But God makes His judgments based not on human logic but on Divine judgment, which includes Yishmael's situation at that moment, his depth of prayer, and his sincere repentance. God's judgment is based on the internal, invisible, intimate knowledge of a person to which we humans have no access. God knew that Yishmael's repentance was sincere at that moment, and this repentance cut across the frame of reference of *pikadon* (deposit). God's system of banking is to return goodness to a person who has a deposit of good deeds, but to suspend a person's deposit of bad deeds if he repents.

Human Judgment and Divine Judgment

At this point, we comprehend the underlying theme of the three sections of our reading: Sarah's conception of Yitzchak, Yishmael's banishment, and the wandering of Hagar and Yishmael in the desert. While we humans make decisions and judgments based on our perception, that vision is limited by our humanity. What we can see are merely the externalities. We see what appears to be happening, what seems to be truth and reality. What we fail to see is the internal — the deposits, the repentance, the struggles, the fulfilled or unfulfilled potential, and, most of all, God's plan. Our vision of reality is, in fact, only partial vision and is, at best, limited.

God, on the other hand, has unlimited vision of the intimate inner workings of our hearts and souls. He knows our deposits, our repentance, our resolve. He is aware of our fears, our hopes, and our struggles. And, of course, He knows His plans for us.

As human beings, we make judgments using the only tools we have, intellect and intuition. We have no choice but to decide and act, even though we are operating with limited information. When Sarah decided to banish Yishmael and when Avraham opposed Sarah's advice to send Yishmael away, they both based their decisions on a limited vision. Despite the fact that it is impossible for any of us to be aware of the results of our judgments, we must move ahead with our plans. At the same time, we must be aware of the limitations of our perceptions.

When we look at the externals of a situation or a person, we become judgmental of other people, thinking we know who they are, what they think, and how they feel. When Hagar judged Sarah to be unworthy, she was unaware of the deposits, and when she abandoned Yishmael, she assumed that God's plan was indeed what it appeared to be; she assumed Yishmael would die. Based on her vision of the external reality of Yishmael's weakened state, she judged that life was over for him.

All too often, we make another type of prohibited judgment: We judge God's actions, as if we can understand His thinking and His interaction with this world. If His actions fail to live up to our human vision of fairness, we judge God as unmerciful, unkind, unfair.

Yishmael refused to judge his life-and-death situation with

the finality that seemed obvious. He prayed in the hope that God would see that which was impossible for a human to see — his internal repentance and resolve to change. Yishmael hoped there could be another kind of judgment, a judgment made by He who sees everything and knows everything; He who sees our hearts and reads our minds; He whose judgments are based on our deeds and deposits, but also on our repentance.

The Power of Repentance

We learn about the power of repentance from Yishmael. Yishmael, abandoned by his father and mother, did not give up on God. He did not make the mistake of giving up because of the past or the future. He held on to the hope that, based on the present, there could be a future. He didn't condemn himself to certain death, but prayed for his life. Yishmael lived in the "now." He prayed to God and cried "now." And the angel of God answered him.

The angel represents to us total, radical mercy. We learn that there is no such thing as a rejection that includes God's rejection. No matter how bad it seems in this world, how alone we might feel, the final arbiter of our fate is God. "Yishmael" means "God will hear," showing that Yishmael's strength came from the power of his prayer.

God accepted Yishmael's prayer and then revealed His mercy to Hagar. The Torah tells us:

> God opened [Hagar's] eyes, and she saw a well of water. She went and filled the flask of water, and she gave the lad to drink.
>
> (Bereishis 21:19)

The Torah doesn't say, "God made a miracle and there was a well." It says, "God opened [Hagar's] eyes, and she saw a well of water." The well was there all the time, but she didn't see it until

God opened her eyes and showed her a world filled with Divine kindness. Although until this point she functioned with limited perception, God now allowed her to see Yishmael's salvation.

The Midrash explains that Hagar hadn't seen the well because "we are considered blind until God opens our eyes" (*Bereishis Rabbah* 53:19). This applies to all of us — how often do we think we "get it," only to find that we misunderstood all along? We are not able to recognize the obvious unless God opens our eyes.

And sometimes we think we have all the facts, that we see all we need to see, but actually we lack clear vision, limited by a blindness imposed on us by God. At times, God imposes blindness as a challenge. A well — or any kindness from God — may be in front of our eyes, but we don't see it. Many of us have the same type of vision as Hagar: we can see God's strict justice, that is, we can see when things are difficult, but we aren't able to see God's kindness and mercy. The blindness is a challenge which can be overcome if we, like Yishmael, understand that God never abandons us, there is always hope. Perhaps we don't, after all, know everything.

Rosh HaShanah

When we read this section on the first day of Rosh HaShanah, we cry because of Yishmael and not because of Yitzchak. We identify with his tremendous sense of abandonment — no mother to protect him, no father to guide him, alone were it not for the presence of God. It is as if Psalm 27 was written as Yishmael's prayer:

> Your Presence, God, do I seek.... You have been my Helper. Abandon me not, forsake me not, O God of my salvation. Though my father and mother have forsaken me, God will gather me in.
>
> (Tehillim 27:8–10)

On Rosh HaShanah, most of us do not come to stand before God like Sarah, who had a deposit in the bank. We don't feel confident enough to say, "I did so many good things, God, pay me back." Most of us come to stand before God feeling like Yishmael. We come feeling that our good deeds are few in number. And yet, we hope anyway. When we come to shul on Rosh HaShanah, we come with prayer. We come in repentance. Even though we have come with few good deeds, there is still hope for us.

We are who we are at any given moment. Yesterday, perhaps, we were undeserving, but today we pray to God for help, for life, for forgiveness. We are who we are, where we are, right now. We live neither in the past nor in the future, but in the present, in this moment of judgment. Rosh HaShanah is the day that our limited vision of reality and God's unlimited vision meet, and the connecting point is our prayer.

To See Good Is to Feel Good

Each of the patriarchs — Avraham, Yitzchak, and Yaakov — had a quality that he developed to such a great extent that the quality became rooted permanently in the soul of Israel, becoming part of our spiritual DNA, so to speak. Avraham developed the quality of *chesed* (lovingkindness). Not only was Avraham a person who gave, who was caring and loving — but he became a *baal chesed* (a master of kindness). In other words, this quality was internalized to such an extent that it became part of his essence and was transmitted to every one of his descendants. All Jews, to this day, have this same ability to be kind. Similarly, Yitzchak developed the quality of *gevurah* (self-control and discipline), and Yaakov embodied the quality of *emes* (truth). These are the three pillars on which we, the Jewish people, stand.

Just as the patriarchs established vital character traits for their descendants, so too, did the matriarchs implant spiritual genes into our souls. The pillar that Leah built — that is, the quality that she developed in herself to such a great magnitude that she rooted it into the genetic makeup of the Jewish people, is *hodayah* — the ability to thank. Leah mastered this quality to such a great extent that all of her descendants have been born with the capacity to feel gratitude.

> Leah conceived and bore a son, and she called his name Reuven.... She conceived again and bore a son and...she called his name Shimon. Again she conceived and bore a son and...called his name Levi. She conceived again and bore a son and declared, "This time let me gratefully praise God." Therefore she called his name Yehudah....
>
> (Bereishis 29:32–35)
>
> Leah seized the quality of thanks and acknowledgment. Thus, her descendants were masters of thanks and acknowledgment. [For example,] "Yehudah recognized it, and he said, '[Tamar] is more righteous than I' " (Bereishis 38:26). David said, "Give thanks to God for He is good" (Tehillim 18:1). Daniel said, "To You, the God of my fathers, I give thanks and praise" (Daniel 2:23).
>
> (*Bereishis Rabbah* 71:8)

The *midrash* tells us that Leah "seized" the quality of thanks and acknowledgment, and thus she had descendants who were masters of thanks and acknowledgment. Leah said, "I will praise the Lord"; her descendant David wrote a whole book, the book of Tehillim, which gives thanks to God; and her descendant Daniel gave thanks and praise to God in the darkness of the first Jewish exile. However, it is difficult to understand where Yehudah fits in. There is no indication that Yehudah gave thanks; he merely stated that Tamar was more righteous than he. Why was this statement an outgrowth of Leah's ability to thank? Furthermore, how did Yehudah's ability to make such a statement relate to his descendants David and Daniel? The *midrash* implies a chain of development, from Leah to Yehudah to David to Daniel — what is the connecting link between them?

In addition, why does the Torah tell us that Leah gave thanks when she bore her fourth son? Surely she thanked God after the births of each of her first three sons as well. Finally, what exactly is this "quality" of thanks and acknowledgment, and how does it affect Leah's descendants today?

HaKaras HaTov

In Hebrew, the expression for gratitude is *hakaras hatov*, which literally means "seeing good." Before a person can experience gratitude, he must learn to recognize good. Obviously, if a person can't see that something is good, he won't know to be grateful and he won't be grateful. However, once a person defines and recognizes good, his life becomes filled with gratitude. Rabbi Shlomo Wolbe, in his book *Alei Shor*, teaches three reasons why it is imperative to recognize good.

First, *hakaras hatov* enables a person to live a positive life. *Hakaras hatov* is defined by an appreciation of small things as well as large things, and, through this prism of recognizing good, ordinary favors and ordinary goodnesses don't seem so ordinary. Recognition of and appreciation for these small and sometimes large things leads to a feeling of happiness and contentment.

In order to learn to see good, a fundamental concept must be grasped: It doesn't matter who does the good (the favor or kindness) for a person, and it doesn't matter how the good comes about. The one and only thing that matters is did something good come to him. In other words, it is not the external (or the giver) that defines *hakaras hatov*; "seeing good" is a perception of the recipient of the good.

The Rabbis teach the mitzvah of seeing good through a simple example: "Do not throw a stone into a well of water from which you drank water" (*Bemidbar Rabbah* 22:4). Why? Because we must feel grateful to the well, and throwing a stone into it would be an expression of ingratitude. What a strange example — the well didn't intend to do anything good; it is an inanimate object! Furthermore, the well doesn't care whether the person who drank its water feels gratitude or not. Nevertheless, one is not to throw a stone into that well. Seeing good does not relate to the well, but rather to the person who benefits from it. Regardless of whether the well "intended" to do good, a person who drank from it received good. What is relevant, then, is this person's awareness that goodness came to him through the well.

In short, the mitzvah of seeing good, or gratitude, depends on an individual's perception of what happens to him. If a person wants to live a positive life, he has to make a conscious decision to look for and recognize good. When he goes to the store and buys bread in the morning, he needs to recognize that the grocer who sold him the bread did him a favor. The grocer may not have intended it to be a favor; he intended to make money. Nevertheless, the one who bought the bread received good, and he has to recognize good.

If this same person goes home with his bread, eats breakfast, and then gets on a bus and travels safely to the other end of town, he must recognize that another favor was done to him. The bus driver didn't intend good for him — he was just doing his job. Nevertheless, when the passenger arrives at his destination he must see that a good thing happened; he must acknowledge that something good occurred in his life. If he doesn't see good, he can't acknowledge it, but once he opens his eyes, he begins to recognize that the majority of his life, despite all the troubles, is actually good. People are helpful, services are rendered, stores supply the items he needs, and he must be grateful.

This is more difficult than it should be because we live in a world where people are very cynical. We often hear, "He's only doing his job" or "She didn't mean to do me a favor — she meant to do herself a favor." True, but was good received? Was a favor done or not? If good was received or if a favor was done, then we have an obligation to recognize it. Our recognition of good enables us to lead a positive life.

The second reason why *hakaras hatov* is important is that it creates love between fellow Jews. When a person gives his friend a gift, there are actually two gifts received. The first gift is the given item, whether it is a physical item or someone's time or effort; and the second gift is the thoughtfulness and love that comes along with it. There's a big difference between receiving flowers from a friend or buying flowers for oneself. When another person sends the flowers, he or she sends a little bit of love along, too. The flowers a person buys for herself may be more to her taste, but she won't enjoy them as much because they do not bring with them friendship and love. More important, when we receive a gift of love and recognize it, we experience a feeling of love in return.

We learn this lesson from God, who made a point of informing the Jewish people of the gift He was about to give them:

> The Holy One, blessed be He, said to Moshe, "I have a good gift in My treasure house, and Shabbos is its name, and I would like to give it to Israel. Go and notify them." From here Rabban Shimon ben Gamliel says, "Someone who gives bread to a child must notify his mother."
>
> (*Beitzah* 16a)

It is not enough to give something; a person should also inform his friend that the gift is from him. Why?

> Make the child a sign, so that if he eats [the bread] before he comes to his mother, she will see the sign and ask, "Who did this to you?" He will say, "So-and-so [did this] and he also gave me bread." From this, [the child's] father and mother will know that [the giver] loves them and it will increase love and friendship in Israel.
>
> (*Rashi, Beitzah* 16a)

In other words, when the mother sees the sign, she will understand that someone loves her child and she'll feel very good.

This will increase love and friendship in Israel. We don't believe in anonymous gifts (except in one instance, the gift of *tzedakah*; *tzedakah* is better if given anonymously so that the recipient won't be embarrassed). Anonymous gifts may be romantic or exciting, but they don't increase love. If a Jew gives a gift, he signs his name because that will bring gratitude, and gratitude will bring more love into the world.

The third reason given by Rabbi Wolbe for *hakaras hatov* is that it is the basis for all good relationships. If a person wants to maintain friendship or love with another person, he must be grateful for every good that person gives him.

> As face answers to face in water, so the heart of man [answers] to man.
>
> (Mishlei 27:19)

In other words, people are reflections of each other. If one person smiles at another, the second person usually smiles back. If one person frowns at another, the second person usually frowns back. When a person expresses gratitude to another, love is awakened in response. The opposite is also true; if someone is not grateful for the good that another person gave him, the friendship and love between them won't last.

A classic example of this occurs in marriage (although it's not only true of marriage). People get married. They're in love, it's so nice, he's the best guy, she's the best girl, isn't it wonderful. About a year later, annoying habits begin to grate. He's always late, she's not so orderly. Every person has bad qualities, just as every person has good qualities. Noticing the annoying things is easy, but this should not be one's focus.

The basis of a good relationship between a husband and a wife is no longer the romance and the love of the engagement period. The basis is a recognition that the husband and wife help each other and appreciate each other. If she puts dinner on the table, or if he does, the effort should be appreciated. If the husband goes to work every day and comes home with money to pay the rent, the wife should appreciate it; if the wife earns a living, the husband should appreciate it. Who does which job is not important, but the appreciation is extremely important. The basis of a relationship continuing in a positive way is *hakaras hatov*; it's recognizing every good thing and not taking anything for granted.

The following story from the Gemara shows that *hakaras hatov* applies even in difficult circumstances:

> Rav Chiya was constantly tormented by his wife. Nevertheless, whenever he obtained anything suitable, he wrapped it up in his scarf and brought it to her. Rav said to him, "But surely [you are not obligated to do this, for] she is tormenting the master!" He replied, "It is sufficient for us that they [our wives] raise our children and deliver us from sin."
>
> (*Yevamos* 63a)

Rav Chiya's wife was evidently a difficult person to live with, yet he would still buy gifts for her. His students couldn't understand why he would express his love and his gratitude to a woman who tormented him. Rav Chiya, however, chose to focus on the positive and not on the negative. When he focused on the good he received, he generated love and gratitude within himself. Rav Chiya thus demonstrated that the good a person does for us stands alone and must be recognized, whether or not unpleasant things are also part of the package.

The basis of every good relationship must be a recognition of and appreciation for the good that the other person does. "You took out the garbage? Thank you so very much." "It's very kind of you to do the mending." "Oh, dinner's on the table? Thank you!"

Seeing good and feeling gratitude enable us to lead a more positive life, increases love and friendship in Israel, and it is the basis for all good and lasting relationships.

The Wide Scope of HaKaras HaTov

When he lived in Egypt, Moshe Rabbeinu killed an Egyptian who was beating a Jew (Shemos 2:12). Pharaoh found out about it and wanted to kill him, so Moshe was forced to flee. He settled in the land of Midian, where he met the daughters of Yisro (who was also known as Re'uel) by a well and helped them.

> The minister of Midian had seven daughters. They came and drew water and filled the troughs to water their father's sheep. The shepherds came and drove them away. Moshe got up and saved them and watered their sheep.
>
> They returned to Re'uel, their father. He said, "How could you come so quickly today?"
>
> They replied, "An Egyptian man saved us from the shepherds...."
>
> (Shemos 2:16–19)

Why was Moshe referred to as the "Egyptian man"? The simple explanation is that Moshe was dressed like an Egyptian man, but the Midrash teaches us something more:

> This can be compared to a person who was stung by a scorpion. He ran to put his foot in the water, and as he did, he saw a child drowning in the water. He stretched out his hand and saved him.
>
> The child told him, "If it were not for you, I would be dead."
>
> He answered, "I did not save you — the scorpion that stung me saved you."
>
> Similarly, the daughters of Yisro said to Moshe, "May you be given strength because you saved us from the hands of the shepherds."
>
> Moshe answered them, "The Egyptian I killed is the one who saved you."

This is what the daughters told their father: "The Egyptian man, that is to say the one that Moshe killed, is the one who caused this to happen."

(*Shemos Rabbah* 1:39)

Obviously, the Egyptian man didn't literally save them, but the Torah is teaching that *hakaras hatov* includes recognizing even good that comes in an indirect manner. Regardless of the source, something good occurred and that good exists.

This concept can be applied to all of us. If our grandparents or our great-grandparents came to the United States, we have to be grateful to them and to the United States. The fact that we derive good from this country at this point in time is because it provided refuge for our grandparents. Although the good coming to us is indirect, we still have to be grateful. If we go further back in our history, we become aware that we must be grateful to God, because God took us out of Egypt. If God hadn't taken our ancestors out of Egypt, we wouldn't have been born in the United States — we would have been born in Egypt. Every year the Jewish people observe Pesach to celebrate our gratitude for something that happened thousands of years ago, because we continue to derive good from it. Ultimately, all good comes from God, and the failure to recognize it is, in effect, a denial of God's *chesed*.

Hakaras hatov extends even to mishaps or accidents. If somebody tries to do a favor for his friend and it doesn't work out too well, the person's effort nevertheless must be appreciated, and *hakaras hatov* must be expressed. When God gave Adam HaRishon a wife and she gave him fruit they were forbidden to eat, God's gift didn't seem to be such a big favor. Yet Rashi says that Adam was ungrateful when he said to God, "The woman whom You gave to be with me — she gave me of the tree" (Bereishis 3:12). Adam's words implied: *The good You gave me didn't turn out to be good*. However, if somebody intends good for a person, the recipient must be grateful for the intention, even if the outcome is not as he would have hoped.

Hakaras hatov is required every time we receive good, or when someone merely intends for us to receive good. The good might come to us indirectly (even very indirectly); it might come because of something that happened generations ago (or even a millennium ago); and it may be that the giver did not even intend good, but the recipient nevertheless benefited. Gratitude is required for all of these situations, because the quality of gratitude, seeing good, should permeate one's entire personality and character.

Why HaKaras HaTov Is Difficult

Hakaras hatov is a difficult mitzvah; people don't want to feel grateful. Often, a person will respond to a favor or a kindness by thinking, *That favor wasn't so much; after all, my friend didn't actually go out of his way and it didn't cost him anything.* Sometimes a person will go so far as to (subconsciously) deny that he received good rather than allow himself to feel grateful. For this reason, most people would rather pay for a service and not feel grateful; then they can feel quite comfortable thinking, *There is no reason to be grateful because I've paid for the services rendered.* The question is: Why do human beings feel such a strong resistance to gratitude?

Rabbi Wolbe gives this practical explanation: Everyone is born helpless, and our first perception in this world as infants is "Everything is coming to me. My mommy will take care of it. My daddy will take care of it. What do I do when I want something? I cry." Babies cry instinctively when they are wet or dirty or hungry or uncomfortable. A baby thinks the whole world revolves around him, and he's right! In order for that child to grow up healthy and whole, he has to know that when he cries, his mother responds. A child needs this envelopment, this total caring, in order to grow up emotionally healthy. As the child grows, he learns intellectually, no longer instinctually, and he understands that if he has a need, his parents will take care of it. He learns intellectually that whatever he wants, he gets, because he is the center of the world. Everything is created to serve him, and he knows it.

As the child gets older, it takes a lot of effort for him to be weaned from this early perception. For the first few years of his life he perceives that everything is coming to him, but after a while he learns that this is not always the case. He learns that some things he has to earn, and that some things he's not going to get, and that when he receives something, he's supposed to say thank you. And he has to learn that everything he has is really a gift. As he gets even older and becomes an adult, he has to realize that whether the things come from other people or directly from God, not everybody gets them; so whatever he gets is truly a gift. He learns that even life itself is a gift, that when he wakes up in the morning, that's a gift. If he has clothes to wear and food to eat, that's a gift. But it takes a long time for a person to learn this.

When a person says something like, "I didn't ask to be born," he is being ungrateful for the gift of life. Immature adults say, "Well, after all, they are my parents, don't you think they should at least pay for my higher education?" If someone pays for an education, that's a gift and the child should be thankful for it. It's difficult to get away from the infantile perception that if you cry, your mommy will feed you. Although it's difficult for a person to make the switch from infantile understanding to adult awareness, that switch must be made. The bottom line is that nothing is coming to us. When a person can finally understand his life this way, he will live a positive life because he will be grateful for the education and the clothes and the care given to him by his parents. He will be grateful for the small kindnesses of strangers, for health, for financial stability, for friendship.

Another reason that the mitzvah of *hakaras hatov* is very difficult is because when someone receives good from another person, on some level, he is aware that he now owes that person. He feels beholden, and he feels the need to pay back. Human beings are born with an instinct for independence. We all want to feel that we are in charge of our lives, that we don't owe anybody anything, and that we don't need any favors.

Our egos demand a certain amount of self-sufficiency, and an acknowledgment that a favor was done is an acknowledgment of neediness. Nobody wants to feel that he needs another person. When a person acknowledges that his friend gave him something, he acknowledges that possibly he couldn't have acquired it on his own. This creates a feeling of vulnerability. The verbal expression of thanks is not the obstacle; once a person acknowledges in his heart that he received a favor, he has succeeded with the difficult part. The problem is in acknowledging the needing. If a child receives candy from an adult, he'll snatch the candy and hide behind his mother. His mother tells him, "Say thank you." The child will often shrug his shoulders, refusing to thank and be grateful. Why is it so hard for him to say thank you? Because he feels vulnerable, and he doesn't want to acknowledge that he wanted that candy and some stranger came along and gave it to him.

One assumes that the greater the gift, the greater the *hakaras hatov* felt. In other words, a gift of a hundred dollars is not the same as a gift of five thousand dollars. Why did Leah, for instance, have more *hakaras hatov* after the birth of her fourth child than she had after her first three births? Leah knew through *ruach hakodesh* (prophetic inspiration) that there were going to be twelve tribes in Israel. She also knew Yaakov would have four wives, so she assumed her share of the children would be three. When her fourth child was born, she said, "This time I'll thank God. This is bigger. I got more than I expected." The greater the gift, the more we should acknowledge it.

However, usually the opposite occurs — the greater the gift is, the less we want to acknowledge it, because it means a greater admission of our neediness and vulnerability and a greater obligation. Sometimes a person does something very big for another person, and afterwards the recipient no longer speaks to him! It's very painful to be the giver in this situation. The reason this happens is because nobody wants to remember a time when he was so vulnerable that someone else had to step in and save him. If a doctor saves a person's life, he pays the doctor and feels that the obligation is finished. Nothing further needs to be acknowledged. But if a person's friend pulls him out of a very bad domestic or financial situation, he often doesn't want to remember or acknowledge it. It's more comfortable to deny, to forget. Why? Because he doesn't want to remember the time in his life when he was very vulnerable and needy.

The closer the relationship between giver and receiver, the more difficult it is to admit dependence or to acknowledge good. People in a close relationship become used to the good that the other person does, to the extent that they don't really notice it. We begin to think that the other person owes us good and it's part of our contractual arrangement. "You have to make dinner because I worked all day. I should be grateful you provided me with a hot meal? I did my share!" If the other person is merely doing what he owes us, why should we be grateful? Not only that, if the person doesn't do his usual kindness, we become angry. This attitude sours relationships; it causes the deterioration of *shalom bayis* (peace in the household) and creates resentments. To maintain good relationships, gratitude for the small things is crucial. "As face answers to face in water, so the heart of man [answers] to man."

Gratitude Toward God

Ultimately, all *hakaras hatov* boils down to being grateful to God. We learned that *hakaras hatov* involves tracing goodness to the source and being grateful all the way back to the beginning.

Ultimately, all the good that we get in this world comes from God. If we have bread to eat, it's because a farmer grew the wheat, but that wheat was created by God and grown in God's earth and nurtured by God's rain.

In order to be people of ethics and morals, we must be grateful to the Creator for everything we have. Everything that we have said so far about interpersonal relationships applies equally, if not more so, to our relationship with God.

> [If] one rejects kindness [done to him], it is as if he has rejected God.
>
> *(Koheles Rabbah 7:4)*

Anyone who denies the good given to him by his friend will deny the good given to him by God. In essence, people behave the same way to God as they do to other people. If a person is aware of other people, he'll be aware of God. If he can acknowledge other people, he'll acknowledge God. If a person trains himself to see good in people, which is sometimes very difficult, he will see good in God, even when he is confronted with trouble or difficulties. Ultimately he will see that everything in his life — direct or indirect, intentional or not — comes from God.

God continues to give us good, but we no longer have Moshe Rabbeinu to remind us of His many gifts. God has given us the ability to understand that everything comes from Him, and our job is to train ourselves to look, to see, to admit that God is the source of good. However, it is impossible to be grateful to God without being grateful to other people, because the other people are the messengers of His beneficence. If a person's parents pay for his higher education, they are acting as agents of God. If someone doesn't recognize the kindness provided by his parents, he won't have the ability to recognize God. When a man's wife makes dinner, he has to recognize that God sent him his wife to begin with. He is not alone in the world because God sent him a spouse. But if he doesn't recognize that his wife is kind to him, why should he be grateful to God? He'll repeat the behavior of Adam, saying, "What good did You do for me?" Or he'll say, "Perhaps You intended good, but she can't even cook a decent dinner!"

Even after we grow up, we think things are coming to us. People often say things like, "I deserve a raise. I deserve health. I deserve success." And when they don't get what they want, they say, "It's not fair." A family friend passed away recently after suffering from cancer, and his daughter said to me, "My father deserved more than this." Who said this is true? Nobody asks for suffering, but the father never said, "I don't deserve this." Instead, he said, "I had a very good life and I'm grateful for it. How should I prepare myself for death?"

What, in fact, do we "deserve"? Anything that God gives us is a gift. Every extra day that we have is a gift, and my dying friend understood that. We must not think, like the little baby in his mother's arms, that everything is coming to us.

We also like to think of ourselves as independent, capable of achieving without God's help. The Torah warns us,

> And you will say in your heart, "My power and the might of my hand have gotten me this wealth."
>
> (Devarim 8:17)

We must look at our lives truthfully and train ourselves to see that, ultimately, everything we own and everything we accomplish is due to God's blessing. God provides the intelligence, talent, health, and energy we need to succeed. Acknowledging God means admitting to ourselves that we can't accomplish anything without God's help.

This brings up another difficulty, and it's a big one: If we acknowledge that God helps us, then — we owe Him. And if we owe Him, we have to pay Him back. How can we pay God back? We will have to do mitzvos. It's easier to say, "What God? I did it all myself!" because if we acknowledge that God is constantly giving to us and helping us, we are obligated to do mitzvos.

We will do just about anything to avoid owing a human being — when we can't reciprocate, we deny that anything was done for us, we forget about it, or we find reasons why we shouldn't be grateful. We do the same thing in connection to God. Since it is difficult for us to accept our dependence on God, we convince ourselves that we can manage on our own. Only in a crisis do we face the fact that we need God's help.

Deep down, though, we know that our entire existence as individuals and as a nation depends on God. Our business in this world is to thank Him. When we wake up in the morning, the first word out of our mouth is acknowledgment and thanks: We say "*modeh* — thank You, God!"

> I gratefully thank You, O living and eternal King, for You have returned my soul within me with compassion — abundant is Your faithfulness.
>
> (*Modeh Ani*)

We get up, wash, get dressed, and daven:

> As long as the soul is within me, I gratefully thank You, Hashem my God and the God of my forefathers, Master of all works, Lord of all souls. Blessed are You, Hashem, who restores souls to dead bodies.
>
> (*Shacharis* Prayer)

As long as our souls are within us, we have to thank God. The number-one business of our lives is thanking God and always being aware that we can never thank Him enough.

> Were our mouth as full of song as the sea, and our tongue as full of joyous song as its multitude of waves, and our lips as full of praise as the breadth of the heavens, and our eyes as brilliant as the sun and the moon, and our hands as outspread as eagles of the sky and our feet as swift as hinds — we still could not thank You sufficiently, Hashem our

God and God of our forefathers, and bless Your Name for even one of the thousand thousand, thousands of thousands and myriad myriads of favors that You performed for our ancestors and for us.

(Nishmas Prayer)

In short, we are incapable of expressing sufficient thanks for our lives. The best we can do is be aware that this is so and tell God that we are aware.

Yehudah

Let us return to our original question about Yehudah. Yehudah didn't thank God; he acknowledged that he made a mistake. The Torah (Bereishis, ch. 38) relates that Yehudah had three sons. His firstborn married Tamar, but he died without issue. Yehudah instructed his second son to marry Tamar and fulfill the mitzvah of *yibum* (levirate marriage), having a child in memory of the brother who had died. But the second son also died leaving no issue.

According to the halachah of levirate marriage, Yehudah should have given his third son in marriage to Tamar — but he didn't out of concern that his third son would die like the others. Tamar knew through prophecy that she was meant to give birth to a son from the family of Yehudah. She took matters into her own hands, disguised herself as a prostitute, and waited on the road where Yehudah would be passing. God caused Yehudah to have an irresistible impulse to consort with her, although he did not know her identity.

Yehudah and Tamar agreed on a price, and he left her a pledge of his signet ring, cloak, and staff. However, when he later tried to pay her and redeem his pledge, Tamar had disappeared.

Soon Yehudah found out that his daughter-in-law, Tamar, was pregnant. Because she was betrothed to his third son, this was tantamount to adultery, and Yehudah therefore convened a panel of judges who sentenced her to death. Then Tamar decided to reveal to Yehudah (privately) what happened. She sent him the pledge, and "Yehudah recognized it. He said, '[Tamar] is more righteous than I' " (Bereishis 38:26).

What did Yehudah recognize? He recognized the pledge, but he also recognized Tamar's righteousness and his guilt. He recognized the unpleasant fact that he had been wrong in denying Tamar his third son.

How is this related to *hakaras hatov*? *Vayaker*, he recognized, has the same root as *hakaras*, recognizing. *Hakaras hatov* means "seeing good," recognizing the good as such. Both *hakaras hatov* and Yehudah's recognition are acknowledgments of reality. Yehudah recognized his belongings as well as his failings; in both cases he manifested the ability to see truth, even unpleasant truth.

Yehudah confessed, saying, "[Tamar] is more righteous than I." The Hebrew word for confession is *vidui*, and it comes from the same root as *hodayah* (thanks). Yehudah's confession of his guilt and his admission of an unpleasant reality was an extension of his mother's ability to thank (Rav Chaim Goldvicht).

What is the common factor between thanksgiving and confession? When we thank God, we are acknowledging the facts, including the "unpleasant" fact that we are dependent on God, that our very existence is from Him. We are admitting that we need help, that we are vulnerable. As we discussed earlier, it is incredibly difficult to acknowledge that in every aspect of our lives we are dependent on God to nourish us and to provide for us. It is incredibly difficult to give the credit for our accomplishments and success to God instead of to ourselves. It was our mother Leah who taught us and gave us our ability to thank.

> From the day that the Holy One, blessed be He, created His world, there was no man that praised Him until Leah came

and praised Him, as it says, "This time let me gratefully praise God" (Bereishis 29:35).

(Berachos 7b)

This *midrash*, however, provokes another question. Surely sacrifices and prayers had been offered to God before Leah's time. Why is Leah proclaimed the matriarch who seized the quality of thanksgiving?

Although many others sacrificed to God as an expression of gratitude, Leah took this quality to new heights. She was originally destined to marry Eisav, not Yaakov. In addition, she was born barren. But Leah prayed to be spared her destiny and to have a different life. God answered her, and Leah married Yaakov and gave birth to many sons.

Leah, more than any who preceded her, recognized and acknowledged her vulnerability, her dependence on God. She understood how significantly her life and her role within the Jewish people had been changed due to the kindness of God. She confessed that she was beholden to God, and she declared herself grateful for His kindness. Although human beings are born with a resistance to feeling gratitude, especially for a great favor, Leah broke through that barrier when she thanked God for her fourth son. This is why she is the matriarch who seized the quality of thanksgiving and implanted it in her children.

Yehudah took this ability to acknowledge and admit vulnerability and developed it further when he used it to face his daughter-in-law honestly. Since Tamar revealed the truth to him privately, Yehudah could have gone into denial and accused Tamar of obtaining the pledge by some other means. Or he could have allowed her to go to her death by convincing himself that his judgment was right and she was just a harlot. But he didn't do that. Instead, he saw the truth and confessed the truth. Where did he get the strength to do this? From his mother, Leah.

Tamar gave birth to twins, Peretz and Zerach. In Megillas

Rus (Rus 4:18–22), we learn that Peretz was the ancestor of King David, the next one mentioned in our original *midrash*.

David and Daniel

King David wrote the book of Tehillim, in which he poured out his heart to God. He constantly expressed his gratitude to God, in difficult times and in calmer moments, for both good and bad emanate from God. Both are a means to bring us to good. David recognized that were it not for God, he would have no salvation, no rescue. And David never hesitated to recognize and acknowledge his own faults, his sins, knowing that his obligation was to serve God.

When David was in trouble, he admitted that he was vulnerable and that there was no one in the world who could save him but God. He turned to God, asked for help, and offered thanks.

King David received the quality of thanksgiving from Leah and the ability to recognize, admit, and confess from Yehudah; and he expressed these eloquently in the book of Tehillim. King David was able to synthesize the components of *hakaras hatov* that he had inherited from Leah and Yehudah.

The last of Leah's descendants mentioned in our opening *midrash* is Daniel. Daniel was captured by the Babylonians during their conquest of Israel, and he was brought to the king's court. There he was raised to a position of honor, elevated to the status of advisor to the king. When King Nevuchadnetzar had a dream that none of his advisors could interpret, he threatened to kill all of them. Daniel was given the key to the dream in a night vision, and he thanked God for the wisdom granted him. "I thank You, God of my fathers, who has given me wisdom and might and has made known to me now what we desired" (Daniel 2:23). Recognizing that his status and his wisdom were a gift from God, Daniel expressed his gratitude even while in dark exile.

Leah

Leah mastered the quality of *hodayah* to the extent that it became a permanent feature of the Jewish people. However, this feature was given to us only in potential. In order to reveal and express this quality, we must learn to see the good in every aspect of our lives and to trace it back to its source, which is God. This requires effort, but the potential is already within us. We need only the desire to make it happen. We must make a decision to be happy, to see good, to be positive. Our lives are filled with manifold kindnesses from other people and from God. Let us work at seeing that God is good and does good.

May it be the will of God that we recognize all of the bounty and all of the good that He has given to us in the past and that He gives us now, at every moment. May we recognize that even those things which seem unpleasant or difficult in our lives are gifts from God. May we be able to admit our vulnerability and our dependence on God, and may we develop the humility to also admit our mistakes and shortcomings. Finally, may we develop this quality to such an extent that we grow as individuals and bring love to Israel.

The Sound of Silence

Everyone enjoys a good conversationalist. Certain people are very witty, or very good at expressing complicated ideas, or just fun to talk to. We can tell a lot about a person by the language he uses, whether it's refined or coarse, whether he uses sophisticated words or too many platitudes and clichés. And we all know, of course, that "it's not just what you say, it's how you say it."

So much for speech on a simple level. But what is speech really about? Why did God restrict the gift of speech to human beings? And what about the times when we don't speak — what are we to make of silence? If a person says very little, does it indicate an emptiness or a lack of wit? Why is silence uncomfortable for us?

God has given us instructions regarding the use of speech and its antithesis, silence. Just as there is a time to rejoice and a time to weep, so, too, there is a time to speak and a time to be silent. We can learn to distinguish the times appropriate for speaking from the times appropriate for silence by studying the story of Queen Esther.

> Esther did not tell her nation and her origin for Mordechai had commanded her not to tell.
>
> (Esther 2:10)

In the days of King Achashveirosh, when the Jewish people were in exile in Persia, a Jewish woman named Esther was forcibly taken into the king's palace. The king was gathering all the attractive women in his domain, planning to choose one of the maidens for his queen. Esther was advised by her uncle Mordechai, a Torah sage and leader of the Jews, not to reveal that she was Jewish. In addition, she told no one that she was of royal lineage, a direct descendant of King Shaul.

From the verse quoted above, it would appear that Esther kept her genealogy hidden because Mordechai had directed her not to tell. According to the Midrash, however, it was Esther herself who chose silence:

> "Esther did not tell her origin." This teaches that she seized silence for herself like Rachel her ancestress, who seized the art of silence, and all her prominent descendants arose with silence. [How do we see that] Rachel seized the art of silence? She saw all her betrothal gifts in the hand of her sister and she was quiet. Binyamin, her son, [also] seized the art of silence: His stone on the breastplate of the high priest was called *"yashfeh,"* [hinting to the fact] that he knew about the sale of Yosef and remained silent. *Yashfeh* [is read] *"yesh peh — he had a mouth"* — *and yet he was silent [and did* not tell his father] about the sale. Shaul, her descendant [seized silence as well, as it says]: "And the matter of the kingship he did not tell" (Shmuel I 10:16). Esther "did not tell her origin."
>
> (*Esther Rabbah* 6:16)

Esther's ancestors understood silence. Rachel was silent when her father, Lavan, gave her sister to Yaakov as a wife on Rachel's intended wedding night. When his brothers sold Yosef, Binyamin was silent and did not reveal to his father, Yaakov, what had happened. Later, Shaul was anointed king of Israel by the Prophet Shmuel, but he did not tell his own family about it until his kingship was made public. Thus, when the *midrash* tells us that Esther seized the quality of silence, it does not mean that she was a quiet person or that she kept quiet in this particular situation. Silence was her defining characteristic, her self-definition. Esther *developed* the quality of silence that she inherited from her ancestor Rachel by building on the pillar of silence that Rachel had erected long before.

What is the quality of silence? How does it manifest itself? How should we use it today?

Speech

> And the Lord God formed the man of dust from the ground, and He blew into his nostrils the breath of life; and man became a living being.
>
> (Bereishis 2:7)

> And Hashem formed the man, dust from the ground, and He blew into his nostrils a breath of life, and the man became a speaking spirit.
>
> (*Targum Onkelos*, Bereishis 2:7)

The human being is made up of two elements: dust of the earth, his physical body; and the breath of God, his spiritual soul. When the body and soul come together he is described as a "living being." Onkelos translates "living being" as "a speaking spirit." Speech defines our humanity. When body and soul come together, when God blows the breath of life, the soul, into the body of the human being, the person becomes a speaker. Speech is the definition of his humanity (*Maharal, Gevuras Hashem*, ch. 28).

Man's roots are in two seemingly contradictory sources. He has a soul that is blown into him by God, a soul with no physical likeness. The soul is a "piece" of God Himself; it contains Divinity. And man also has a body which, on its own, without the soul, would not be human. When the soul enters the body, a human being is created.

Each of the two components, body and soul, has its own method of expression and its own needs. The soul does not need what the body needs and the body does not want what the soul wants. The connecting point between these two components, says Onkelos, is speech. The soul without the body requires no expression. When the soul enters the body, however, the soul and body must interact and speech is the mechanism through which they coalesce. Speech brings ideas, spiritual thoughts, and connection to God into physical reality, using the tongue, teeth, and lips.

The higher the level of speech, the closer we are to our true humanity, which is our "piece" of Divinity; the lower the level of speech, the closer we are to mere physicality. If a person uses speech to express his connection to God, he is using speech on a high level. If, on the other hand, he uses speech in a crude manner, his speech reflects a soul that is stuck in crudeness. For example, if a person speaks *lashon hara* (gossip), he is using speech in a negative way, in effect nullifying his Divinity.

It is possible to reach such a low level of speech that we reflect only the animal part of ourselves, that is, the physical body detached from its Godly component. In fact, this is one way we can understand Bilaam's speaking donkey. *Chamor* in Hebrew means donkey, but it comes from the word *chomer*, meaning material or physical. When Bilaam's donkey opened its mouth, it became the expression of Bilaam's understanding of humanity, which is that we are nothing more than talking donkeys.

On the other hand, the highest expression of speech is Torah and prayer. When we sing at a wedding about "the voice of joy, the voice of happiness, the voice of the groom, the voice of the bride," we are speaking about spirituality. The voice is that of building a home, of building *Yiddishkeit*, of building Torah. When the Torah describes the speech of the matriarchs Sarah and Rivkah, we are told that they had a "voice" (*kol*). That is, they had prophecy; there was something spiritual in their words. When used properly, "voice" is an external expression of an internal spirituality.

When Yaakov disguised himself as Eisav and went to his father for a blessing, Yitzchak commented, "The hands are the hands of Eisav, but the voice is the voice of Yaakov" (Bereishis 27:22). What was the voice of Yaakov? "The voice in the *beis midrash* and the shuls" (*Bereishis Rabbah*). Yaakov's speech was on the highest level, on the Torah level. His voice was the sound of the voices heard in the yeshivos and in the shuls.

Torah

> "Oh, that I were as the months of old, as in the days when God watched over me" (Iyov 20:9). What are the days that make up months and do not make up years? The months of pregnancy. [The fetus] is also taught all the Torah from beginning to end. As soon as it sees the light, an angel approaches, slaps it on its mouth, and causes it to forget all the Torah completely.
>
> (*Niddah* 30b)

When a child is born — when he comes into contact with the air of this world — the angel who taught him Torah comes to him and taps him on his mouth, causing him to forget the entire Torah. The expression "tapped on the mouth" means that he receives speech. In short, he forgets all his Torah learning and in exchange receives the ability to talk. The Maharal explains that the soul and the body of the child are totally separate until the moment of birth. The moment that the child descends into the birth canal and comes out of the mother's womb is the exact moment that his soul enters his body, and at this exact moment he receives speech (*Maharal, Gevuros Hashem*, ch. 28).

I was privileged to be my daughter's labor coach, and I remember vividly the moment when the child was coming out of the birth canal. The head descended looking like that of a clay dummy — it was blue and lifeless. I was afraid because there seemed to be no life in the child. And then there was another push and the rest of the baby's body came out. The baby turned pink and began to cry. I didn't know the above statement of the Maharal at that time, but I said to myself, "I have just seen the soul enter the body."

When the child is in the mother's womb, he is able to learn all the Torah. This ability exists because he is not limited by his body. His soul is separate and, free from the limitations of physicality, it is able to absorb the Torah from beginning to end.

The minute the child comes into a physical reality and is born, he forgets all his Torah. The soul is now trapped by the body, so to speak. The baby can no longer retain all of the Torah that he learned in his mother's womb because he is no longer an infinite being; he is now a limited, physical being. As a physical being, he is no longer capable of absorbing so much "light," and by necessity the Torah is forgotten. In its place, the baby is given the power of speech, the ability to connect the spiritual and physical. Speech becomes the expression of his potential, and also of his limitation.

Silence

Although speech is the highest level of expression of humanity, there is an even greater level of connection: Silence. At first glance, silence is merely the absence of words. But in truth, silence is the foundation on which all speech is built. The Gemara poses a question: "What should a man's pursuits be in this world?" The answer given is: "He should be silent." Then a *Tanna* asks, "In all cases?" The answer is "Except when he speaks words of Torah" (*Chullin* 89b).

Silence is the higher connection to God; it is an internal connection to our source, the breath of God. "Being silent" means that one exists in a place that doesn't have to be spoken out — for instance, during those moments when a person experiences a very deep emotion, so deep that there are no words, so deep that words would limit the emotion. Silence means existing in a place where speaking would limit one's connection with God. Silence doesn't mean that one is nowhere; silence means that one is in the Oneness of God. Wisdom (*chochmah*) is the highest level of silence, because wisdom is Godliness.

When the child is in the womb, accessing all of the Torah from beginning to end, he is in a place of silence. There is no speech there; rather, there is a holistic connection with God. The Torah that the child learns in the womb is not the same Torah that we hear in the yeshivos. The Torah heard in yeshivos involves talking, obviously, whereas the Torah that the child learns in the womb is pure, raw Torah, a Torah that can't be spoken. When the child emerges into this world and the angel taps him on his mouth, thus giving him speech, he loses that holistic connection to Torah.

Speech is the mechanism through which we bring God into a physical reality, yet we do not have to let go of silence:

> Shimon...said, "All my life I was raised among Torah scholars, and I have found nothing better than silence."
> (*Avos* 1:15)

Shimon grew up among Torah scholars, the Sages of the Mishnah — yet he never found anything better than silence. How is silence greater than words when language used to express Torah is the highest expression of a person's humanity? The Maharal explains that a person can't think and talk at the same time. If a Torah Sage is learning, he has to think. Thinking abstract ideas of Torah connects a person back to his source, the breath of God. Speaking words of Torah brings that connection to God into this world — which is what this world is all about. But in bringing Him into this world, and verbalizing the abstract ideas of Torah, one by definition limits those ideas (since God is infinite and the world is finite).

In other words, there is a process which links the spiritual with the physical, the unlimited with the limited. The foundation of Torah is thinking. But once a person brings his thoughts into this world, and he brings God into this world, he limits the thought to a particular idea. A speaker can have ten ideas in his head, but when he comes to a conclusion and states it, he's limited the concept. This happens to me personally when I give a Torah lecture. I might give the same lecture to different audiences at different times and different places, but there is no way the lectures can be identical. Sometimes I mention new ideas that were never before included in the lecture, and sometimes I emphasize different points. Whatever form the lecture takes is a limited version of the entirety of my ideas and thoughts on the subject.

Although a person may desire to bring down Torah thoughts into this physical world, he also wants to retain his connection to the ineffable and unlimited original spark of insight, to the *chochmah*. After his thoughts are expressed verbally, he is not finished with those ideas, and, as he continues to think about the subject, he may be inspired with new insights or more details. So the process begins with thinking and silence, then moves to limitation and speech, and then returns to the realm of silence.

The Sound of Silence

In the modern world, we have become uncomfortable with silence. We mistrust it. We always need to fill an empty void somehow, to speak. We're afraid to be left in a vacuum of silence, because it makes us feel alone. This happens when we are disconnected from our internal selves, disconnected from our source, from the breath of God. If a person defines himself as living outside of his internal self, then he must speak in order to be noticed and in order to exist. Sometimes, desperate to have something to say, a person will talk about other people; he'll gossip or criticize or speak nonsense. This kind of empty speech means that the speaker defines himself by what others are listening to — if he says nothing, perhaps he is nothing, and, fearing this, he resorts to gossip. There is absolutely no connection to God when a person speaks improperly; it is, in fact, spiritual exile, and that, in turn, brings physical exile.

In other words, if a person is connected with his internal self, he doesn't have to talk, because he knows who he is — he's connected to God. He doesn't need to speak so someone will notice him and let him know that he exists, that he's important. He already knows he exists because he feels a connection to God. When he speaks *lashon hara*, however, he detaches himself from God; he brings himself down from the pure plane where the spiritual and physical coalesce to the mundane, material plane where he is completely physical, in the realm of *chomer*, and he becomes a talking donkey.

> It happened...that Moshe grew up and went out to his brethren and observed their burdens. He saw an Egyptian man striking a Hebrew man, of his brethren.... He struck down the Egyptian and hid him in the sand.
>
> He went out the next day and behold two Hebrew men were fighting. He said to the wicked one, "Why would you strike your fellow?"
>
> [The man] replied, "Who appointed you as a dignitary, a ruler, a judge over us? Do you propose to murder me, as you murdered the Egyptian?" Moshe was frightened and thought, *Indeed, the matter is known!*
>
> When Pharaoh heard about this matter he sought to kill Moshe....
>
> (Shemos 2:11–14)

When Moshe Rebbeinu sought to disrupt the fight between the two Israelites, they scorned his words and taunted him. Moshe realized that his life was in danger because "the matter is known." A simple reading of the text implies that it was known that he killed the Egyptian and Pharaoh could find out, which meant that Moshe's life was in danger.

Rashi looks more deeply into these words and explains that what became "known" was the reason for the exile and slavery in Egypt. What frightened Moshe was not that he would be called before Pharaoh; what frightened Moshe was that the exile and the suffering of the Jewish people came as a result of their transgressions.

When Moshe heard the men speaking of his secret, he understood that something that should have remained hidden had been disclosed. When the Jewish people exile themselves from their Godly connection by speaking inappropriately, by breaking silence and choosing improper speech, they create a spiritual exile. Physical exile always results from spiritual exile; hence the reason for the exile and enslavement in Egypt was "known" (*Maharal*).

To Speak or Not to Speak

Some things should be temporarily hidden, and some matters should never be revealed. Keeping silent on things that should be hidden, as Rachel and Esther did, leads to redemption. When we are one with ourselves and with God, when we define ourselves internally as connected to God, then silence is an expression of ourselves, and it is an expression of our connection to God. Therefore, we should speak only when we have something to say, remembering that not everything thought should be spoken.

In interpersonal relationships, sometimes not saying something is more important than saying it. We must learn to measure our words, to ask ourselves if the words are worth saying and if we are speaking to the right person. It is a mistake to share every feeling and thought with every person. In addition, words of revenge or anger must not be uttered. And finally, silence is the foundation of *shalom bayis* (peace in the home). It's not only what is said, it's what is not said that makes a peaceful and happy home.

Just as speech can be used to express a person's connection with God on the highest level, or mere earthiness on the lowest level, so, too, silence can be used to connect with God or to disconnect. Silence is a value when silence is mandated, but improper silence can have a harmful effect. Silence in the face of injustice or *chilul Hashem* (desecration of God's Name) would be a form of agreement with evil. For example, when Pinchas saw evil in the camp of Israel, he refused to remain silent; holding his peace at such a moment would have been improper. The prophets of Israel were never silent when they witnessed the desecration of God's Name. How else would the people come to repent and return to God?

"Do not hate your brother in your heart" is a Torah prohibition. A person who is hurt or wronged should speak up (calmly, gently, and constructively) in order to allow his brother to rectify whatever harm he has done.

Holding back words of love or affection or communication could be harmful in an interpersonal relationship. Of course, as we said, words must be measured and weighed, but what must be said should be said.

What is difficult about silence is that we get no feedback, no praise for it, no positive reinforcement. No one says, "I'm so impressed because you didn't gossip," or "I noticed how you didn't speak inappropriately." No one hears the words we choose not to say. Also, no person can possibly intuit how difficult it was for his friend to remain silent. But God notices. More than that, when a person is appropriately silent, he sits within the Oneness of God; Godliness defines him and he is again a breath of God.

Silence

We have discussed silence as a connection to God, but silence, *shetikah*, means something else as well. *Shetikah* means holding back not only words, but also personal desires. When Rachel was silent on the night of her sister's wedding, this was not merely an absence of words. She put her own needs aside so that God's agenda could be fulfilled. Rachel understood that although she wanted to marry Yaakov, that was not what God wanted; He did not want Leah to be embarrassed. *Shetikah* means allowing God's will to be our will, too; it is an expression of humility, allowing God to determine the agenda. In remaining silent, Rachel laid the foundation for all of *klal Yisrael*, because without her silence and holding back, we would not have six of the tribes of Israel.

We erroneously believe that something is more important than nothing. Nothing, in our modern vocabulary, is empty, nonexistent, zero. Yet when that nothing is *shetikah*, it creates an "empty space" for God to enter, and then "nothing" is very significant — in fact, that "nothing" becomes the ultimate.

> Rabbi Yitzchak said, "What is the meaning of the verse, 'Indeed in silence speak righteousness; judge uprightly the sons of men' (Tehillim 50:8)?" ... Rabbah (others say it was Rabbi Yochanan) said, "That which Moshe and Aharon said is more significant than that which Avraham said. Avraham said, 'I am but dust and ashes' (Bereishis 18:27), whereas Moshe and Aharon said, 'And we are nothing' (Shemos 16:8). Rabbah (others say it was Rabbi Yochanan) also said, "The world exists only on account of [the merit of] Moshe and Aharon, for it is written here, 'And we are

nothing,' and it is written there, '[God] hangs the world upon nothing' (Iyov 20:6)."

(*Chullin* 89a)

What does "in silence speak righteousness" mean? Which is it — silence or speech? It is actually a recognition that silence also "speaks." The silence of righteousness is not empty; it creates a space for God. Our father Avraham created a space for God because he nullified himself to dust and ashes. Moshe and Aharon did even more — they created a completely empty space, and God filled that space. Space created by withholding speech is not empty — it is the foundation of the world.

The perfect example of "nothing" is Shabbos. Rabbi Joseph Polak, the *av beis din* in Boston, points out that the *Shulchan Aruch* is full of halachos for Shabbos. Most of them do not concern what we do on Shabbos, but what we don't do. A person who never kept Shabbos might ask, "What do you *do* on Shabbos?" And we answer, "Nothing!" He says, "Well, what do you want to do on Shabbos?" And we reply, "Nothing, we want to do nothing. It's the best!" The "nothing" of Shabbos — refraining from action — is not empty, it is full. The break from activity on Shabbos is what defines the entire week. All week long, we wait for Shabbos, we count the days until Shabbos will come. Shabbos defines us as Jews, reminds us that God is the Creator and reminds us that it is He who sets the agenda for the rest of the week. The one day we *stop* is the day we get back in touch with the purpose of the rest of our lives, which is to serve God.

The Jewish people have been in many exiles, all over the world. The host countries that have taken us in (in accordance with their various national agendas) always ask us, "What do you want?" And we always answer: "Nothing. What we want is 'nothing' — we want only Shabbos!"

"Something" and "nothing" — speech and silence. Just as the "something" of the weekdays is defined by the "nothing" of Shabbos, so all of speech should be defined by silence. All of the speech that is important in this world should be defined by the silent thought process that goes into the speech. Speech should be defined by thinking first, aligning our speech with God's will, holding back, creating space for God.

Rachel and Yaakov

The secret of the intensity of the relationship between Rachel and Yaakov is that they were two sides of the same coin. Rachel embodied silence and Yaakov embodied speech (as explained by Rav Aaron Kotler). Rachel is defined by holding back her words and her desires, thereby creating a space for God to enter. Yaakov is defined by the words of Torah that enter space, that fill space with God. "The voice is the voice of Yaakov," and the silence is the silence of Rachel.

Our Sages refer to Rachel as the *akeres habayis*, the main force of the home, because silence, *shetikah*, is the foundation upon which speech is built. Yaakov built all of his Torah on Rachel's holding back, on her silence. Sometimes, something that seems to have no continuity or reality, like silence, is really the *ikar*, the foundation on which all else is built. When you look at a building, you see the walls and the windows — everything above ground. You don't see the foundation under the ground. Nevertheless, if the foundation of a building is bad, the building is bad. *Shetikah* is the foundation of speech; without remaining silent, without holding back and letting God define us, everything that we say and do is meaningless. Rachel's silence was the foundation of Yaakov's speech, and that was the secret of their marriage.

Rachel's Descendants

Rachel's descendants also had this quality. Binyamin was silent when his brother Yosef was sold, because he understood that some things should not be said. *Klal Yisrael* needed to go into exile, into Egypt; it was their destiny. God had informed Avraham of this exile, which was a precursor to the giving of the Torah. Binyamin understood that despite his father's pain and tears, Yosef's exile was the key to God's agenda. So he held back his desire to comfort his father, and for twenty-two years witnessed Yaakov's grief, knowing that this, too, was part of God's plan.

King Shaul, the first king of Israel, was crowned in a private coronation ceremony. Then he returned home to his farm and didn't mention it to anyone. Later, when the public coronation ceremony took place and the prophet Shmuel was looking for him, Shaul was hiding among the baggage. Why this humility? Shaul understood that the kingship did not belong to him, but to God. He did not want that which was not truly his (Rav Tzadok, *Likutei Ma'amarim*). God appointed him king because of this great humility. The foundation of kingship in Israel isn't about power; it's about leading the nation in the direction that God wants it to go, being a servant of God, and serving as a role model to the nation. Ultimately, Shaul's kingship, his silence and humility, was the foundation for the kingship of David. Shaul laid the foundation of humility, and David built the grandeur of royalty on that humility.

Why was Queen Esther given her name? Esther is from the Hebrew word *nistar*, which means hidden, silent. Esther hid her words. She was silent before she was selected to be the queen, as per Mordechai's instructions, and she also decided to remain silent in the court of Achashveirosh even after she was made queen.

> Then the king made a great feast. He made a feast for her, and she did not tell him [who she was]. He remitted taxes, and she did not tell him. He sent gifts, and she [still] did not tell him.
>
> (*Megillah* 13a)

For all the years that Esther was queen until the time the lives of the Jewish people were threatened, she was silent. Her silence paved the way for the miraculous salvation of the Jewish people in Shushan; it was the foundation of redemption. Until the moment when she had to reveal herself, Esther remained silent because there was no need to speak. Esther is hidden because the reality in which she lived was her internal closeness to her source, to God. She had no need to speak, no need for external expression; she lived in *shetikah*, in the connection with God.

The Still, Silent Voice

In its highest form, speech is a connection between the physical and spiritual, the translation of one's connection to God into a physical reality. The highest expression of speech is the articulation of words of Torah. There are other expressions of speech that are considered holy, such as words of consolation, words of comfort, words of kindness, and words of friendship. In its lowest form, a person uses speech to draw attention to himself so that he can feel that he exists. Negative speech is an exile from the source, the breath of God, because it is an external self-definition instead of an internal one.

Silence in its highest form is a connection with God and an acquiescence to Him; living within a self-definition that is not our agenda, but His agenda. Silence is the foundation of all speech and all action. It is not the mere absence of words, nor is it a state of passivity, a lack of presence, or a lack of actions. Rather, silence and holding back are the foundation, sometimes undervalued because we don't see or hear them. This is what God taught Eliyahu HaNavi.

Eliyahu was a very zealous prophet; he didn't hesitate to tell the Jewish people what he thought. He warned them, scolded them, and exhorted them to repent. He would demonstrate his prophecies with action in addition to words — for instance, he had a public showdown with the prophets of Baal on Mount Carmel. Eliyahu's zealousness for God brought drought and famine into the land. Yet still, the Jews did not listen to him. When he could no longer tolerate the insolence of the Jewish people toward God, he ran away to Mount Sinai.

> God came to him and said to him, "Why are you here, Eliyahu?"
>
> He said, "I have acted with great zeal for Hashem, God of Legions, for the children of Israel have forsaken Your covenant. They have razed Your altars and have killed Your prophets by the sword, so [that] I alone have remained, and they now seek to take my life."
>
> [God] replied, "Go out and stand on the mountain before Hashem."
>
> And behold, God passed by, and a great, mighty wind rent the mountains and shattered the rocks before God, but God was not in the wind. After the wind [came] the earthquake, but God was not in the earthquake. After the earthquake [came] a fire, but God was not in the fire. After the fire [came] a still, silent voice.
>
> (Melachim I 19:9–12)

Where is God to be found? God lies in a still, silent voice. What is this silent voice? Malbim explains it to be the combination of silence and speech. God is in that still, silent voice of each one of us. When we speak as God wishes and when we are silent as He requires, when we hold back our desires and act according to the desires of God, when we find the perfect voice, then that still, silent voice within us, our soul, expresses its origin in Divinity.

Creating a Relationship with God

The Destiny of Rachel

The wisdom of the Torah is infinite, spanning from esoteric and mystical knowledge about the essence of creation to practical, everyday, "how-to" information. The latter type of wisdom is particularly evident when we read about the problems and struggles of our ancestors, the great matriarchs and patriarchs of Israel. One source of unhappiness experienced by our ancestors was their initial inability to have children. Their words and actions in response to this unhappiness are terse in the Torah, but they have deep ramifications which can be internalized by modern readers and can enable us to handle our personal difficulties.

When bad things happened to good people, our ancestors did not shrug their shoulders and say, "Things happen because they happen." Instead, they probed deeply into their situations, attempting to understand God's message to them, and then sought solutions. This is especially evident in the story of Rachel.

> Yaakov worked seven years for Rachel, but he loved her so much, it seemed like no more than a few days.
>
> Finally Yaakov said to [her father] Lavan, "The time is up. Give me my bride and let me marry her."
>
> [Lavan] invited all the local people and made a wedding feast. In the evening, he took his daughter Leah and

> brought her to [Yaakov], who consummated the marriage with her....
>
> (Bereishis 29:20–23)

Rachel and Yaakov knew that Lavan was a deceiver who wouldn't hesitate to substitute Rachel's sister Leah for Rachel at the wedding. Therefore, Rachel and Yaakov devised a password to exchange with each other under the *chuppah* (wedding canopy). When Rachel saw that her father was indeed going to substitute Leah, she imagined Leah's embarrassment should Yaakov refuse to go through with the ceremony. Leah would be shamed and humiliated before all the townspeople. Out of compassion for her sister, Rachel sacrificed her own happiness and told Leah the secret password (*Bava Basra* 123a).

Rachel did an amazingly kind thing — she allowed her sister to marry her betrothed on her own wedding night. Soon afterwards, Rachel was also married to Yaakov. However, whereas Leah bore child after child, Rachel was barren.

> And Rachel saw that she had not borne children to Yaakov, so Rachel became envious of her sister. She said to Yaakov, "Give me children — otherwise I will die."
>
> Yaakov's anger flared at Rachel, and he said, "Am I instead of God who has withheld from you fruit of the womb?"
>
> She said, "Here is my maid, Bilhah. Consort with her so that she may bear upon my knees and I, too, may be built up through her."
>
> (Bereishis 30:1–3)

The Torah says that Rachel "became envious" of her sister. This is puzzling because had Rachel been the jealous type, she would not have allowed Leah to take her place under the *chuppah*. Furthermore, jealousy is forbidden by Torah law. How could our righteous matriarch have been jealous? This passage presents additional difficulties:

The Destiny of Rachel • 83

1. Why did Rachel ask Yaakov for children, as if this were totally in his control? Surely Rachel knew that having children was up to God, not Yaakov.
2. Why did Rachel say she would die if she didn't have children? Isn't this drastic? Does life have no meaning without children?
3. Why did Yaakov become angry at Rachel? We would expect Yaakov, a righteous man who himself had suffered greatly, to understand and participate in his wife's pain, to feel empathy. Yet instead he became angry at her.
4. Rachel's response to Yaakov's anger was to give him her maidservant, Bilhah, so that Yaakov could consort with her, "that she may bear upon my knees and I too may be built up through her." This is a strange response to Yaakov's anger, especially for someone who was just described as envious.

As so often happens, the Torah's recounting of biblical conversations cannot be understood without a working knowledge of Jewish philosophy and the Oral Torah. What at first glance appears to be puzzling or unkind language turns out to have a deep and eternal message for us all.

Suffering

Rachel stated that if she didn't have children, she would die. When a person prefers death to continuing his life as it is, that person is experiencing something extreme and tragic; he is suffering. What is suffering actually about?

There are two world views about suffering. The first view is that suffering is sent to a person by God as a means of pushing him away, of punishing him. It is a manifestation of God distancing Himself from the sinner. Therefore, the person suffers not only the pain, but the distance from God as well.

This is not the Jewish point of view. The Hebrew word for suffering is *yissurim*, which connotes both chastisement and teaching. It implies that there is a purpose to suffering, a lesson to be learned, an indication that growth must take place. *Yissurim* also includes smaller disappointments, including everyday struggles and obstacles. Our Sages say that suffering can consist of a minor incident, for instance, when you put your hand in your pocket and expect to find a couple of coins, but instead find only one (*Arachin* 16b). Disappointment and unfulfilled expectations are a form of suffering, *yissurim*. These *yissurim*, large and small, come to teach us and to help us become better people.

The Jewish view is that suffering comes to a person because God is expressing His desire to bring him closer. The suffering is a revelation of God's presence and love, and an expression of His desire to forge a deeper connection. The person who is suffering acquires depth from his pain and distress, and if, in his anguish, he turns to God, he builds a stronger spiritual connection. The suffering thereby becomes a ladder to perfection and proximity to God.

A person's reaction to suffering will depend on his world view. If he believes God is pushing him away and punishing him, he will feel lonely and discouraged and will find no answers. The suffering will be intensified by the pain of the perceived rejection by God.

If a person believes that suffering is something sent by God as a means of bringing him closer to Him, that the suffering is for his own good, and that the suffering is a message of love, he will feel encouraged. He will understand that suffering in this world has a purpose and there will be some acquisition for his pain.

We spend much of our lives acquiring possessions. Some possessions come to us as gifts, but in order to obtain certain other possessions we must expend effort and hard work. Our appreciation of the acquisition will depend on whether or not we earned it, and if so, how hard we had to work to get it. Generally speaking, an acquisition that was obtained through our labor will be more valued than one received as a gift (Rav Chaim Goldvicht, *Asufas Ma'arachos, Yissurim B'Maaseh HaKinyan*).

A gift obligates the receiver to the giver. There are always strings attached, even if not verbalized, and, therefore, a gift received doesn't bring with it a true sense of ownership. On the other hand, a possession accrued through hard work is not only valued more, but it also truly "belongs" to us. This applies to nontangible acquisitions as well — to truly "own" spiritual acquisitions, one must work hard for them. Just as physical acquisitions must be paid for, so must spiritual acquisitions. The value of a material possession is stated on the price tag; the more valuable the item, the more money must be paid for it. So, too, the more valuable a spiritual "item" is, the more one must pay for it. The payment for these acquisitions is obviously not money — instead it is suffering, *yissurim*.

Our Sages teach that there are three spiritual acquisitions that are so valuable that they can be acquired only through suffering. "Israel is acquired through suffering, Torah is acquired through suffering, the World to Come is acquired through suffering" (*Berachos* 8b). There is a huge price tag because these three "items" have a value beyond our imagination.

Destiny

There is a difference between the idea of fate and the idea of destiny. Fate means that whatever happens is random: it happens because it happens. You happened to be at the wrong place at the wrong time. Coincidence. Bad luck. The luck of the draw. This is not a Jewish concept. Destiny, a very future-oriented idea, is a Jewish concept. Destiny means that God creates a situation specifically for each person. Therefore, each person receives whatever he needs, including whatever trials he needs, to grow and perfect his character and his service of God. Absolutely nothing is random; there is always a reason behind what happens.

Human beings have a limited vision of the world, and, because of this, there is no way we will ever understand God. We don't and can't always understand why God sends us a specific form of pain, although if we examine ourselves carefully, it is sometimes possible to gain insight into His reasons. What we do know for certain is that our suffering contains within it potential growth, and that we can build something out of our pain and distress, thus using *yissurim* for spiritual growth. We can't understand God's plan, but we can understand that our lives are in the hands of Heaven, and that what happens to us is part of our destiny, a destiny carefully and lovingly mapped out for us by God Himself. So although we may not have control over our destiny, we do have control over our perception of our suffering, and we can make the decision to build from it.

Fate would say to Rachel: "Too bad, you were born barren, no children, luck of the draw. Learn to live with it." Destiny said to her, "God created this problem for you for a reason. God wants you to come closer to Him. What can you do with your suffering? How can you fill the vacuum created by your lack of a child? God wants you to talk to Him — what spiritual ladder will you climb?"

The Jealousy of Rachel

The Torah tells us that "Rachel became envious of her sister." Says Rashi, "She envied her good deeds. She said, 'Were she not more righteous than I, she would not have merited sons.'"

God forbids us to be jealous. The definition of jealousy is wanting something that belongs to someone else. This is forbidden because everything a person has in this world comes from God. God gives each person exactly what he needs to maximize his potential. Every day in *Ashrei* we say, "You open Your hand and satisfy the desire of every living creature" (Tehillim 145:16), confirming that, in fact, God does give each being what he needs. If someone is dissatisfied with his lot and wants that which belongs to his neighbor, he is in effect saying, "God did not distribute things properly. God makes errors. God's benevolence is off-kilter. I know better who should get what."

This is not to say that we can't desire something similar to that which our neighbor has. This type of urge makes society progress, because it causes people to strive to be better and to have better lives. Therefore, if a man lives in a house with a leaky roof and drafty windows, and he sees that his neighbor has a warm, cozy house with a solid roof and secure windows, he might be motivated to repair his house because he desires comfort similar to that which his neighbor enjoys. But it would be forbidden for him to sit in his cold house feeling angry that his neighbor has a better house, thinking, "Why does so-and-so deserve such a great house while I've been given this dump? It's not fair! I should have that nice house, not he."

In short, we are forbidden to be jealous, but we may allow ourselves to be motivated by what others have. However, the Torah does not say that Rachel was motivated by Leah; we read that Rachel was envious of her sister.

There is one exception to the jealousy rule: We are allowed to be jealous of the Torah and mitzvos of others. "The jealousy of those who learn Torah increases wisdom in the world" (*Bava Basra* 21a). Whereas it is forbidden to be jealous of the material possessions of another, we are allowed to be jealous of another person's spiritual acquisitions, his learning and mitzvos. When a person feels jealousy, this emotion causes him to experience a more intense desire for the object of his jealousy. If that object is Torah and mitzvos, the desire has merit because it will ultimately bring more Torah and learning into the world.

Why should one type of desire provoked by jealousy have

merit and the other be forbidden? The difference is that we have no control over what God gives us, but what we give to God is within our control. Material blessings are directed from God above to the world below. Human beings have no control over this type of blessing for it is God's domain. It is His decision to bestow on us or deny us as He so wills. On the other hand, we have total control over spiritual acquisitions; if our desire is to do more mitzvos and acquire more learning, we have the free will to achieve it. Moreover, we have control over our reactions, our beliefs, our speech, and our intention to act. Our Sages express this difference in the saying, "Everything is in the hands of Heaven, except the fear of Heaven" (*Berachos* 33b). What we have in terms of material or physical blessing is dependent upon God; how we react — our emotional response — is within our control. It makes sense that we are allowed to feel jealous of another's Torah, mitzvos, and spirituality. These things are totally within our domain, and if this type of jealousy motivates a person to learn more Torah, to be more spiritual, to strengthen his relationship with God, this is productive jealousy.

Rashi states that Rachel envied her sister's good deeds. This is permissible jealousy. In her pain, Rachel looked to her sister Leah. Pain creates a vacuum, a vacuum that must be filled. Rachel may not have known why God sent her this pain, but she knew it was part of her destiny. She knew it had a purpose and had to be used to attain spiritual growth. So Rachel looked to Leah's spiritual accomplishments, so that she could imitate her to fill the hole in her heart and to strengthen her relationship with God.

The Importance of Prayer

Through the veil of her suffering, Rachel turned to her husband, Yaakov, and said, "Give me children, otherwise I'll die." The gift of children is in the hands of God, not man. Surely Rachel knew this. Rashi explains that Rachel was asking, "Did your father not pray for your mother when she was barren?"

Rachel told Yaakov that if he would not pray for her and she would not have children, she would die. Rashi explains that a person who has no children is as if dead. He feels as though he has no continuity — a light has been extinguished. This feeling is a feeling of darkness, of death. Surely we empathize with the feeling (although, when a person has no children, his mitzvos become his children, his continuity).

Far from the response we expect, Yaakov became angry with Rachel and replied, "Am I instead of God who denied you fruit of the womb?" Rashi explains this verse as follows:

> "You say that I should do like my father. I am not like my father. My father had no children when he prayed, but I do have children. It is from you that [God] has withheld, and not from me."

This sounds cruel. We know that Yaakov suffered greatly in his life, so why did he have no empathy for his beloved wife? A righteous person prays for others — for example, Eliyahu and Elisha prayed for strangers (Melachim I 17:20–21; Melachim II 4:16) — so how are we to understand Yaakov's unwillingness to pray and his seeming lack of compassion?

Sifsci Chachamim, quoting Maharshal, gives a beautiful insight: Yaakov couldn't pray the same way as his father prayed, because when Yitzchak prayed for his barren wife, he had the same pain as she. Just as Rivkah was barren, so was he. Just as she lacked a sense of continuity, so did he. Her pain was his pain. Therefore, when Yitzchak prayed for Rivkah, he prayed for himself as well. Yaakov did pray intensely for Rachel, but he saw that his prayers were not answered. His pain was not exactly the same as Rachel's, so his prayer was not and could not be the same as his father's.

Yaakov was trying to tell Rachel that God sends suffering to each person for a reason, and the suffering isn't random. In this case, the suffering involved a lack of children. Yaakov already had four sons from Leah. He had experienced different forms of suffering in his past, but this pain of Rachel's was not something directed by God to him — "God denied you fruit of the womb, Rachel; you, not me." It was directed specifically to Rachel, it was her custom-made *yissurim*. It was a message from God to Rachel: "Come a little closer, Rachel!"

Regardless of how much empathy and love we have for another person, ultimately each of us stands alone in this world. If not for God, we would be alone in our pain also. When a person suffers, a friend or loved one can hold his hand, but he can't feel the identical pain. The only one who knows exactly what the pain is, what it feels like, where it is hurting, is God. Yaakov was trying to tell Rachel, "God denied you a child. He is calling you. He wants you to pray to Him, He wants you to attain spiritual growth. This, Rachel, is an opportunity for you to draw close to Him, to fill your vacuum with your prayer. I have already prayed for you, Rachel, but the gates to Heaven were closed for me (*Sifsei Chachamim*, quoting *Maharshal*). It is not my prayer that God desires. It is your prayer."

Ramban explains that Yaakov was angry because he felt that Rachel wasn't using prayer properly. Yaakov meant to say, "Rachel, you misunderstand the nature of prayer. Prayer is not a magic potion. You can't manipulate God. Just because you pray for something doesn't mean it will happen. Prayer is a way of drawing closer to God, a way of growing, a way of overcoming your *yissurim*. Through your prayer you have a chance to create a deeper connection with God. And perhaps through that connection, you will merit a new destiny. It's a major opportunity, Rachel, so grab it."

Rachel wasn't the only one to have a problem conceiving. All of our matriarchs were barren: Sarah did not give birth until she was ninety years old, and Rivkah waited for twenty years to have a child. There is no mention of Leah's infertility in the Torah, as she conceived immediately after her marriage to Yaakov. Yet when the Torah says, "And God saw that Leah was hated and He opened her womb" (Bereishis 29:31), we learn from this that she, too, was biologically barren, and required a miracle to conceive (*Seforno*).

Leah

> Leah was destined to marry Eisav and Rachel was destined to marry Yaakov. Leah would sit at the crossroads and ask people about Eisav — what kind of man he was, what were his deeds. She found out that he was an evil man, a murderer, a robber, that he did every abomination to God. When she heard this, she cried and said, "Rachel and I are sisters from the same womb. Rachel will marry Yaakov the Righteous, and I will marry Eisav the Evil?!" She cried and afflicted herself until her eyes became tender. Therefore, it is written, "Leah's eyes were tender" (Bereishis 29:17).
>
> (*Tanchuma Vayeitzei* 4)

Later, when Leah married Yaakov, she is given children immediately. The Torah explains why:

> God saw that Leah [was] hated and He opened her womb, but Rachel remained barren.
>
> (Bereishis 29:31)

What does the Torah mean that Leah was hated? Our Sages say that this verse means that the actions of Eisav were hated by her ("Leah hated"). Leah hated the evil behavior of Eisav, so she wept and prayed that she would be spared from marrying him.

> Rachel, on the other hand, knew she would marry the righteous Yaakov. Her heart was happy and light. When both sisters married Yaakov, God said, "She who cried and afflicted herself and hated the evil deeds of Eisav prayed to

Me, so it is only right that she should not be distanced from the righteous [Yaakov]. I am going to give her children first."

(*Tanchuma Vayeitzei* 4)

The matriarchs were born biologically barren because God desired their prayers. Since they would become deeper, stronger, more spiritual people through suffering, God sent them *yissurim*. It was essential that Sarah, Rivkah, Rachel, and Leah developed to their maximum potential, because the Jewish people were to descend from them. Suffering refines a person and results in a closer connection to God, as well as a deeper understanding of and empathy for others. To be a mother of Israel, to prepare for the birth of the Jewish people, a matriarch had to become totally aware of God's presence in the world. The suffering sent to our matriarchs was specifically designed to strengthen this foundation; through the experience of intense suffering, these righteous women matured into the matriarchs they were destined to become.

Leah's suffering, her entreaties to God, and her intense prayer prepared her for her marriage to Yaakov and for motherhood. She had achieved a close relationship with God because, through her prayer and through her tears, she made herself a deeper person, a person capable of bearing six progenitors of the tribes of Israel, a person worthy of her role as matriarch. By the time she married Yaakov, God had no reason for her to wait to conceive, so despite her biological infertility, He immediately sent her children.

Rachel, too, had known *yissurim*. She too had borne the weight of pain. She had grown up in the home of an evil father, had been forced to wait seven years to marry her soulmate, Yaakov, and then, on her wedding night, she had looked on while Yaakov married her sister. While that was her own decision, her gift of compassion, it was nevertheless great suffering. Rachel's role as matriarch of Israel, however, required even more. If she was to become Rachel Imeinu, the mother of the Jewish people, she needed to be deeper, more spiritual, more intensely connected to God. She needed to fashion herself into a vessel deep enough to hold the tears of Jewish sorrow, the pain and suffering of two thousand years of exile. This type of depth comes only through the pain of *yissurim*.

Woman

There are two names for women in the Torah's creation story. One is *isha*, which means "woman," and the other is Chavah, which means "mother of life." We learn from this that women have two purposes in the world. The first purpose is similar to the purpose of men, since the Hebrew word for "man" is *ish*, similar to the word *isha*. God asks that all human beings know Him and become knowledgeable in matters of wisdom and righteousness. The word *isha* indicates that a woman, like a man, was created for the purpose of becoming pious and wise and serving God (Rav Yitzchak Arama, *Akeidas Yitzchak*).

The second purpose of a woman, indicated by the name *Chavah*, is to give birth. A woman who does not give birth is thus denied one of her two purposes in life, but she remains worthy of doing good and turning away from evil, just like a man who has no children. To a barren woman and a barren man God promises:

> And I will give them in My house and within My walls a memorial better than sons and daughters.
>
> (Yeshayahu 56:5)

Unquestionably, the most important aspect of the lives of the righteous is good deeds (see *Rashi* on Bereishis 6:9). This is why Yaakov became angry at Rachel when she said, "Give me children, or else I will die." It was to rebuke her and teach her this great matter, which is that she was not

dead with respect to the shared purpose [of men and women] when she was prevented from having children.
>
> (*Akeidas Yitzchak* on Bereishis 30:2)

Disappointment, Yaakov told Rachel, should not be equated with worthlessness; a woman has value outside of her motherhood.

Yaakov made a very good case, but, nevertheless, he was later punished for his lack of empathy:

> Because he became angry at Rachel upon her saying to him, "Give me sons," Yaakov Avinu was told by Hashem, "Is this the way to answer those who are oppressed? Upon your life, your sons will stand before her son!"
>
> (*Bereishis Rabbah* 71:10)

In Egypt, the sons of Yaakov bowed down to their brother, Rachel's son, Yosef, submitting themselves to be to him as slaves. Yosef, echoing his father's words to Rachel, told them, "Fear not, for am I instead of God?" (Bereishis 50:19).

This time the words were said with love instead of with anger.

Rachel and Bilhah

Rachel looked to Leah's spiritual accomplishments to find a way to fill the vacuum of her infertility, to use spiritual growth as a way of meriting a new destiny. Hoping to change her destiny through climbing the spiritual ladder, Rachel brought her maidservant, Bilhah, into her home. She said, "If I can't have my own child, let me raise another woman's child as my own." Rachel knew that this had been done by Sarah, who, unable to have a child, had given her maidservant, Hagar, to Avraham in the hope that Hagar would conceive.

Rachel was hoping that by giving Bilhah to Yaakov, she would succeed on two levels. First, if Bilhah was able to have a child, another son of Yaakov would be born. And second, perhaps, as Sarah gave birth to Yitzchak after bringing Hagar into her home, so would Rachel have a child as a result of this act (*Rashi*).

When Bilhah gave birth to a child, "Rachel said, 'God has judged me and He has heard my voice and given me a son.' Therefore she called his name Dan [judgment]" (Bereishis 30:6). This indicates her acceptance of the judgment of God, as Rashi explains, "He has judged me and found me worthy. He has judged me and found me meritorious." With the birth of Dan, Rachel accepted that not everything in this world is as we would choose it to be, but God's judgment is wisest and best, although it sometimes hurts. More than that, she saw both her suffering and Dan's birth as a gift. Although Dan was not her biological son, he would be a tribe of Israel, and she would raise him and love him as her own. "God has given me merit."

Prayer, spiritual growth, action, and acceptance of God's will filled the vacuum of Rachel's pain.

Rachel's Tears

In the end, Rachel did have children of her own:

> God remembered Rachel; God hearkened to her and opened her womb. She conceived and bore a son.
> (Bereishis 30:22-23)

What did God remember? Rashi explains that He remembered the signs that Rachel had given Leah on her wedding night — the compassion Rachel had felt for Leah.

Why did God remember Rachel now? Why didn't God remember the given-over signs years earlier? Rachel had been in pain and suffering all this time and God didn't remember that act of kindness? Clearly Rachel was never denied children as a punishment. She suffered because God was calling to her, and He called to her by sending *yissurim*. When she worked on earn-ing her spiritual acquisitions, when she turned to God and came closer to Him, when she deepened herself to the point where she could become Rachel Imeinu, then God remembered her for something she had done previously. He remembered the signs.

Sounds like a happy ending. Yet let us not forget that although Rachel gave birth to a child, Yosef, and later to another child, she died in that second childbirth. She called her second son "Ben-Oni" (son of my affliction), a remembrance of the suffering she had experienced. Yaakov renamed the child Binyamin (son of my right hand), perhaps indicating that all strength is the result of affliction.

Ironically, just as her sister Leah had wept, Rachel was to weep many tears, and she still weeps until this very day:

> A voice is heard on high — wailing, bitterly weeping. Rachel weeps for her children.
>
> (Yirmiyahu 31:15)

Rachel was a righteous woman. The redemption of the Jewish people is built around her. Even today, now, she waits in Beis Lechem for her children to come back to the Land of Israel, to return from the final exile. Her *yissurim* were a precursor of our own. If she suffered greatly in this world, perhaps it was to prepare her for our suffering, the suffering of her children; to strengthen her and to strengthen us. As we have wept innumerable times in this exile, so, too, does Rachel sit and weep with us.

> Thus said Hashem: "A voice is heard on high — wailing, bitterly weeping. Rachel weeps for her children; she refuses to be consoled for her children, for they are gone." Thus said Hashem: "Restrain your voice from weeping and your eyes from tears; for there is reward for your accomplishment...and they will return from the enemy's land. There is hope for your future...and your children will return to their border."
>
> (Yirmiyahu 31:14–16)

We never completely understand why God sends us pain and suffering. This is true on a personal level as well as on a national level. We have been in exile for about two thousand years, and we have experienced suffering as a people and as individuals. Nevertheless, we are God's beloved people and we must not forget that our pain, our *yissurim*, comes to us from our God for our good. We must learn to see our disappointments as opportunities to grow spiritually, to become deeper people, to draw closer to God. How we fill the vacuum created by our lacks, by our distress, by our pain, is completely in our hands. May we, like Rachel, use our misfortunes wisely, and merit, as she did, to come close to God. And may Rachel's tears cease to flow, when her "children will return to their border."

Voices in Prayer

Prayer is a major aspect of Judaism. The obvious question we might have about prayer is, why must we pray? Are we fulfilling a duty, like showing up for roll-call? Or is prayer a means of making sure God knows what we want, serving as a shopping list? Or should prayer be a means of elevating ourselves spiritually, escaping from the mundane world and connecting to the Holy One so that we can be holy, too? What should we say to God when we pray — does a set of rules and regulations exist?

The great scholar Rabbi Yehudah Leib Chasman would say the following words every Rosh HaShanah: "My dear Jews — today, on the day of judgment, you come to the house of God. This is a phenomenal opportunity to pour out your hearts to Him. What are you going to ask Him? What are you going to say to Him? What will you say to the One who discerns the hearts of man? Will you say, 'Master of the Universe, give me potatoes! Give me barley! Give me wheat!' Or will you aspire to something higher than that?"

When we stand before God in prayer, must it be to ask for something big? Should we, for example, ask for the cessation of hostilities in the Middle East? Should we ask for an end to hunger and sickness, or for Mashiach to come now? What about little things — is it a chutzpah to ask God for a job or a new car?

What about praying that we get to an appointment on time? Or that God helps us find our keys?

When a person talks to God, how honest is he allowed to be? What limitations are there to prayer? If someone asks God to change something for him, does that imply he's not content with his lot, that he doesn't accept that which God has given to him?

The answers to these questions — and much of what we learn about prayer in general — are found in the story of Chanah. Chanah was the Prophet Shmuel's mother, and her prayer is the quintessential prayer for all time.

Chanah

The book of Shmuel I begins with the story of the Prophet Shmuel's mother, Chanah. In those days, before the Temple in Jerusalem was built, the center of the Jewish world was the city of Shilo, where the Tabernacle stood. Three times a year, Jews would travel to the Tabernacle to bring sacrifices and to pray. In the time of Chanah, Eili was the high priest, and every year Chanah and her husband, Elkanah; Elkanah's other wife, Peninah; and Peninah's children would make the trip to Shilo, gathering other Jews along the way.

> It happened on the day that Elkanah brought offerings that he gave portions to Peninah, his wife, and to all her sons and daughters. But to Chanah he gave a double portion, for he loved Chanah and God had closed her womb.... This is what he would do year after year....
> (Shmuel I 1:4–7)

Peninah had many children, but Chanah had none. She desperately wanted a child and would cry bitterly about it. Nothing would console her.

Elkanah, her husband, said to her, "Chanah, why do you

cry? ... Why is your heart broken? Am I not better to you than ten children?"

(Ibid., 8)

Elkanah's words did not comfort Chanah, and she went to pray at the Tabernacle.

> Chanah arose after eating in Shilo and after drinking; and Eili the Kohen was sitting on the chair, near the doorpost of the Sanctuary of God. She was bitter in spirit, and she prayed *on* God, weeping continuously. She made a vow and said, "God, Master of Hosts, if You take note of the suffering of Your maidservant, and You remember me and not forget Your maidservant, and give Your maidservant male offspring, then I shall give him to God all the days of his life, and a razor shall not come upon his head."
>
> It happened as she continued to pray before God that Eili observed her mouth. Chanah was speaking *on* her heart — only her lips moved, but her voice was not heard....

(Ibid., 9–13)

This account raises some questions. Why do we need to know what Chanah's words were — isn't it enough to know she wanted a child and prayed to God? And why couldn't she pray through thought — why did her lips move? In addition, the language describing her prayer is difficult to understand — why does the Navi say "She prayed *on* God" and "Chanah was speaking *on* her heart"? Finally, why did Chanah pray at all? She was a *tzadeikes* (righteous woman); perhaps she should have accepted God's will graciously. Was her prayer legitimate, or was it a form of complaint against God?

Introduction to Prayer

Prayer reflects the emotional state of the person who prays. The Midrash (*Yalkut Shimoni Va'eschanan*) tells us that there are thirteen different types of prayer, each corresponding to a difficult emotional state. One type of prayer is called *rinah* (joy). When a person feels tremendous happiness, he will call out to God and say, "Thank You! This is wonderful. My soul cries out to You in joy!" Another type of prayer is *pilul*, in which a person expresses *deveikus* (a deep desire to connect with God). More usual, however, is the kind of prayer where we call out to God in a state of crisis or distress. This, indeed, is the foundation of prayer.

In order to understand prayer, we must understand ourselves as human beings. God created us in such a way that we usually feel some sort of lack; we rarely feel that we have everything we want in life. Unlike animals, whose requirements are met in nature, we are left in a constant state of worry. A person worries about what he lacks today, and when a person lacks nothing today, he worries about what he'll be missing tomorrow. The human soul is therefore in a constant state of stress, although the degree might vary.

The deficiencies and concerns of the human being consist of physical, emotional, and spiritual needs. Even when we have enough money for our physical needs (food, clothing, and shelter), there's always something else: better food, a nicer home, fancier clothes. In addition, if I have an apartment and a job and a salary today, I worry that I'll lose my job and I won't have the money to pay for even basic necessities tomorrow. So having my needs met sufficiently now fails to provide me with tranquillity; I have no guarantees about the future.

In addition, human beings have emotional requirements, the desire to love and to be loved, to give and to receive, to forge relationships. We all need a variety of relationships and it is necessary to communicate with other people within those relationships. Mundane dialogue isn't enough; our need is for meaningful expression, a chance to share burdens with one another.

Equally important is our spiritual need. We want to be

loved by God and to have a relationship with Him. There are billions of people in this world, but each person wants to feel that God looks at him specifically, that He looks at him and says, "I'm interested in you. You are very special. You are very dear." Each person has an intense desire to know that God is interested and involved in his life.

None of these needs, physical, emotional, and spiritual, are ever 100 percent fulfilled. A person never feels totally content for more than a day. A person never feels that all his needs are met, that nothing is lacking. We are usually experiencing some lack, some crisis, some stress, at any given moment.

In the western world today, most people have all the material requirements. Most people have food, clothing, and shelter. Are the millions and millions of people who have enough, or even plenty, content? Advertisers know we are not content, not at all, and they play on this human weakness, which is the feeling of lack. Madison Avenue would never succeed if people didn't have a basic human drive to want more.

Although God created a world in which we experience deficiency, He does not fulfill all of our needs. Surely, if He chose to, He could give us anything we desire. In fact, He could have created us in such a way that we would feel contentment instead of discontent. Why did he give us so many needs?

God created the world in deficiency in order to force the human being to form a relationship with Him. When a person feels stress or lack, he calls out to God for help. There was a saying during World War I: "There are no atheists in the foxhole." When a person is really scared, and there's no one who can help, there's no one to call upon, what does he do? He cries out to God. Always. Even an emotionally closed person prays when he or his children are in danger. Even a person who doesn't like to pray, or who doesn't "believe," will pray when he's experiencing tremendous pain.

Pain creates a vacuum in us and from that vacuum we call

out to God. There is a renewal of connection between man and God. Our Rabbis teach: "Why were all our forefathers barren? Because God desires the prayers of righteous people" (*Yevamos* 64a). When we read this Gemara, we might think, *What kind of sadistic God is that? Is it because He wants my prayers that He gives me stress and suffering? What's in it for God when He causes me to suffer?*

When a human being feels pain or worry, he immediately calls out to God, "Help me." This creates a relationship. Because God wants a relationship with each of us, we all experience this feeling of worry. Distress and worry will also come to a very righteous person, someone who already has a relationship with God. This is an indication that God is initiating a deeper, more intense relationship with that person. Not every righteous person suffers, and not every evil person doesn't suffer. There is no consistent correlation that we can see, but people who are in deep distress are often righteous. Stress or pain or suffering, in varying degrees, create a vacuum in a human being, causing him to call out to God, "I need help!" This cry for help, this acknowledgment that God exists and He can help, this turning to God, is what creates the religious personality.

A former student of mine with three small children developed a very unusual kind of cancer for a Jewish woman, cancer of the cervix. She went through treatment, doing whatever she could do medically. But each time she went to the hospital, she understood that her recovery would depend on God, and she prayed. Thank God, she recovered, but she said to me about a year after she was cancer-free, "You know something? You're not going to believe this, but sometimes I miss the illness because with it came an intense relationship with God."

In other words, pain forces us to talk, to begin a dialogue. How do we create a deep relationship with another person? We tell him about our pain. We don't talk about what to have for breakfast or about spiritual beliefs. We talk about our pain, we unload our burdens. The closer the relationship we want, the more pain we reveal; if we want the deepest kind of relationship, we share our deepest pain.

The Manna

> Why didn't the manna fall for Israel [only] once a year? [We can understand this through] a parable. A human king had one son. He allotted his food to him only once a year, and [the son] only came to see his father this once a year. The king decided to allot his food once a day, and [the son] then came to see his father every day. So it was with Israel. One who had four or five children would worry and say, "Maybe no manna will fall tomorrow, and they will all die of hunger," and thus all of them directed their hearts to their Father in heaven.
>
> (*Yoma* 76a)

Manna fell in the desert every day. Each person could only collect enough for that day; if he collected more, the manna would rot. The Rabbis ask why God sent the manna in such a way that only a daily portion could be collected. Why couldn't He send enough for a year, so the people could have "manna in the bank"? And the answer is so that each person would worry. And when a person worries, he prays, thereby beginning to create a relationship and learning to depend on God. God creates in us a state of worry, of crisis, of need, in order to open up the possibility of dialogue. When God sends us pain, He is calling us. He is saying, "I want to have a talk. I want you to come close and tell Me about your pain. I want to have a relationship with you through that pain."

Can't we pray from joy and thanksgiving? If God fulfilled all our needs and desires, couldn't we pray in gratitude? Isn't that *rinah* prayer? And wouldn't it do the job of creating a relationship with God?

Yes, we could pray in joy and gratitude and praise. When

the Jews crossed the Sea of Reeds after the Exodus from Egypt, their souls sang out with abundant joy and connection to God. But, in truth, it is more common to forget God when all is going well. Human nature is such that when we are satisfied, we usually feel no need to reach out to God.

Think about the common situation of a mother losing her child while shopping in a store. She looks around for the child and calls his name, but he's nowhere to be seen. Her heart begins to pound. It's very natural for her to start praying at this point, begging God to help her find her child. As she searches frantically and asks the salesclerks for help, she prays to God with all her heart. Suddenly she spots her child playing behind a display. The natural reaction at this point is to rush to the child, hug him, heave a sigh of relief, and...forget all about God. How many of us would voice a prayer of *rinah* at this point?

Speaking

Secular science teaches that everything in the world belongs to one of three categories: Animal, vegetable, and mineral. The Torah, on the other hand, divides existence into four categories. In addition to animal, vegetable, and mineral, there is a category of speakers. Human beings uniquely belong to this category. We are not animals, because we have the power of speech — that is, when a person has an idea, a feeling, or an intellectual moment, he can express himself through speech.

When God created the human being, He created him from two elements:

> And the Lord God formed the man of dust from the ground, and He blew into his nostrils the breath of life; and man became a living being.
>
> (Bereishis 2:7)

The dust of the earth refers to the body, and God's "breath" is the soul of the human being. Body and soul together are called "a living being." Onkelos, the great Torah Sage, defines the living soul as "a speaking spirit." In other words, what makes a person a "living being" is his ability to speak. The soul formulates ideas and emotions which are then translated by the body: Through speech, the body and soul work together to translate a thought into reality. How is it, though, that speech defines us as human beings?

What is special and unique about the power of speech is that it enables a person to "stand before the Creator in prayer and Torah" (*Zohar Tazria* 46). In other words, the fundamental difference between a person and an animal is the human being's ability to translate a spiritual reality into a physical one — to pray and communicate with God.

When a Jew prays, he speaks. God created us with His breath and we still connect to Him with breath — the breath of our words. Sometimes we pray in a loud voice, sometimes we pray in a whisper. But in either case we pray with words and we must emit breath. (A person who is unable to speak is exempt from praying with words, but even a mute person should move his lips, if possible, when praying.)

What about meditation or thinking a prayer? Why must we speak out loud for prayer to be heard by God? Can't He read our minds?

Yes, God can read our minds, absolutely. When creating human beings, however, God chose to give us the defining characteristic of speech. This was the medium He chose to unite body and soul, dust of the earth and breath of the Divine. The highest level of speech is prayer, so that when we stand before God in prayer and Torah, we connect with Him on the most sublime level of our humanity.

Speech creates a relationship. This is true among human beings and it is true of our association with God. Standing before God in speech forms a connection. Although it's true that

God knows what we're thinking without our speech — He's the ultimate mind-reader — thinking, which obviously serves other purposes, does not activate this particular relationship. The procedure for developing this specific connection to God is like turning a faucet on: All the pipes are in place, but we must do something before water pours out. We must turn on the tap, and the "tap" is speech.

So What Do We Talk About?

Often, the pain we feel is caused by something external to us — financial setbacks, sickness, death. But sometimes we have internal pain, pain not caused by a physical calamity or emotional disappointment. This pain is caused by an existential loneliness, a deep feeling that we are alone, that nobody truly understands us. There exists a place, deep down inside every person, that is an absolutely private place; it is a very raw place. That part of us is our separateness from every other individual, a point we cannot share with anyone else, and that point, that area of our personalities or our souls, wants to connect with God. This is the point from which we should pray.

After the snake in the Garden of Eden caused Chavah to sin, it was punished by losing its legs and being forced to slither on the ground and eat dirt for the rest of his life. Says the Gemara:

> The Holy One, blessed be He, does not act like human beings. The way of a person who is angry with his neighbor is to persecute him as far as depriving him of his livelihood, but it is different with the Holy One, blessed be He. Although He cursed the snake, [He did not deprive it of its livelihood]. When it goes up to the roof, there is its food; if it goes down, there is its food.
>
> (*Yoma* 85a)

Wherever the snake goes, there's something to eat, because it only eats dirt. The snake is secure in the food department — no hunger, no starvation, no worries about tomorrow's dinner. So why is this such a terrible curse?

The curse is this: Since the snake experiences no lack, it has no reason to call out to God. The ultimate in divine disconnection is having everything. Lacking something creates a situation in which we are forced to look for solutions, and when we have difficulties finding solutions, we turn to God for help.

Judaism is not achievement-oriented, it is process-oriented. The process of building a communicative relationship with God goes like this: I lack, I pray, I get. God then sends another lack. I lack, I pray, I get. This continues until the end of our lives. Sometimes we lack, we pray, and we don't get. This is a disappointment, but our Sages teach us that "no prayer is returned empty" (*Berachos* 32b). This does not mean that God always answers our prayers the way we would like. Sometimes we pray with tremendous focus and intention, but our wish is not granted. Sometimes an entire nation can pray, but we hear no answer.

Several years ago, a young Israeli soldier named Nachshon Wachsman was captured by terrorists. His parents, strong in their faith, understood that his fate was in the hands of God. True, the Israeli government was negotiating, and the army was preparing a military strike, but success or failure ultimately depended on God. The Wachsmans asked the Jewish people, religious and secular, in Israel and abroad, to pray for Nachshon's safe return. *Tehillim* were said in yeshivos, children in schools prayed, Jews around the world gathered and held prayer vigils. The whole country of Israel put aside their differences for this week, and even tough newsmen suspended their cynicism and prayed. On that Friday night, the day the terrorists said they would kill him, the country rang with prayers. We heard prayers in the shuls, in the homes, ringing through the dark, Jews praying for a boy they had never met but loved nevertheless.

The next day, we learned that Nachshon had been killed. The military rescue had failed. News reporters gathered at the Wachsman home and asked Nachshon's father, "What do you say now? God didn't answer our prayers." Mr. Wachsman answered, "Sometimes, our Father says no."

What does this mean? Was God not listening? Did He not notice, not hear? God certainly heard, but a different plan was in effect. God had decided Nachshon's fate. Yet can anyone say that millions of Jewish prayers were wasted? Except for one, all of the young soldiers who bravely tried to rescue Nachshon from his murderers survived the dangerous mission. Perhaps our Father saved these other boys in the merit of our supplications. No prayers come back empty.

All prayer has meaning, because even when our requests are not fulfilled, we have strengthened our relationship with God. We are then able to accept our lack or our sorrow because we can understand that the difficulty is not in our control; we prayed but God said "no" this time. We can accept a disappointment or even a tragedy because the process of praying reminds us that it is not we who run the world. God is in control and in His wisdom He sometimes decides to deny us something. When we pray, God may say no, but He gives us the strength to handle our distress.

The highest level of prayer is to pray for something that will further connect us to God. When a person prays for the fulfillment of desires that are interwoven with doing mitzvos, his prayers correspond to God's desires. At this level, a person asks for food so he'll have the strength to learn Torah, a home so he can have guests, money so he can run his yeshivah. Even "mundane" desires can be connected to God's will. For example, a person may pray that God will help him get to his doctor's appointment on time, because it's a mitzvah to take care of one's body. A person may pray for good health so that he will be able to do mitzvos: take care of an elderly parent, build a sukkah, or teach Torah to his grandchildren.

People often make the mistake of thinking, *I'll handle the little things myself, and I'll leave the big things to God. I don't want to bother God over something small.* This attitude is a grave error. All prayer, including a prayer for something we deem to be "minor," is an expression of the deep belief that God cares about us and that He intervenes in the world. Failure to pray is a denial that God can, and desires to, intervene in the world, that He cares, and that everything we do is important to Him. If I'm stuck in a traffic jam, and I really must get to my doctor's appointment at the other end of town, I remember that God cares about me. Therefore, it's not out of line, and in fact it's appropriate, to pray, because if He wants to, God can get me out of that traffic jam.

Once, when I was lecturing in Toronto, I borrowed a twelve-year-old Chevrolet to get from place to place. Before going to speak, I stopped at a kosher restaurant for dinner, and when I was ready to leave the car wouldn't start. I didn't panic. Instead, I said, "Okay, God. I need a partner. I can't get the car started. I have to get to the lecture and raise funds for my school. Could You please send some help?" I tried to start the car again, but still nothing happened. So I went to call the owner of the car, hoping he could tell me how to start it.

Standing at the pay phone, I heard a voice say, "Holly, is that you?"

I turned to see one of the very few people I knew in Toronto. I told her what happened, and she said, "Oh, I know how to fix that."

Sure enough, she was able to get the engine running. I asked her, "Where were you about ten minutes ago?"

She answered, "I was deciding what restaurant to go to."

I can't promise you that God said, "Go to 'Milk and Honey.' " But I can't promise you that He didn't.

This story illustrates that there is no need to wait for a life-and-death situation to pray. It wouldn't have been the end of the world if I had been late for the lecture, but when I'm in trouble, major or minor, my instinct is to ask God to help me. If we begin with little troubles, we begin to build a trusting relationship and in this way keep our communication system with God functioning smoothly. The faucet is ready to be turned on any time. We need not wait for the set prayer times; we pray when we can — in the kitchen, at work, or in the car.

Remember, though, that not all prayer is asking for help. Jewish people pray three times a day, and much of it is not kvetching. The prayer we say in the morning is, "Thank You for giving me back my soul." There is much thanks and much praise. Consistent with the prayers for help, these prayers indicate an awareness that God is in the world, giving us another day of life, good health, and many other blessings.

How Does Prayer Work?

What is the difference between destiny and coincidence? Destiny implies that everything that happens has a purpose. The word *mazal* is commonly incorrectly translated as "luck." This is wrong because luck is the same as coincidence or random fate, while *mazal* means "something that flows from heaven to earth," something God sends. Sometimes He sends something that feels good, so it's *mazal tov*. Sometimes He sends something that feels bad, so it's *mazal ra*. (It may not really be bad, but it could seem bad.) *Mazal* means: Everything that happens comes from God.

Sometimes God sends a particular hardship for the sole purpose of forcing a person to pray, thereby building a relationship with Him. When this is the purpose of our suffering, then our prayer will affect our *mazal*. The relationship He desired is established, and thereafter God removes the pain. But sometimes God sends us a difficulty that is to be a permanent part of our life. This difficulty will define and refine us, be part of us forever, part of our destiny. In this case, prayer will not be effective in changing the *mazal*; instead, prayer may lead to acceptance of our destiny and it will create a closer connection to God (*Michtav MiEliyahu*).

We cannot know which type of hardship is happening. We don't know whether the hardship sent to us is permanent or temporary. But we do know that in either case, God wants us to speak to Him.

Chanah's Prayer

Chanah's pain about her childlessness was very deep. She could not be comforted by her husband because her pain came from that point within her that nobody else could touch. Seeing other people in Shilo with their families intensified this pain until she could no longer bear it. She turned to the only Being to whom she was able to turn, the only One who could understand her suffering, God.

> Chanah arose after eating in Shilo and after drinking; and Eili the Kohen was sitting on the chair, near the doorpost of the Sanctuary of God. She was bitter in spirit, and she prayed on God, weeping continuously. She made a vow and said, "God, Lord of Hosts, if You take note of the suffering of Your maidservant, and You remember me and not forget Your maidservant, and give Your maidservant male offspring, then I shall give him to God all the days of his life, and a razor shall not come upon his head."
>
> It happened as she continued to pray before God that Eili observed her mouth. Chanah was speaking on her heart — only her lips moved, but her voice was not heard — so Eili thought she was drunk.
>
> (Shmuel I 1:9–13)

Chanah's lips moved but her voice wasn't heard because

she whispered her prayer. From this we learn that "one who prays must frame his words distinctly on his lips," but he needn't shout, for God hears even a whisper (*Berachos* 31a). Speech, however soft, creates the connection.

Why does the text say she was bitter in spirit? Spirit (in Hebrew, *ruach*) normally involves a religious or spiritual connection. What Chanah lacked was a baby — why describe her lack as a spiritual one?

For Chanah, having a child was the ultimate expression of her relationship with God. It was as a mother, she felt, that she could serve God best. Therefore, her bitterness was a spiritual distress, an expression of spiritual loss. This prayer, then, was not merely about her own needs, but about her ability to serve God.

Previously we asked why the text says that Chanah "prayed *on* God." The Gemara explains that "she hurled her words upwards" (*Berachos* 31b). In the words of the Maharsha, she complained about God. She was saying, "I have a complaint against You, God. I have a need. My need is about myself, but it is also about You. I have to tell You how I feel." Chanah did not hold back her feelings. She was open, even when her openness expressed her anger toward God. The place of her pain was open for Him to see; she showed Him everything — her anger, her suffering, and even the place of her deepest, private loneliness.

A few verses later, the same unusual wording is used — "Chanah was speaking *on* her heart." The Gemara asks, Why does the text say "on her heart" when it seems to mean "in her heart" or "from her heart"?

> *On her heart* means "about the matters of her heart." She said before Him, "Master of the World, of all the things You created in a woman, You did not create a single one without a purpose: Eyes to see, ears to hear, a nose to smell, a mouth to speak, hands to do work with, legs to walk with, breasts to nurse with. These breasts that You

put *on* my heart, are they not for nursing? Give me a child, so that I may nurse with them."

(*Berachos* 31b)

Chanah was saying, "I have a purpose. My arms have a purpose, my legs have a purpose. Why did You give me breasts, if not to nurse a child? I stand before You as a woman. I stand before You as a mother, but how can I be a mother when I have no child? Give me this opportunity to serve, enable me to complete the task for which I was brought into this world."

Pain creates a vacuum. For Chanah, the vacuum was her empty womb. She wept bitterly. What are tears? When a person cries, what does it mean? Tears are water on the soul, an expression of vulnerability. In this way, tears are an aspect of prayer. The Gates of Tears are never closed (*Berachos* 32b), and God always listens to someone who is crying. When we weep before God, though, we must speak through the tears. Words and tears together express our deepest loneliness, our desire to turn to God, and our neediness which only He can understand.

When Chanah felt "bitter of spirit," she turned to God and cried. She also did more than that — she made an oath. She swore that if God would give her a child, she would give the child to God. In other words, she expressed her motivation: "I'm not asking only for myself, God. My yearning is about my desire to serve You. I want You to give me a child and make me a mother because that will be the ultimate path for me to come close to You." Chanah's yearning was to give birth to a Jewish child, to bring a Torah Jew into the world. Without someone to continue her path in Torah, she felt herself to be an inadequate servant of God. Countless other Torah mothers in the course of our history have made the same oath as Chanah, toiling and sacrificing so that their children would continue in the Torah path. Perhaps their strength and determination came from Chanah. Chanah, here, expresses the universal deep desire of the Jewish woman to perpetuate the Torah.

Chanah called herself a "maidservant." In fact, she used the word *maidservant* three times. This word makes a statement about Chanah's self-definition. She was subservient to God, understanding that He is the One who runs the world and that He has a purpose and a plan. Although she came very close to God, opening herself totally to Him, she approached Him in awe and with complete respect.

This is the paradox of prayer: We stand before God in awe, in reverence, and at a distance. He is our Master and we are His servants. Yet, at the same time, we stand before Him in proximity and closeness, open with our feelings, as a child to his parent, for He is our Father. If we are to serve our Master, we need the "tools" — so we ask for whatever we need to serve Him to our greatest capacity. As His children, though, we stand in nearness and love, and we ask simply, and with humility, for His help.

Chanah called God "Lord of Hosts." The word *host* refers to each and every thing created by God.

> From the day that God created His world there was no man who called Hashem "Lord of Hosts" until Chanah came.... Chanah said before the Holy One, blessed be He, "Master of the World, of all the hosts that You have created in Your world, is it so hard in Your eyes to give me one son?" A parable that this is similar to: A king made a feast for his servants. A poor man came and stood by the door. He said to them, "Give me a bite," but no one paid any attention to him, so he forced his way into the presence of the king and said to him, "Your Majesty, out of all the feast which you have made, does it seem to you so difficult to give me one bite?"
>
> (*Berachos* 31b)

In essence, Chanah was saying, "You, God, created a world with billions of components — molecules and atoms and particles so small they cannot be seen in a powerful microscope. The world is a feast of hosts. I, Chanah, am but one lowly person and I am asking for one little baby. It is nothing compared to everything else You do! You are like the rich king who serves everything at his banquet. For You it is nothing, but for me it is everything. It is a crust of bread for a starving peasant, the difference between life and death. I have knocked on the door and Your servant, nature, has turned me away. So now I have walked into the palace, right into Your inner chamber, and in Your presence I beg for a crust of bread — for a baby."

Another interpretation of "Lord of Hosts," is that Chanah meant:

> "God, You created the system of the world wherein the celestial beings, angels, live forever, but they don't reproduce. The terrestrial beings die, but they have means of continuity, children. Which am I? If I'm a terrestrial being, give me a child. If I'm not a terrestrial being, if I'm an angel, let me live forever."
>
> (*Radak*, Shmuel I 1:11)

What are angels? They are celestial beings who do the will of God constantly, consistently, without questions. They have no free will; they always serve the purpose for which they were created. Human beings are different. We, like angels, were created to serve God, yet we have the free will to do so or not. Angels do not procreate, but they live forever to serve their Master. A person's service of God ends with his death unless he has children raised in Torah to continue his service of God. And this was Chanah's argument. "Give me a child who will continue in this path, or let me live forever to serve You as an angel; let me be purposeful one way or another." For Chanah, the inability to serve God completely was an intense source of suffering.

Chanah had on her boxing gloves when she spoke to God; her prayer had no barriers, no holding back. Sometimes prayer to God doesn't mean "please help me." Sometimes a person prays to ask God, "Why are You doing this? I want to understand. I want to talk to You." Chanah's prayer went even further. She left no stone unturned. In fact, she even threatened that she would become a *sotah*.

A *sotah* is a married woman who secludes herself with another man, despite being warned by witnesses not to do so. If her husband suspected her of illicit behavior, she could be brought before the high priest for a miraculous test of her fidelity. If she was indeed guilty, she and her lover would die. But if it was a false accusation, God would give her a child. The Talmud tells us:

> Chanah said before the Holy One, blessed be He, "Sovereign of the Universe, if You will look, it is well, and if You will not, I will go and shut myself up with someone else with the knowledge of my husband, Elkanah. Because I will have been alone with someone they will make me drink the water of the suspected wife, and You cannot falsify Your law, as it says, 'She shall be cleared [of suspicion] and shall conceive seed' (Bemidbar 5:28)."
>
> (*Berachos* 31b)

If God Is Calling

This is not to suggest that we should threaten God, because we are not Chanah with her sublime relationship with Him. In fact, many commentators ask how even she could get away with this seemingly outrageous behavior. When a person is in deep pain, when there seems to be a gaping hole in his life, it is possible that he will say things that are not meant to be said. Chanah was so distressed that she knew no boundaries when beseeching God. He who knows everything empathized with her deep yearning and pain, and she was therefore allowed to express every aspect of her suffering and bare her soul.

Ultimately, the story had a happy ending. Chanah gave birth to an extraordinary son, Shmuel, who was a prophet and leader of the Jewish people. She raised him until he was two and then, as she had promised, she dedicated him to the service of God and brought him to the Tabernacle to minister to the aging priest, Eili. Chanah was blessed with six more children.

But not every occasion of prayer ends as happily. Many times we pray and it does not seem that our prayer is answered. There are women who do not have children, although they desperately lay their cases before the Arbiter. Sometimes God answers, sometimes the *mazal* changes, but often this is not the case. How do we go on? How do we know whether the *mazal* sent to us is a pretext God uses to draw us close, or an intrinsic part of the service He expects of us in this world?

We don't know. We cannot know. But we put our trust in God, nevertheless. "Put your hope in God. Strengthen and fortify your heart, and put your hope in God" (Tehillim 27:14). Twice we are told to hope in God, but in between these two commands is the instruction to be strong, to accept. Like bookends, the hope surrounds the acceptance. Why this repetition? The Torah conveys to us that all of our hope must be placed in God. We must rely on Him that He will answer our prayers. If He doesn't answer us the way we wished, we must pray again. We shouldn't give up, because nothing is impossible for God. On the other hand, we must accept His will. We work on two tracks simultaneously — trust Him completely, and never give up because God can do anything. We accept that His decisions for us are right and appropriate and just (even if they are painful), and we strengthen and fortify our hearts.

The Realm of Prayer

When we stand before God, must it be to ask for big things? May we ask for little things, even barley and potatoes? Keeping in mind that our larger goal is to be "speakers" — to connect with God in the fullest sense — it is nevertheless fine, even good, to ask God for help every day. Every prayer creates a connection, but, like Chanah, our yearning should be to ask Him for what we need to extend our service to our fullest potential.

The fundamental purpose of prayer is to develop a relationship with God. When we turn to God, when we plead with Him to alleviate our suffering, and when we thank Him for our blessings, we are expressing our awareness that God is involved in every aspect of our lives. To create a close relationship, we must pray with emotional openness, for there is nothing we can't tell Him. He understands our inner fears and hopes and desires. He knows the point of our deepest insecurity and hopelessness. He will listen and care. If we feel empty or distressed, it's because God is calling us. If God is calling us, should we not answer?

How Did Miriam Know to Bring a Tambourine?

The story of Miriam is extremely difficult to understand on a cursory level. It seems as if every incident about Miriam raises questions. Yet, with the help of the Oral Torah and the commentaries of our Sages, we can take the disparate incidents about Miriam and see that a thread runs through her story, connecting the events of her life and forming a picture of a great leader of Israel.

At the Sea

After the sea split and the Jewish people escaped from the Egyptian bondage, Moshe, together with the men, sang a song to God. Miriam, the sister of Moshe and Aharon, sang separately with the women.

> Miriam the prophetess, the sister of Aharon, took her tambourine in her hand and all the women went forth after her with tambourines and with dances. Miriam spoke up to them, "Sing to God for He is gloriously sublime, having hurled horse with its rider to the sea."
>
> (Shemos 15:20–21)

When we read this passage from the book of Shemos, everything seems clear: the men sang, the women sang, everyone joyfully praised God. Upon reflection, however, we have a question. How did Miriam and the other women know to bring tambourines out of Egypt? We learned in *parashas Bo* that the Jewish people left Egypt in a hurry: "Egypt imposed itself strongly upon the people to hasten to send them out of the land" (ibid. 12:33). As they were rushing about, hastily preparing their children, gathering their things, throwing their unleavened dough over their shoulders, and fleeing for their lives, did Miriam and the women say, "Hold everything. We've got to get our tambourines — we can't possibly leave without them"?

Searching for a clue, we reread the passage. Instead of finding an answer to our question, however, we come up with additional questions: Why is Miriam called a prophetess here? This is not the first time she is mentioned in the book of Shemos, so why was she not called a prophetess earlier? And why is Miriam called the sister of Aharon in the passage, rather than the sister of Moshe?

Rashi addresses this issue:

> When had she prophesied? When she was the sister of Aharon alone, before Moshe was born. She said, "My mother is destined to bear a son who will deliver Israel."

Why didn't the Torah tell us Miriam was a prophetess when she first prophesied — why did it wait until more than eighty years had passed? And what about the tambourines?

In the Desert

Hoping to uncover the solution to these questions, we continue reading the Torah, and we discover something else about Miriam. Throughout their forty-year sojourn in the desert, the Jewish people were sustained through the miracles of manna from heaven and water from a traveling well. At the end of this forty-year period, prior to entering the Land of Israel, these miracles ceased.

> The children of Israel, the whole assembly, arrived at the Wilderness of Tzin in the first month, and the people settled in Kadesh. Miriam died there and was buried there. There was no water for the assembly.
>
> (Bemidbar 10:2)

Rashi explains that the well disappeared upon Miriam's death because it had been there in Miriam's merit. What did she do that gave her this merit? "Merit" always connotes measure for measure, so she must have done an exactly fitting good deed — but what?

Rabbeinu Bachya explains that Miriam merited the well because when she placed Moshe's ark in the Nile River, she stood at a distance to see what would happen to him. The connection on a simple level is that water equals water — the reward is exactly the same as the mitzvah. But the Torah is never so simple; there is always a deeper implication. If Miriam merited a well, it is because water has a deeper spiritual meaning, an internal significance, as does her action of waiting by the water to see what would happen. Aside from the water connection, what did Miriam do when she stood by the water that caused God to give the Jewish people a well in her merit so many years later?

The Midrash gives a different reason why Miriam merited the well:

> There were three pedagogues: Moshe, Aharon, and Miriam. In the merit of Moshe, [the Jewish people] ate the manna, something our holy fathers never saw.... In the merit of Aharon, I [God] surrounded you with the clouds of glory.... And the well was in the merit of Miriam, who sang a song at the water, as it says, "And Miriam answered, 'Sing to God for He is gloriously sublime' " (Shemos 15:21).
>
> (*Bemidbar Rabbah* 1:2)

This gives us a second connection between Miriam and water. We have Miriam standing at the water, Miriam singing at the water, and a well of water that exists for her sake. Our *midrash*, however, merely solidifies the concept of water equals water; we still want to understand the deeper significance of Miriam's merit.

In Egypt

> The king of Egypt summoned the Hebrew midwives — of whom the name of the first was Shifrah and the name of the second was Puah — and he said, "When you deliver the Hebrew women and you see them [the babies] on the birthstool, if it is a son, you are to kill him, and if it is a daughter, she shall live." But the midwives feared God and they did not do as the king of Egypt commanded them, and they gave life to the boys.
>
> (Shemos 1:15–17)

Our Sages tell us that the midwife referred to as "Puah" was Miriam, and the midwife referred to as "Shifrah" was Yocheved, her mother (*Sotah* 11b). They refused to kill the male children, and they also gave life to the babies. The Midrash suggests that "they gave life" means they gave the babies food, they prayed for them, or they played with them and spoke gentle words to them. This teaches that in addition to refraining from killing the children, there was something that they actively did for the babies (*Shemos Rabbah* 1:6).

> God did good to the midwives, and the people increased and became very strong. And it was because the midwives feared God that He made them houses.
>
> (Shemos 1:20–21)

Rashi explains that these "houses" were not mere physical dwellings. They were houses of grandeur in Israel: the houses of the priesthood and kingship. The priesthood came from Yocheved, and kingship from Miriam. King David, the beginning of the royal dynasty, descended from Miriam. Miriam's fear of God was returned to her as God's gift of royalty.

Again, we want to understand the internal connection between Miriam's fear of God and kingship. God runs the world in a measure-for-measure fashion; what did Miriam do to deserve the kingship?

The answers to all of our questions begin with understanding the meaning of wells of water.

The Wells

All three of our patriarchs had connections to wells.

> [Avraham] said, "You will take these seven ewes from me, that it may serve me as testimony that I dug this well."
> (Bereishis 21:30)

> Yitzchak dug anew the wells of water which they had dug in the days of Avraham, his father, for the Philistines had stopped them after Avraham's death; and he called them by the same names that his father had called them.
> (Ibid. 26:18)

Yaakov, unlike his father and grandfather, did not dig a well. Instead, he encountered a well:

> So Yaakov lifted his feet and went toward the land of the easterners. He looked, and there was a well in the field. And behold three flocks of sheep lay there beside it, for from that well [the shepherds] would water the flocks, and the stone over the mouth of the well was large.
> (Ibid. 29:1–2)

What is the difference between digging one's own well and uncovering a preexisting one? Before we answer this question,

How Did Miriam Know to Bring a Tambourine? • 125

let us look at another interesting fact — wells played a big part in the meeting of Rivkah and Eliezer (the servant who had been sent to find a wife for Yitzchak), Yaakov and Rachel, and Moshe and Tzipporah.

> [Eliezer] said, "Hashem, God of my master Avraham, may it happen for me today and do a kindness for my master Avraham. Behold, I am standing at the well of water, and the daughters of the people of the city are coming out to draw water. The maiden whom I will ask to give me water and she will answer, 'Drink and I will give your camels to drink, too,' shall be the one whom You have chosen for Your servant Yitzchak...."
> Before he finished speaking, Rivkah came out.
> (Ibid. 24:12-13)

> Rachel had arrived with her father's flock, for she was a shepherdess. And when Yaakov saw Rachel, the daughter of Lavan his mother's brother, and the flock of Lavan his mother's brother, Yaakov came forward, rolled the stone off the mouth of the well, and watered the sheep of Lavan his mother's brother.
> (Ibid. 29:9-11)

> Moshe fled from before Pharaoh and settled in the land of Midian. He sat by a well. The minister of Midian had seven daughters; they came and drew water and filled the troughs to water their father's sheep.... Moshe desired to dwell with the man; and he gave his daughter Tzipporah to Moshe.
> (Shemos 2:15-21)

Why did our ancestors find their wives at wells? What is the significance of the wells?

The Land of Israel has very few bodies of water. Most water in Israel comes from rain. This rain seeps into the land, deep into the earth, where it forms underground aquifers which flow throughout Israel. It is by digging into the earth that we have access to the water.

A well is created by digging deep into the earth, deep into the physical world. Deep, deep down we find water. The water in a well was always there, but the only way to access it is by digging. In Midrashic literature, water is a metaphor for spirituality, for Torah, so digging the well is a metaphor for finding God and Torah within the physical world. By digging, a person can find the Godliness that exists within the material world.

A well has an opening at the top, with light in the opening, but the deeper one goes, the darker it gets. It's the same with spirituality — the truth in the Torah is hidden. Torah is not easily accessible, and a person who wants to uncover the secrets in the Torah must dig deep into it. The truth contained in the Torah is like water hidden in the earth and tapped when a person digs a well. A well represents the hidden Torah, while the light at the top of the well represents revelation (*Sefas Emes, parashas Toldos*).

In fact, the water of the well is connected to the primordial waters:

> And God said, "The waters shall be drawn together under the heaven unto one place, and let the dry land appear." And it was so.
>
> (Bereishis 1:9)

Before the creation of the physical world, only God existed. There was no physical world, only spirituality. This spirituality is represented by the primordial waters. When God created the physical world, He buried spirituality — the waters — deep within the material earth. Human beings are able to see only the physicality, but under the physicality, so to speak, is the spirituality, the foundation of the world (*Sefas Emes, parashas Toldos*).

To Find

How can a person find spirituality? How does a person grasp Torah? He has to dig.

> If a person says to you, "I labored but did not find it," don't believe [him]. [If a person says to you,] "I didn't labor and I found it," don't believe [him]. [If a person says to you,] "I labored and I found," believe [him].
>
> (*Megillah* 6b)

If a person claims he worked hard to learn Torah, but he did not find its wisdom, don't believe him. If a person claims he didn't work hard to learn Torah, but he found its secrets, do not believe him. Only if a person claims he worked hard and learned Torah should he be believed. Learning Torah is the same as digging a well because neither can be achieved without hard work (*Rav Tzadok, Likutei Ma'amarim*). But just as a person who digs a well discovers water that was always there, a person who toils at Torah discovers his connection to God, which was always buried beneath the surface.

Interestingly, our Sages use the word "find" when describing this difficult learning process because "find" connotes getting something that's waiting to be discovered. If a person walks down the street and comes across a coin, he "finds" it. He did not work hard and weary himself to obtain that coin; the coin was there. This seems to be in contradiction to the labor discussed above, but it is not. Like the coin one finds on the street, the "underground water," that is, the deep truth in the Torah, is already there, waiting. However, it can be accessed only by working hard, by wearying oneself over it. On the one hand, we toil, sweat, and labor; but on the other hand, ultimately it is God who enables us to "find," to encounter that which was always there. We labor intensely to grasp the meaning of Torah, but there is also a Divine miracle in our discovery.

On one level, the well represents the Oral Torah. The

Written Torah is easier to access. A person can read the written Torah from the beginning to end and feel that he has finished learning. In order to learn the Oral Torah, however, a person has to work hard and long. It is a job that is never completed. Nevertheless, although the Written Torah is easier to access, a simple "reading" of the Torah from beginning to end does not produce a true understanding of it. If one desires to comprehend the Written Torah in a nonsuperficial manner, the Oral Torah is required. The meaning of the Written Torah is hidden beneath the surface and can only be accessed with toil, struggle, and digging.

On a more general level, the well is an expression of all human effort to reach God:

> The water is from below — this is the well, as it says, "Arise, O well" (Bemidbar 21:17). The bread is from above, [as it says,] "Behold, I rain down upon you bread from the heaven" (Shemos 6:4).
>
> (*Shemos Rabbah* 25:6)

The manna was given to the Jewish people from heaven, from above to below, and represents God's flowing abundance to us. The well, on the other hand, represents human effort that digs into the earthiness of this physical world in order to encounter God. This creates a relationship in which God gives to us from "above to below," and we "give" to God, from "below to above."

With this new understanding of the deeper meaning of wells, we can now interpret the significance of the patriarchs' wells. Digging wells represents their digging into this physical world to discover God and create their own relationships with Him.

In order to dig a well, a shovel is required. When Avraham dug a well, the "shovel" that he used to dig with was *chesed* (lovingkindness). When Avraham developed the quality of kindness to its ultimate level, he was in fact digging into the world to unearth Godliness. When Yitzchak dug a well, the "shovel" that he used was *gevurah*, the quality of awe, self-control, sacrifice, and introspection. With this quality, he unearthed Godliness in this world. Avraham and Yitzchak used different means to uncover spirituality by digging and redigging the same wells, albeit using different tools. Yaakov, however, dug no well. The well he encountered was already there, but he had to uncover it, to roll off the huge stone that sat on top of it (*Sefas Emes, parashas Toldos*).

> So Yaakov lifted his feet and went toward the land of the easterners. He looked, and there was a well in the field. And behold three flocks of sheep lay there beside it, for from that well [the shepherds] would water the flocks, and the stone over the mouth of the well was large. When all the flocks were assembled there, they would roll the stone from the mouth of the well and water the sheep; then they would put the stone back over the mouth of the well, in its place....
> And when Yaakov saw Rachel, the daughter of Lavan his mother's brother, and the flock of Lavan his mother's brother, Yaakov came forward, rolled the stone off the mouth of the well, and watered the sheep of Lavan his mother's brother.
> (Bereishis 29:1–3, 10)

What was Yaakov's method of uncovering Godliness? Yaakov's quality was the *emes* (truth) of Torah. One can encounter God as Avraham and Yitzchak did, by digging into the physical world to encounter spirituality. Or one can encounter God through Torah. The Torah, given to us by God, must be labored at and uncovered; the stone has to be rolled off, and it takes a lot of effort.

Why does the Torah tell us that "when *all the flocks were as-*

sembled there*, they would roll the stone from the mouth of the well"? Why did the shepherds have to wait for everyone to arrive? This indicates that it took the strength of all the shepherds together to budge the stone, since it was a huge, heavy stone. When Yaakov was able to remove the stone by himself, he showed superhuman effort. This superhuman effort is what it takes to roll off our spiritual stone — our *yetzer hara*, which is our inborn resistance to Torah (*Sefas Emes, Parashas Vayeitzei*). God created human beings with this resistance in order to give us free will, and it's not easy to strengthen ourselves sufficiently to roll it away. It takes effort and labor. Yaakov had to roll off his *yetzer hara* in order to uncover the well of Torah, and although he always had the potential to roll that stone off, he didn't actually demonstrate it until he saw Rachel.

It was necessary for Yaakov to uncover the well. There is no Torah without kindness and without discipline and awe, so Avraham and Yitzchak first had to dig. Once that was done, Yaakov's job was to uncover, to reveal the light.

Male and Female

Kabbalah teaches that everything in the physical world possesses either male or female traits. Male traits are not exclusive to men and female traits are not exclusive to women. Rather, in spiritual language, "male" and "female" refer to particular characteristics.

The male trait in Kabbalah is raw, untapped potential, whereas the female trait is actualization of potential. In the male-female relationship, the male gives seed, which is raw potential, and the female actualizes the seed — she forms something from the seed, a baby. In this relationship, the male is the giver, and the female is the receiver. In addition, the male is the aspect of "from above to below," and the female, as recipient and actualizer, is the aspect of "from below to above."

In the relationship between God and the Jewish people, God is "male," bestowing good upon His beloved people from above to below, and we are "female," receiving God's benevolence and reaching toward Him from below to above. As the metaphor follows, God remains unactualized potential until the Jewish people bring Him into this world through Torah and mitzvos. He remains, as it were, exiled from the world He created until we release Him from exile and create a space where He can dwell in this world (*Maharal*). Shir HaShirim is based on this metaphor of God as male, the Jewish people as female.

In Hebrew, *well* is a feminine noun and represents human effort, digging to find God, spirituality, and Torah. The well represents "from below to above" because through the digging process, the search for God, we find Him, thus bringing into being His "potential." When the Midrash states that Miriam's merit brought the gift of a well to the Jews in the desert and that Moshe's merit brought the manna, it is teaching that Miriam's quality was the ability to dig, to search and find God, to reach up to Him from below to above in all situations, despite all adversity. Conversely, Moshe represents God's benevolence to us, His role as giver, bestowing on us the Torah.

Another feminine entity is the womb — the place where the seed develops from its potential into its fruition and the place from which a child enters this world. Perhaps this is why Miriam is identified as a midwife. A midwife enables life to enter this world, and, as such, she is the quintessential actualizer of potential.

At this point we can understand why three leaders of the Jewish people met their wives at wells. The well represents the human ability to actualize. Male is an expression of potential and female develops this potential. Until a man marries, he remains "potential"; when he marries, his mate enables him to express this potential in practical terms. The wells in the Torah illustrate this idea: Yitzchak's wife Rivkah was first seen at the well, because without her Yitzchak could not have become the patriarch of Israel. Likewise, Moshe was not developed enough to be a leader of Israel until he met Tzipporah at the well. And Yaakov, upon seeing Rachel, was able to move the stone off the well and thereby reveal light.

Miriam

Miriam's name comes from the Hebrew word *maror*, which means "bitter."

> Egypt enslaved the children of Israel with crushing harshness. They embittered [*vayemareru*] their lives with hard work.
>
> (Shemos 1:13-14)

Miriam was given her name because she was born at the most intense time of the bitterness of exile (*Shemos Rabbah* 26:1). The most intense time of the exile, however, was also the beginning of the redemption. When a point on a wheel spins downward and reaches the bottom, there is nowhere to go but up. Bitter becomes sweet. Miriam later sang the song at the sea — she was there for the redemption.

The book of Shemos opens with a concise description of the harsh trials of the Jewish people in Egypt. The Egyptians enslaved the Jewish people and embittered their lives by degrading them. Pharaoh ordered the Hebrew midwives to kill the male babies. When they refused, he decreed that all the male babies should be thrown into the Nile River. Next comes the episode of the birth of Moshe:

> A man [Amram] went from the house of Levi, and he took a daughter of Levi [Yocheved]. The woman conceived and gave birth to a son. She saw that he was good, and she hid him for three months. When she could no longer conceal him, she took a wicker basket and smeared it with clay and

pitch, placed the child into it, and placed it among the reeds at the bank of the river. His sister stationed herself at a distance to know what would be done with him.

(Shemos 2:1–4)

Amram and Yocheved are the parents of Miriam, Aharon, and Moshe. But how are we to understand the language of this story? Why does the Torah say that a man "went" and "he took"? Where did he go? And how does this baby, Moshe, have an older sister already?

The Midrash explains that "the man went" is not to be understood that he went from one place to the other, changing geographic locations. It means that he went from one mindset to another, that he changed his opinion.

> Where did he go? Rav Yehudah Bar Zavina says, "He went on the advice of his daughter." [Amram] was the greatest man of his generation. Since the evil Pharaoh decreed that every male that was born should be thrown into the river, [Amram] said, "We are toiling for nothing." So he went and divorced his wife. [Then] all [the other Jews] went and divorced their wives.
>
> [Miriam] said to [her father], "Your decree is harsher than Pharaoh's. Pharaoh only decreed on the males. You decreed on the males and the females. Pharaoh only decreed in this world, you decreed also in the next world. Pharaoh's decree may or may not be fulfilled.... But you are a *tzaddik*; surely your decree will be fulfilled."
>
> So he remarried his wife, and they all remarried their wives.
>
> (*Sotah* 12a)

Amram's decision to divorce his wife was based on his reasoning that it was better not to have children than to have his children murdered. Bringing forth life was not worth the pain and agony of seeing the children destroyed. Since Amram was the leader of his generation, his action was a precedent, in effect a decree, on his fellow Jews.

Miriam urged her father to return to her mother, arguing, "Pharaoh's decree applies only to the boys, but you, Father, deny life to the girls as well. There is a fifty-fifty chance a child will be a girl, and who knows, maybe God will send more girls than boys. How can you deny this chance to a potential daughter of Israel? Pharaoh's decree applies only to life in this world, but you have denied the soul access to the next world. Even if a child lives a short life, his life is worthwhile because every soul must enter this world before having eternal entry to the next world. Pharaoh's decree may or may not be fulfilled: He could die, he could change his mind, there could be a revolution. Pharaoh is an evildoer, and God may overturn his decree. But you, Father, are righteous, and God will fulfill your word, for He listens to the righteous."

Miriam's message to her father was "Father, you are not in charge of this world. We are required to do our part as best we can, but whether we succeed or not is up to God. Our job is to make the effort, to reach from below to above. We are not responsible for the result; God alone determines whether we succeed or fail, whether or not there will be existence today or tomorrow. We can control our attempts to have a baby, but we can't control the length of its days; that's up to God. We misunderstand our function in the world if we base our activities on what might or might not happen in the future."

Miriam also told Amram her prophecy that he and his wife would give birth to the savior of Israel, the man who would save the Jewish people from the hands of the Egyptians.

Amram went with his daughter's advice and "took" — that is, he remarried — his wife. They had a son, and they saw that he was good. But after three months, Yocheved could no longer hide the baby. The Midrash says that Amram rebuked Miriam when he thought that this baby would die like the others.

[Miriam's] father rebuked her, saying, "My daughter, where is your prophecy now?" But she still believed in her prophecy, as it says, "And his sister stationed herself at a distance to know what would be done to him." [The word] *stationed* refers to prophecy [i.e., she stood by her prophecy].

(*Mechilta, parashas Beshalach* 10)

Miriam did not lose faith. She held on to her prophecy; she was sure that her baby brother would not have a tragic end. This is why she stood firm by the river and watched to see how God would save that baby. Miriam's vision was clearer than Amram's. When all appeared lost and the end seemed near, Amram lost heart, but Miriam did not give up. She understood that although human beings make tremendous efforts in this world, they face tremendous resistance and opposition. In the end, it is God alone who determines whether our efforts will succeed, and nothing is impossible for Him.

Waiting for the Redemption

Eighty years later, Moshe led the Jewish people through the sea. The Egyptians were destroyed and the redemption from Egypt was complete. Miriam rejoiced and sang because the crossing of the sea was the proof that her prophecy was true. Throughout the bitter exile, Miriam never gave up on life. She never quit. Until the end, she believed that we must do our *hishtadlus*, make efforts and do our part, and the rest we should leave to God.

Trapped between the army of Pharaoh and the Sea of Reeds, the job of the Jewish people was to jump into the water — that is, to act with faith, knowing God would do the rest.

Miriam knew that without participating in redemption it would not happen or it would be delayed. The job of the Jewish people was, and still is, to act with faith, to reach out to God, to affirm life by bringing more of it into the world, despite adversity and opposition. This reaching out is, in fact, the only means we have to bring the potential redemption into reality. Our job as the Jewish people, as "female," is to reach up to God, to "actualize His potential" through our actions and through our faith in Him, from below to above. When we proceed with courage and faith, when we stand firm in our trust, God responds from above to below. The creation of this relationship between male and female, God and the Jewish people, is expressed through the concept of digging, searching, creating a well, seeking God in this world.

We can now understand why the women took those tambourines out of Egypt.

> The righteous women in that generation were confident that God would perform miracles for them and they accordingly had brought tambourines with them from Egypt.
>
> (*Mechilta*; cf. *Rashi*, Bereishis 34:25)

"Bring the tambourines," said Miriam, "and wait for the miracle. Wait for the prophecy of salvation to be fulfilled. The instruments are an expression of our faith — they are an action that confirms our belief that God will respond to us, if we but reach up to Him."

Why did Miriam merit the well? We had two answers: because she watched for Moshe on the Nile River, reaching up to God from below, knowing that nothing is impossible for God; and because she sang at the sea, after witnessing the final affirmation that God responds to the relationship created by the Jewish people through their efforts.

Water at the Nile River and water at the Sea of Reeds bring forth the water of the well. The external link of water was obvious. We now also understand the internal links. Miriam was rewarded specifically with a well because the well represents the effort we make to connect with God through the deep and hidden waters of our holy Torah. Miriam dug her well and God responded by giving her water.

Miriam was identified as a prophetess more than eighty years after she prophesied because this was the time that her prophecy was fulfilled. This was the moment when, after her continuous, optimistic "digging," she found water. Miriam's name means "bitter," but life was never bitter for Miriam. For Miriam, life was song. Her faith was that life is good; if it is bitter and difficult and even tragic now, there will be a redemption. The last two letters of Miriam's name in Hebrew are *yud* and *mem*, which spell *yam*, sea. There may be bitterness (*mar*) in life, but in the end there is also that sea — redemption.

The Jew's job is to continue digging, continue believing, continue acting. In this way we bring God into the world. Out of the depths of the well's darkness comes water. The Gemara tells us that if a person says, "I labored and I found," he should be believed. Miriam's song is "I found" — "Sing to God for He is gloriously sublime."

The House of Kingship

We can now understand why Miriam merited the well, but why was Miriam also given the house of kingship? The Torah tells us this was her reward for defying Pharaoh's decree and giving life to the Jewish babies in Egypt (Shemos 1:20–21). However, just as the well has a deeper implication, so does the concept of kingship.

"There is no king without a kingdom" (*Pirkei d'Rabbi Eliezer*, ch. 11). Every king needs a kingdom to acknowledge his rule, or else he is not a king. This is no less true for God than it is for an earthly king. Even God, if He is to be King, needs a people who accept Him as King, who willingly embrace subservience to His rule. This is the theme of Rosh HaShanah, which is, in essence, the coronation ceremony of God as our King.

In this relationship between God as King (*Melech*) and the Jewish people as subjects, we are called the "kingdom" (*malchus*). As King, God gives from above to below; He is the Divine from whom all abundance flows. As *malchus*, kingdom, we reach up to our King and create the "space" for Him to enter. These efforts are from below to above. God is the giver and we are the receivers. God is the potential King and we, so to speak, bring Him into this world, "actualizing" Him, because without subjects He cannot be King.

What is the Jewish concept of an earthly king? The Jewish king serves in two roles — he is both the king, *melech*, and the kingdom, *malchus*. As king to the earthly kingdom, he serves as giver, endowing his subjects with good. As the subject of the Divine King, he is the recipient, recognizing that all good emanates from God. In his role as the receiver, *malchus*, the Jewish king takes action and makes efforts, yet at the same time he recognizes that everything he has in the world comes from God, not from himself.

The concept of a Jewish king is defined by King David, and his name, in Hebrew spelled *daled vav daled*, provides us with an understanding of what a human king must be. The *daled* stands for the Hebrew word *dal* (poor). The king understands that he is poor except for whatever God bestows upon him. The *vav* looks like a vertical line; it represents the vertical connection between Heaven and earth, from above to below and from below to above. Thus, the king represents both roles, the giver and receiver, *melech* and *malchus*, at the same time. The third letter again is *daled*, because despite his ascension to the throne and the vast power and honor he receives, the Jewish king acknowledges that he remains poor except for whatever God gives him.

David was directly descended from Miriam through his mother's side (*Shemos Rabbah* 1:21, 40:4). God promised to give Miriam the house of royalty through King David as a reward for her fear of God. When Miriam allowed the babies to live and actively sustained them despite Pharaoh's orders, she accepted her role as a subject of God. Her actions indicated her awareness that no earthly king can depose the Heavenly King, and when it came to following orders, she would obey God, not Pharaoh or any other earthly king. Measure for measure, the house of David, the dynasty of the Jewish kings, came from her.

Miriam, born during the most bitter time of the Egyptian exile, understood that the harshest suffering was but the precursor for the redemption. She waited for the redemption, never wavering, tambourine in hand, ready to sing. May we all share Miriam's strength, determination, and trust, and accept that the bad, frightening moments we experience as our exile winds down foretell of the time when we will also "sing to God, for He is gloriously sublime." May this time come speedily in our days.

What's in a Name?

Sometimes the Torah presents a little story that is very pleasant to read, but seems to be without great significance. For example, Melachim II tells the story of the Shunamite woman, a woman from the tribe of Yissachar, who lived during the days of Elisha the Prophet. In the merit of opening her home to Elisha, she was granted a son, and when this son passed away Elisha brought him back to life. It's very exciting to read about a resurrection, but is that all there is? Read the story carefully for yourself, and ask questions as you go along. You'll discover that even a "simple" Torah story has a great deal of wisdom in it.

It happened one day that Elisha traveled to Shuneim. There was a great woman there and she pressed him to eat a meal; and so it was, whenever he passed by, he would turn there to eat a meal.

She [once] said to her husband, "I now know that he is a holy man of God who passes by us regularly. Let us make a small, walled attic and place there for him a bed, a table, a chair, and a lamp, so that whenever he comes to us, he can turn in there."

One day...he turned to the attic and lay down there. He said to Geichazi, his attendant, "Summon that Shunamite woman." He summoned her and she stood before him. He then said to [Geichazi], "Please say to her, 'You have undertaken all this exertion on our behalf — what [favor] can be done for you? Can something be said on your behalf to the king or the army commander?'"

She replied, "I dwell among my people."

So he said [to Geichazi], "What can be done for her?"

Geichazi said, "Actually, she has no child, and her husband is old."

He said, "Summon her." He summoned her, and she stood in the doorway. [Elisha] said, "At this season next year you will be embracing a son."

She said, "Do not, my master, O man of God, do not disappoint your maidservant!"

The woman conceived and bore a son at that season the next year, as Elisha had told her. The boy grew up. One day, he went out to his father, to the reapers [in the field]. [Suddenly] he said to his father, "My head! My head!"

[His father] said to the attendant, "Carry him to his mother." He carried him to his mother. He sat in her lap until noon, and then he died. She went up and laid him on the bed of the man of God, shut [the door] upon him, and left.

She then called her husband and said, "Please send me one of the attendants and one of the donkeys, so that I can hurry to the man of God and return."

He said, "Why are you going to him today? It is not a Rosh Chodesh or Shabbos!"

She replied, "It is well."

She saddled the donkey and said to her attendant, "Lead and go, and do not impede me from riding unless I tell you." She set out and came to the man of God at Mount Carmel.

When the man of God saw her from afar, he said to Geichazi, his attendant, "Behold — it is that Shunamite woman! Please run to her and ask her, 'Is all well with you? Is all well with your husband? Is all well with the boy?' "

She told [Geichazi], "All is well." Then she came before the man of God at the mountain and grasped his legs. Geichazi approached to push her away, but the man of God said, "Leave her, for her soul is bitter within her. Hashem has hidden it from me and not told me."

She said, "Did I request a son of my master? Did I not say, 'Do not mislead me?' "

He said to Geichazi, "Gird your loins; take my staff in your hand and go. If you meet a man, do not greet him, and if a man greets you, do not respond to him. Place my staff upon the lad's face."

The lad's mother said, "[I swear] as Hashem lives and [I swear] as you live, I will not leave you!" So he [the prophet] arose and went after her.

Geichazi went ahead of them and placed the staff on the lad's face, but there was no sound and nothing was heard. He returned to [Elisha] and told him, "The lad has not awakened."

Elisha came into the house and [saw that] the lad was dead, laid out on his bed. He entered and shut the door behind them both, and prayed to God. Then he lay upon the boy, placing his mouth upon his mouth, his eyes upon his eyes, and his palms upon his palms. He stretched himself out over him and warmed the flesh of the boy. He withdrew and walked through the house, once this way and once that way, and then he went up [again] and stretched himself over him. The lad sneezed seven times and opened his eyes.

[Elisha] called Geichazi and said, "Summon this Shunamite woman."

He summoned her and she came to him. He said, "Pick up your son!"

She came and fell at his feet and bowed down to the ground; she then picked up her son and left.

(Melachim II 4:8–37)

The story has a happy ending, and on a superficial level it is simple to understand. However, if we consider the story more deeply, there are several puzzling aspects to it.

1. The Shunamite woman is called a "great woman." What was the source of her greatness?
2. If she was a "great woman," why does she remain nameless? Throughout the story she is referred to only as "the Shunamite woman."
3. The Shunamite woman stated, "I now know that he [Elisha] is a holy man of God" — how did she know?
4. Elisha was a great prophet. Yet we see no public prophecy in this chapter. In fact, throughout the story he is called "a man of God" or a "holy person," but he is not called a prophet. Was Elisha acting as a prophet, or did he play a different role in this story?
5. When Elisha asked the Shunamite woman if he could do something for her, she answered, "I dwell among my people." How does this response answer Elisha's question?
6. When the Shunamite woman's son died, why didn't she tell her husband? Why was she so secretive? And why did she run to Elisha, assuming he could revive the child?
7. Why is there no background information about this woman? We assume she wanted a child and prayed for children. In other Torah stories about barren women, most notably the stories of Sarah, Rachel, and Chanah, there is much written about their desire for children. In the story of Rivkah and Yitzchak, there is at least a verse describing their prayer for children (Bereishis 25:21). Why is there no

reference this time to the Shunamite woman's longing for a child?

Greatness

A person who is considered great or prominent by society is usually someone who possesses great wealth, power, or fame. The Shunamite woman is called a great woman. Yet there is no description of her wealth or power in this story. She and her husband appear to be well-to-do, but the wealth is her husband's, not hers per se. Her fame is nonexistent; we don't even know her name, nor is there any indication of her power. Yet she stands in the center of this chapter; her husband is merely in the wings.

Although she had no public power or fame, the Shunamite woman was the central force within her home — it was her initiative and activity that gave her home its essence. Her home was a center of dedication to good deeds and acts of kindness. The kindness that she did for Elisha became central; at the beginning of this story she changed an occasional visit by the prophet into a permanent relationship of kindness, making his visits the central focus of her home.

Why did she choose Elisha as the object of this kindness? Again, we want to define greatness. Elisha was certainly a great, notable personality. He was the number-one disciple of Eliyahu the Prophet, and he was himself a great prophet. But this was not the reason she desired to extend hospitality to him; she wanted him as a permanent guest because "I now know that he is a holy man of God." How did she recognize that this man was holy? Because of his actions? Did she intuit something?

The Gemara explains that "you learn from this that a woman recognizes the character of a guest better than a man" (*Berachos* 10b). A woman who watches her guest can intuit his character, because women have the ability to sense the internal essence of a person. They have more *binah* (intuition) than men do. Thus, the Shunamite woman knew Elisha was holy because she had the ability to see his internal essence.

Rav and Shmuel, two famous Sages of the Babylonian Talmud, each give a different explanation for her perception. Rav said she knew Elisha was holy because she never saw a fly land on his table. Shmuel said she knew he was holy because she had spread a white linen sheet on his bed, and she never saw a nocturnal emission (*Berachos* 10b). How do these opinions explain the Shunamite woman's certainty that Elisha was holy?

Rabbi Chaim Shmuelevitz (in *Sichos Mussar*) explains that holiness is something that exists in reality, but human beings do not always see it. If a person doesn't know about the existence of holiness, he may not notice it. Why? Because a prerequisite for awareness of holiness is knowledge of purity and belief in sanctity. Each person has free will to see holiness or not to see it. For instance, two people can look at a pair of tefillin. One person sees the holiness, and the second person sees only some black leather straps and boxes. One lives on a spiritual plane, and the other doesn't.

Animals, on the other hand, have no free will. A fly could sense the holiness of Elisha because that sanctity was real, it existed. A fly, like any other animal, is a simple servant of God, programmed by God to behave in a certain way. A fly in Elisha's presence would know that holiness emanated from him, and it would respond to that holiness by staying away from the prophet's table — its instinct would not allow it to tread into a sphere of holiness. The Shunamite woman observed the actions of the flies and, using her intellect, understood that Elisha was a holy man.

In Shmuel's opinion, the Shunamite woman put a white sheet on Elisha's bed and never saw a nocturnal emission. Here was a human being who had perfect bodily control, even after days of travel. The Shunamite woman understood that this was an indication of the man's high spiritual level, and from this she understood he was a *tzaddik*, a man of righteousness and holiness and purity.

When two Sages answer a question with different opinions, both answers contain different aspects of the truth. In this case, each Sage addressed a different aspect of Elisha's character. Rav's opinion explained Elisha's attainment of a high spiritual level, and Shmuel's opinion addressed Elisha's attainment of physical purity.

There is another opinion on this subject in the *Zohar* (*Beshalach* 44a) which is that in the morning, when Elisha woke up, his hostess could smell the fragrance of the Garden of Eden on his sheet. She deduced that the holiness of his Master was upon him.

It was very clear to the Shunamite woman that Elisha was a man of holiness and sanctity, and she wanted him to be a part of her home. She asked her husband to build a room for Elisha so that her home could be exposed to and affected by his holiness. She asked her husband to provide a bed, a chair, a table, and a light, because all these things were necessary for their guest, the man of God, to feel welcome and comfortable. She directed her traits of kindness and sensitivity and thoughtfulness toward this special guest, doing all that she could for him. She saw that Elisha was a very great person, and she exercised the aspects of greatness in her own personality to serve him as best she could.

Prophets and Prophecy

The sixth principle of Rambam's Thirteen Principles of Faith is "I believe with perfect faith that all the words of the prophets are true." Belief in prophecy is an article of faith because it indicates that we believe that God is involved with and concerned about His people, and that He consequently concerns Himself with our lives and provides guidance. In addition, a belief in prophecy indicates that we have faith that God is infinite and omnipotent and that He can, when He so chooses, reveal the future. Finally, faith in the words of the prophets means that we believe that God can unite Himself with the prophet's mind and communicate that which is beyond the grasp of human logic in such a way that the prophet can nevertheless reveal such knowledge.

Moshe Rabbeinu achieved prophecy on the highest level humanly possible, but there were earlier prophets, including Adam, Noach, Sheim, Eiver, and the patriarchs and matriarchs. After the revelation at Mount Sinai, there were many, many prophets.

> Yisrael had many prophets — twice the number of the people who left Egypt [which is six hundred thousand]. Why, then, are so few mentioned in Tanach? Only those prophecies relevant for all time are written. Those important only for their own generations were not recorded.
>
> (*Megillah* 14a)

Through prophecy one attains a spiritual vision of the greatness of God, His eternity, His kingdom, His independence, His unity, His holiness, and the dependence of everything on Him (Rabbi Yehudah HaLevi, the *Kuzari*). Through prophecy, God gave His people a limited understanding of Himself and His Torah. At the revelation at Sinai, the only national prophecy ever experienced by any nation, the Jewish people were themselves recipients of direct prophecy.

How did a person acquire prophecy?

In order to be a prophet, one had to attain a high level of wisdom, faith, self-control, intellect, and refined character (Rambam, *Introduction to the Mishnah*). Jews of piety, refinement, and holiness would undertake to develop these traits, but God would select only those with the natural gift of a harmonious soul and character, who were in fact able to absorb and interpret their visions (Rabbi Moshe Chaim Lutzatto, *Derech Hashem*).

In the days of prophecy, many were trained to receive prophecy, just as rabbis are trained today. These novices in prophecy were called "the sons of the prophets," and they required not only the wisdom and character traits necessary to be a prophet, but also training by an experienced prophet on how to receive prophecy and how to interpret it. (Much of the prophecy was unclear.) Eliyahyu HaNavi had many such disciples in prophecy, and his closest student was Elisha.

There were thousands of prophets who were the leaders and teachers of their time. Each city had a prophet and individuals would go to him for personal guidance. Many times, a prophet would travel from city to city, as in the case of Elisha and Eliyahu. It was customary to visit the prophet on Rosh Chodesh and Shabbos, as it is customary for many today to visit their rebbes on the holidays. (Hence the Shunamite husband's question: "Why are you going to him today? It is not Rosh Chodesh or Shabbos!")

Prophets would exhort the people to follow the word of God, and they would provide guidance regarding situations not explicit in the Torah. The prophets would advise individuals on their personal affairs or give national advice, such as when to make a political alliance or whether to go to war. Another task was to admonish the people, and the prophets would warn of future punishments that would come if the people failed to repent. Prophets would also reveal good news to come.

Prophets were able to perform miracles (although this was not a validation of prophecy) if the prophecy required such a miracle. When Eliyahu wanted to prove that only God, and not Baal, was God, he publicly performed a miraculous proof of this fact.

Since the prophets were righteous individuals, they could make requests of God that He would fulfill, since "You [the righteous person] would utter a decree and it would be fulfilled for you" (Iyov 22:28). In other words, a righteous person can make demands of God, asking either that He do something or that He refrain from doing something, and God responds.

> I rule man; who rules Me? [It is] the righteous one: for I make a decree and he [may] annul it.
>
> *(Moed Katan* 16b)

The righteous can pray to God for both individual and national blessings and they have done this throughout Jewish history. (However, there are times, obviously, when God's decree is irrevocable, and then nothing, not even the prayer of the righteous, will change the decree.)

Prophecy ended with the destruction of the First Temple, but God did not leave us empty-handed, because He gave us a second way to know Him, the way of wisdom. Wisdom functions differently from prophecy. Although prophecy is on a higher level in one sense, on another level, wisdom is more useful. The Brisker Rav explained this with a parable.

There was once a blind man who desired to enter a house. Not being able to see, he relied, as always, on his sense of touch to find the entrance door. He felt around and found an opening, but the door was so low that in order to enter, he would have to stoop down. He concluded that this was not the entrance to the house. He felt around some more, and found another opening, but this time the opening was in the middle of a wall, and he would have to climb onto a chair in order to enter the house. He concluded that this was also not the entrance to the house. He continued his search until he found some steps which led to the roof. But once again, using his logic, he deduced that these steps did not lead to the main entrance. Finding no other possibilities, he concluded that the most logical entrance was the first one he had felt, even though it was much lower than a regular entranceway. As he finished his analysis, a seeing man approached, quickly assessed the situation, and saw with total clarity that the door to the house was indeed the low one.

In the parable, the seeing man is a prophet. Receiving the light of God's communication, he "sees" the truth clearly, even though, logically, the truth might make no sense (why would anyone live in a house with a doorway that a person has to stoop to enter?). The blind man is the Torah scholar who feels his way around until, using human logic, he draws conclusions. Now, if one lives in a house that is lit up, it is easier to function if one can see. But if one lives in a dark environment, the blind man has an advantage over the seeing, for he is trained in sensory perception and logic, and he is able to make abstract and concrete deductions (whereas the seeing man would encounter difficulties in such a dark environment).

After the revelation at Mount Sinai, prophecy existed for over one thousand years. When the Temple was destroyed and prophecy came to an end, the period of exile, which is likened to darkness, began. In order to connect with God, the men of God had to rely on wisdom, as per the Brisker Rav's parable. Men of wisdom had to use human logic to plumb the depths of Torah knowledge, relying heavily on past prophets and scholars and using the thirteen hermeneutic principles which were given by God as the means of expounding Torah. In addition, they had to know how to convey this wisdom to others. These great scholars were able, through intense learning and spiritual development, to establish an intimate connection with God that surpasses logic and philosophic mediation.

Since the end of prophecy, we rely on Torah scholars and *gedolim* (men of wisdom, purity, and holiness) to guide us because we have become like weak-eyed people who are unable to bear the brightness of direct light and must depend on those with sharp eyes. Similarly, we rely on the prophets who lived before us and were able to receive the direct Divine light (*Kuzari*). Just as the Jewish people relied on prophets to guide them in the days of the judges and the First Temple, so too do we rely on our *gedolim*, our great Torah scholars, to guide us today.

"I Dwell Among My People"

Elisha was grateful for the Shunamite woman's hospitality, and he offered to pray for her in return. This is understandable, but the Shunamite's response is not as easy to comprehend.

> He [Elisha] then said to [Geichazi], "Please say to her, 'You have undertaken all this exertion on our behalf — what [favor] can be done for you? Can something be said on your behalf to the king or the army commander?"
>
> She replied, "I dwell among my people."

The Shunamite woman did not respond with a request or by stating that she had no request. In a refined way, she was saying, "As long as I am among the Jewish people, I need nothing. My people are here, and I dwell with them."

This was another aspect of her greatness. Identification with the community is extremely important for a Jew. If his community is in a state of rejoicing, he should feel the joy. If his community is in a state of pain, he should experience the pain. A person of stature includes himself among the Jewish people, and their position defines his very emotional state.

The *Zohar* (1:69b) tells us that this conversation took place on Rosh HaShanah. When Elisha inquired if he could speak to the "king" for her, he meant the King of Kings. Elisha was asking, "Is there something that I can ask of God for you? Is there some need of yours? I'm willing to make a personal prayer for you, to intercede for you for a separate judgment from the rest of the Jewish people." Her answer was that her place was among her people. Whatever God intended for all of Israel should be intended for her as well (*Malbim*).

This is amazing. After all, she was a barren woman. We

must assume that she desired a child, as most women do.

Yet she had never asked Elisha to pray that she should have a child, and did not ask him now, although it was the perfect opportunity. Surely Elisha knew she lacked a child. He had been her guest many times. Perhaps he had been waiting for her to approach him with this matter first. But she never had, and she did not do so now. A person who believes very strongly in God understands that whatever God does is for the best, even when it is very painful. The Shunamite woman had made peace with her life, so much so that when asked what she lacked, she had no request to make. She had accepted life's disappointments to the point that she no longer thought of them as setbacks; she had moved on and accepted her childlessness. Therefore, it didn't occur to her to ask the holy prophet for a miracle. She had found peace and fulfillment in her role as a member of the Jewish people, as a person who did mitzvos and *chesed*, as a seeker of holiness, and as a promoter of acts of kindness within her home and her community.

The Promise

Elisha, however, did not drop the matter.

> So he [Elisha] said [to Geichazi], "What can be done for her?"
>
> Geichazi said, "Actually, she has no child, and her husband is old."
>
> He said, "Summon her." He summoned her, and she stood in the doorway. [Elisha] said, "At this season next year you will be embracing a son."

When God made a miracle for Sarah and Avraham and gave them a child in their old age, angels were sent with the news, but the promise was from God. Rachel prayed to God and He answered; Chanah prayed to God and again He answered. Here, on the other hand, Elisha, a human being, promised to do a miracle, something completely above nature.

> You [the righteous person] would utter a decree, and it would be fulfilled for you and light would shine upon your ways.
>
> (Iyov 22:28)

God fulfills the requests of the righteous. Despite the Shunamite woman's reticence about asking for a child, Elisha took it upon himself to promise her a son. Her response, however, is quite surprising: She said, "Do not, my master, O man of God, do not disappoint your maidservant!"

Hundreds of years earlier, when Sarah heard the news that she would finally have a child, she laughed. But here in Shuneim, there is no joy, no laughter, not even doubt. Rather, there is tremendous hesitation. We assume that the Shunamite woman had prayed to God, begged for a child, and suffered when her prayers were not answered. True, she had overcome her inner pain, and instead of bitterness and melancholy she had focused her energy on a spiritual devotion to mitzvos. Her mitzvos and good deeds had become her children. Nevertheless, when the prophet came and rocked the foundation of her world by promising a child, renewing her hope, we would expect her to react with joy and animation. Instead, she reacted with caution. Why?

Although the blessing of the prophet was miraculous, it was not a complete blessing, and the Shunamite woman sensed this. Elisha said that the next year she would embrace a child. When Sarah was told that she would finally become a mother, the language was different:

> And he said, "I will surely return to you at this time next year, and behold Sarah your wife will have a son."
>
> (Bereishis 18:10)

The Shunamite woman was told she would embrace a son, not that she would have a son. In other words, she would get to embrace a child, but perhaps he would have no permanent existence. Rashi explains how she understood this:

> "Do not show me something that will cease to exist. It is in your hands to ask for mercy, but please do not give me anything except for a child that will live."

Her reaction was founded on her justifiable fear that this child would never live. Perhaps she had already had a child and lost him. (According to some, including Radak, her first son was Ido, the prophet who was killed by a lion [Melachim I 13:24–31].) Maybe she felt that even a prophet could not promise something that God doesn't want. Somehow she knew that this child who was promised to her might not live.

The Test

The Shunamite woman gave birth to a son, exactly as Elisha had said. The child grew, and there came a day when his mother released him to his father's custody. The child went out to the field, but he began to sicken as soon as he left his mother's home. He cried, "My head! My head!" and was rushed home to his mother. She held him in her arms, and soon afterwards he died.

At this point, we can see that there are two cycles in the life of the Shunamite woman. The beginning of the first cycle is not described, but we assume she was barren and that she had suffered from her childlessness. (We derive this assumption from her reaction to Elisha's promise, a reaction of vulnerability, as if Elisha had opened up an old wound.) The first cycle consists of the pain of barrenness, this pain being surmounted as the Shunamite woman filled her life with good deeds and made her home a place of holiness with Elisha as its central focus, and the cycle ending with a reward from God, the reward of a son. Had this been the end of the story, there would be a clear moral, a religious message. However, there is a second cycle, which makes the message much different.

The second cycle begins with the death of the beloved son, and raises questions of Divine justice and Divine intervention. Why did the Shunamite woman's child die? Why was the prophet's promise not fulfilled in a lasting way? Didn't the Shunamite woman beg Elisha not to disappoint her? We are not given answers, but what stands out is that the Shunamite woman withstood a great test — the test of questioning Divine judgment.

This story is reminiscent of the test given to Avraham — *akeidas Yitzchak*. Avraham was told to take his child, his only child, the child he and Sarah had longed for, and sacrifice him on an altar. Avraham did take Yitzchak and bound him on the altar, thus withstanding the test. Sarah, on the other hand, died when she heard of the test. Yet the Shunamite woman was able to face a terribly painful situation and triumph.

What was specific about the Shunamite woman's test? This was a test of her faith in the prophet and his prophecy. The death of her son destroyed her motherhood. It brought fear; it brought a broken heart. Underlying these feelings, there was a possible threat to her faith. She had believed in the prophet and she had pleaded with him not to disappoint her. The child had been given and then he died; the promise was broken. How would she react? Would this be a crisis of faith for her?

There was to be no crisis of faith. In fact, the Shunamite woman seems to have been strengthened by this test. She saddled her donkey herself (reminiscent of Avraham saddling his own donkey to take Yitzchak to the *akeidah*) and hurried to the prophet. At this point, she acted in a strong and powerful manner. She told her husband all was well, and when Elisha sent Geichazi to greet her, she told him, too, that all was well. Her child was lying dead in her home, but she remain composed, in control, with a strong conviction about how the matter must be handled. She was not even shaken by the fact that Elisha the Prophet had no idea of what had happened, that God had hidden it from him. She made her way to Elisha, grabbed hold of his legs, and confronted him:

"Did I request a son of my master? Did I not say, 'Do not mislead me?' "

This is not really a question. If she entertained a true question, real doubt, she would not have run to the prophet to ask him to save her child. If she doubted the ability of the prophet, if she doubted his greatness and his connection to God, she wouldn't have bothered. So this was not a question; it was a demand that the prophet save her child. It was a renewal of her faith, a demand for another miracle, a demand for a revelation through the hands of this man of God.

From the moment her calamity began, from the moment her son died in her arms, she knew what she was going to do. There was never a moment's hesitation or doubt. She did not tell her husband or her household about her son's death; she said everything was fine. The Shunamite woman's faith in God and in His prophet was very much intact, and she knew that if she wanted another miracle, she had to keep everything secret and private. If she made her situation public, the miracle would never happen.

The encounter with Elisha was a very deep, personal, religious moment, between the Shunamite woman, God, and the prophet, who was the messenger of God. The Shunamite woman did not for a moment cease to believe in the prophet. She told her husband and Geichazi that all was well, because from her point of view, as far as she was concerned, all *was* well. The onus was on the prophet; he had promised her a child and he therefore had to give her a child.

Elisha's initial reaction was to have his servant, Geichazi, perform the miracle like a mechanical action. He instructed Geichazi to take his staff and put it on the child, with no personal involvement by the prophet. But the Shunamite woman refused to let him go. She was aware that he, Elisha, was the man of God, the holy one, and Geichazi was not. Elisha therefore returned home with her and performed the miracle in two parts. First he prayed to God for a resurrection, knowing that a person must make every human effort and then rely on God's intervention. Then he lay down on the boy to bring him back to life, putting his eyes on the boy's eyes, his mouth on his mouth, his hands on his hands. In so doing, Elisha both warmed the body of the child and attempted to breathe life into him, knowing that it was totally up to God to resurrect the child. Perhaps this indicates Elisha's identification with the child. Just as we, when we daven for a sick loved one, put ourselves in the place of the pain of that person, so Elisha did. He used no staff, no tool; he used himself and made a direct connection with the child.

And the procedure worked. The child returned to life. The gratitude of the Shunamite woman was inexpressible — there were no words. She merely bowed and fell at his feet, her heart full of thanks. This *techiyas hameisim* (resurrection) was the reward for her unshakable faith in God, in Torah, and in the prophet Elisha (*Meshech Chochmah, parashas Vayeira*).

And thus ended the second cycle of the life of the Shunamite woman. In the first cycle she was denied children and experienced pain; she overcame her emptiness by filling her life with mitzvos; and she was rewarded with a child. In the second cycle, she again first experienced pain, the death of her child; she surmounted that pain by strengthening her faith in God's judgment and in His prophets; and she was rewarded with the resurrection of her son. Two cycles, very similar, but with different messages.

The Shunamite Woman

The Shunamite woman was called a great woman because she trusted God. When God withheld children, she did not lose faith or question His judgment. When she was not able to do the mitzvos that a mother can do, she turned her energies toward those mitzvos that God granted her the opportunity to perform. She became a master of hospitality, a person who was kind and sensitive to the needs of her guests. She set a tone of holiness in her home, and created an environment of spirituality and good deeds. In addition, she attached herself to her people, to *klal Yisrael*. The Shunamite woman's acceptance of God was so tremendous that she felt as though she lacked nothing. She had an unshakable belief in God's messengers, the prophets, and in prophecy.

Why, then, did the Shunamite woman remain nameless in the Tanach? Perhaps her anonymity teaches us that Elisha came to stay with her not because of her name, her position, or her wealth, but because of who she was internally. Perhaps she remained nameless because of her humility and modesty. She didn't need to be famous, to have the miracles done for her publicized. Her life, her essence, was about serving God, and perhaps a name would be too limiting, too defining, too external to express the intensity of her faith and her attachment to Him.

The *Zohar* says that the Shunamite woman's child was Chavakuk (*Zohar* 1:7b). Chavakuk became a great prophet during the time of the wicked King Menasheh (*Seder Olam* 20).

> Six hundred and thirteen commandments were communicated to Moshe at Sinai. Chavakuk came and based them all on one principle: "The righteous shall live by his faith" (Chavakuk 2:4).
>
> (*Makkos* 24a)

Chavakuk was an outgrowth of his mother's faith. His name comes from the root *chovek* (embrace), since the prophet

Elisha told the Shunamite woman that she would "embrace a child." But there was a second embrace — that of Elisha when he resurrected that child. Chavakuk is named after two hugs, that of his mother and that of the prophet (*Zohar* 1:7b).

The Shunamite woman is not nameless after all. Her name is in her child, in her future. Her importance is as an individual who had faith in God and who built her life around that faith. Her child is the reflection of her greatness and of her strength.

What's in a name? Everything.

Men and Women

Women:
Bridging Heaven and Earth

(Parts I and II are based on a *shiur* I heard
from HaRav Chaim Goldvicht, *zt"l*.)

In the world we live in, some areas of knowledge are held sacrosanct despite evidence of error and revision. However, true wisdom, found in our written and oral Torah, is often misunderstood and thought to be old fashioned. Without the proper tools to analyze and comprehend the Divine word, the lessons of the Torah can, in fact, be misinterpreted. For example, the Gemara lists a number of qualities that descended to the world. Among them is this:

> Ten measures of speech descended to the world. Women took nine of them.
>
> (*Kiddushin* 49a)

What does the Gemara mean by "measures of speech," and why do women have so many more measures of speech than men? Is this a criticism of women?

As is so often the case, our Sages cannot be understood after a simple reading of their words and it is necessary to look more deeply into this concept. By examining three prototypes of women, we will attempt to unlock the secret of the Talmud's statement about speech and reveal that our Sages were speaking of a unique gift which God gave to Jewish women in order to enhance their strength and leadership. What may superficially appear to be criticism is actually a highlighting of the virtue of the Jewish woman.

Sarah

> Sarah died in Kiryas Arba, which is Chevron, in the land of Canaan. Avraham came to eulogize Sarah and to cry for her.... He spoke to [the children of Cheis], saying, "If it is truly your will to bury my dead from before me, heed me, and intercede for me with Efron son of Tzochar. Let him grant me the Cave of Machpeilah which is his, on the edge of his field; let him grant it to me for its full price, in your midst, as an estate for a burial site."...
> Efron's field...and the cave within it...was confirmed as Avraham's, as a purchase in the view of the children of Cheis, among all who came to the gate of his city. And afterwards Avraham buried Sarah, his wife, in the cave of the field of Machpeilah.
> (Bereishis 23:2, 8–9, 17–19)

After Sarah died, Avraham bought burial land — the Cave of Machpeilah in Chevron. At her burial, Avraham eulogized Sarah, who was his beloved wife and life partner. *Midrash Tanchuma* (*Chayei Sarah* 4) tells us that this eulogy was recorded in Mishlei (31:10–31), in the passage which begins with the familiar words "a woman of valor, who will find?"

Each verse in this passage applies to something specific that Sarah did in her lifetime.

Avraham began to cry over her, "A woman of valor who can find? Her husband's heart trusted her" (Mishlei

31:10–11). When [did he trust her]? When he said to her, "Please say you are my sister" (Bereishis 12:13).

"She treats him well, never poorly, all the days of her life. She searches for wool and flax" (Mishlei 31:12–13). [This refers to when Sarah differentiated] between Yitzchak and Yishmael, when she said, "Banish this maidservant and her son" (Bereishis 21:10).

"She is like a merchant's ship" (Mishlei 31:14) [refers to] "The woman was taken to Pharaoh's palace" (Bereishis 12:15) and "Avimelech sent..." (Bereishis 20:2).

"She rises before dawn" (Mishlei 31:15). When? "Avraham rose early in the morning" (Bereishis 22:3).

"She negotiated for a field and bought it" (Mishlei 31:16). She negotiated and bought the field of Machpeilah and there she was buried, as it says, "Afterwards, Avraham buried Sarah" (Bereishis 23:19).

(Midrash Tanchuma, Chayei Sarah 4)

Sarah is credited with the acquisition of the field of Machpeilah, and yet it is clear from the detailed description above that it was Avraham who negotiated, purchased, and acquired the field. Sarah had already passed away at the time of this acquisition. Why does the *midrash* assign the purchase of Machpeilah to Sarah, when she actually had nothing to do with it? In order to answer this question, it is necessary to understand exactly what the Cave of Machpeilah is and what Chevron is, not in terms of their geographic location, but in terms of their spiritual significance. Every city in Israel has a spiritual energy and potential. By identifying the specific quality of the Cave of Machpeilah and Chevron, we can understand why the *midrash* attributes its purchase to Sarah.

The first clue of the significance of Chevron is found in the story of Yosef. Yaakov sent Yosef to the field where his brothers were herding their sheep. When the brothers saw Yosef, they discussed killing him, but instead decided to sell him. He was taken down to Egypt, and thus began the Egyptian exile.

[Yaakov] said to [Yosef], "Go now, look into the welfare of your brothers and the welfare of the flock, and bring me back word." He sent him from the valley of Chevron, and he arrived at Shechem.

(Bereishis 37:14)

The language of this verse is puzzling because it refers to "the valley of Chevron," and Chevron is actually a mountain! Rashi explains:

> Was not Chevron situated on a hill, as it says, "And they went *up* in the south and they came to Chevron" (Bemidbar 13:22)? Why then does it state that Yaakov sent him from the valley, the deep part, of Chevron? Yaakov sent him because of the need to bring into operation the deep thought of the righteous man [Avraham] who was buried in Chevron, in order to fulfill the words spoken to Avraham when the covenant was made between the parts: "Your children shall be strangers..." (Bereishis 15:13).

The key to Rashi's explanation is the word *valley*. In Hebrew, a valley is called an *emek*. Etymologically, *emek* is rooted in the word *amok* (deep), since a valley is a deep space carved out between mountains. Chevron is called a valley, "deep," because of a deep and profound prophecy that was given to Avraham, who is buried there.

Rashi, then, does not read this verse as "the valley of Chevron," because it is not a valley. Rather, he reads it as "the depths of Chevron," meaning the deep wisdom given to Avraham, who was buried in the cave. The deep wisdom is the prophecy of the exile, the prophecy that the Jewish people would descend to Egypt and be strangers there. This exile began with the sale of Yosef.

A righteous person must be buried in a place suitable for his spiritual achievements, and the burials of our matriarchs and patriarchs are therefore described by the Torah in great detail. By defining Chevron in terms of Avraham's burial there, Rashi is telling us something important about Chevron. There is something very spiritually deep about Chevron, and, therefore, only an individual of extraordinary righteousness can be buried there. And if this is true of Avraham, it is all the more so true of Sarah, because the cave was acquired for Sarah's burial.

The word *Chevron* comes from the Hebrew word *chibur*, which means connection (*Zohar, Shelach*). (Similarly, *chaver* is a friend, someone connected heart to heart. *Chavrusa* is a learning partner.) Chevron, then, is a place of connection — but what does it connect?

> [Avraham] ran to bring a calf, and the calf fled from him and entered the Cave of Machpeilah. [Avraham] entered after it and saw Adam and Chavah lying on beds and sleeping with candles lit all around them, and [there was] a pleasant smell around them like the sweet smell [of sacrifices]. Therefore, he desired the Cave of Machpeilah as a burial crypt.
>
> (*Pirkei d'Rabbi Eliezer* 36)

In Midrash, sheep and cattle are always an allusion to something spiritual. Avraham finding the calf in the cave is an allusion to his discovery of a spiritual secret. The cave is no ordinary cave; it has a spiritual connection.

Inside this cave, the burial place of Adam and Chavah, Avraham found an incredible scene, for when he entered the cave, the entrance to the Garden of Eden opened for him. Every entrance connects two different spaces, the outside world and the inside one. This is how Avraham understood that this was a unique place, a place that connects the world of the physical with the world of the spiritual. This was the opening to Gan Eden, the connection between this world and the next world, between temporal life and eternal life (*Sheim MiShmuel, Chayei Sarah*).

When Avraham discovered the cave, he understood its significance. It was for this reason that he sought to purchase the cave as a burial place for Sarah, for this place, the place of connection, was particularly suited to Sarah.

The name of the cave is also instructive. The word *machpeilah* comes from the Hebrew word for "double." Doubles, that is, pairs, were buried in this cave: Adam and Chavah, Avraham and Sarah, Yitzchak and Rivkah, Yaakov and Leah (*Eruvin* 53a). What is the nature of these "doubles"?

Our Sages teach: "A man and a woman who merit it will have between them the Divine Presence" (*Sotah* 17a). In the marital relationship, when there is connection between husband and wife, God is present as well. The word for man, *ish*, is spelled *alef yud shin*. The word for woman, *isha*, is spelled *alef shin hei*. They both contain the letters *alef* and *shin*, which together spell fire. On the other hand, the word *ish* contains a *yud*, whereas the word *isha* contains a *hei*, and together these spell one of God's names (*Rashi*).

The letter *yud* represents the world of the spiritual, and the letter *hei* represents the world of the physical (*Menachos* 29b). Marriage is a union in both a spiritual and a physical way, and the husband and wife who function on a level of physical and emotional intimacy, connecting with God, merit God's Presence. When the man and woman disconnect themselves from God, the letters of His name are taken away, leaving the letters common to both man and woman: *alef* and *shin*, fire. Therefore, a marriage without God's Presence will be a fiery, unstable connection, whereas a marriage that includes serving God will result in spiritual and physical integration.

The couples buried in Chevron forged marriages that represented the total integration of a spiritual and physical connection, and they thereby brought God's Presence into the world and merited burial in a place of connection.

Interestingly, Avraham said of Sarah, "She is like a merchant's ship." When was Sarah like a merchant's ship? When "the woman was taken to Pharaoh's palace."

> God said to Avram, "Go for yourself from your land...to the land that I will show you".... So Avram went as God had spoken to him.... Avram took his wife Sarai.... There was a famine in the land, and Avram descended to Egypt to sojourn there, for the famine was severe in the land....
> (Bereishis, 12:1–5, 10)

God told Avraham (known then as "Avram") to leave his homeland and all that he knew and travel to a new place. Soon after he arrived at this new place, the Land of Israel, God brought a famine, forcing him to go to Egypt. Why? There was something Avraham had to get from Egypt, something he needed before he could live successfully in Israel. He was sent to Egypt to acquire an item, a skill, something he could only learn there.

> When the officials of Pharaoh saw [Sarah], they lauded her for Pharaoh, and the woman was taken to Pharaoh's house.
> (Ibid., 15)

Sarah, being a very beautiful woman, was taken into the house of Pharaoh, the king of Egypt. Pharaoh, however, presumably already had a harem. Sarah was not a young woman, so it's difficult to believe Pharaoh needed her simply as another pretty face. What was it, then, about Sarah that he really wanted?

Egypt was the capital of the material world, a world of hedonism, promiscuity, and physicality. Pharaoh was the king of this very materialistic society, and he was dedicated to its value system. The philosophy of materialism was his belief, yet he retained an interest in learning about the philosophies of others.

Avraham, on the other hand, was a proponent of monotheism and indeed expounded this philosophy wherever he went. He was a believer in the spiritual, and a master of extremely deep concepts. So Pharaoh and Avraham were adherents of philosophies that were the total opposite of each other, but each one was a leader of stature, and each was to learn something from the other. Pharaoh would learn about the God of Avraham, about the spiritual underpinning of the world. And Avraham would learn about the system of Egypt, about materialism and physicality.

How could this interaction take place? Pharaoh, steeped in his world of materialism, had no training, no "language," to understand Avraham's spiritual approach to life. Likewise, Avraham, whose life was dedicated to service of God, to giving to others, had little understanding of the material world which was Pharaoh's domain. If they were to share information, what "language" would they speak? Pharaoh would be speaking the language of the physical, the material, the solid, the grounded, and Avraham would be speaking a different language altogether. There would be no common ground. Therefore, an interpreter was required, someone who could speak both languages, someone who understood the physical world as well as the spiritual world. That person would need to be able to translate idioms, expressions, philosophies — and that person was Sarah.

Sarah understood both worlds and knew both languages. Pharaoh took her because she was like "the merchant's boat." Like a boat that takes merchandise from one continent, transfers it to another, and returns with more merchandise, Sarah brought "merchandise" from Pharaoh to Avraham, and back again. She knew the world of the spiritual and could translate it into the world of the physical for Pharaoh, and she understood that the physical could be translated to the spiritual for Avraham. Sarah was the connection, *chibur*, between Pharaoh's world and Avraham's, between the physical and the spiritual. She represented efficient functioning in this world, but in a very spiritual way.

What tool did Sarah use to interpret? The power of speech. Speech is the seam between the physical and spiritual (*Maharal, Gevuros Hashem* 5:28). Speech is the means of connection, *chibur*, between these two worlds. Speech translates an idea, a feeling, an emotion, into physical reality.

Sarah had more speech than Avraham. When she told Avraham to banish Yishmael and Avraham didn't want to do it, God told him to "listen to her voice." The Sages teach us that Sarah was a greater prophet than Avraham (*Rashi*, Bereishis 21:12). A prophet is someone who communicates with God, bringing a spiritual message down into this very physical world. In order to communicate, the prophet needs the power of speech; speech is the tool of the trade (*Sheim MiShmuel, Chayei Sarah* 5671). Since Sarah was able to bridge the spiritual and physical worlds, Pharaoh took her into his palace to translate Avraham's philosophy for him.

God brought a famine to Israel as soon as Avraham arrived there, because He desired to have Avraham go down to Egypt and acquire something there. That something was contact with the physical world.

The world of Torah requires a physical world in a very real sense. Everything in the physical world has potential for spiritual elevation. The job of the Torah Jew is to find the spiritual core of the physical world and use it. Every mitzvah is connected to the physical — putting on tefillin, using the *mikvah*, and praying all require us to use our bodies. Mitzvos entail eating and drinking and taking pleasure from the physical, while elevating the action to a level of spirituality.

God sent Avraham down to Egypt because He wanted him to see and experience a physical world, to know what materialism truly is. He was then supposed to bring this knowledge back to the Land of Israel, which is the place of ultimate physical and spiritual interaction. For example, the water supply in Israel depends on rain. But rain is solely dependent on our observance of mitzvos; if we do not serve God properly, He withholds the rain. The farmer plows and plants, prunes and harvests, but without rain nothing will grow. Though he must labor, his work is for naught without the blessing of rain. Another example can be found in the laws of *shemittah*, refraining from working the land in the seventh year. Israel was created in such a way that built into the land, programmed into the earth, is a mechanism that detects *shemittah* observance. If a Jew lives in Israel and allows the land to rest in the seventh year, the land will nevertheless produce enough food. This "miracle" is part of the nature of the land. The spiritual triggers the physical.

Avraham wasn't going to be able to live in Israel effectively without an understanding of the physical world and how it works. Avraham grew up outside the Land of Israel — could he have not received his education of the material in his hometown of Ur Kasdim? Not at the deepest level. Egypt was the quintessence of materialism, the prototype for it. Avraham needed to absorb the understanding of it specifically there.

Avraham's sojourn in Egypt was a success. Sarah, as the connection between the two worlds, facilitated Avraham's encounter with Pharaoh. When they left Egypt, the Torah tells us that they took with them much sheep and cattle:

> [Pharaoh] treated Avram well because of her [Sarah], and he acquired sheep, cattle, donkeys, slaves and maidservants, female donkeys, and camels.
> (Bereishis 12:16)

The sheep and cattle represent a grasp of the physical world and knowledge of how to use it and elevate it to its spiritual level. These cattle and sheep came to Avraham "because of her."

Now we understand Avraham's eulogy for Sarah, and why he desired to purchase the Cave of Machpeilah in Chevron for her. Sarah lived a life of bridging. She knew how to connect the physical and spiritual worlds, and, therefore, Avraham knew that Chevron was the appropriate burial place for her. Chevron, which means connection, was negotiated for Sarah, whose life was one of connection, *chibur.*

Why does the Midrash say that Sarah "negotiated and purchased the field of Machpeilah"? Because in living the life she did, she earned the right to be buried there. Though she did not literally buy the cave, she indeed acquired it with the merit of her righteousness and connection.

The Righteous Women in Egypt

Just as Avraham was sent down to Egypt to acquire something he needed in order to live in Israel, so, too, the Jewish people were sent into the Egyptian exile for a purpose. There was something that was needed from there in order to get to Sinai, in order to receive the Torah, and the people could not leave until it was acquired. And just as Sarah lived her life bridging and integrating the physical and the spiritual, so, too, did the Jewish women in the Egyptian exile.

> The Israelites were delivered from Egypt as a reward for the righteous women who lived in that generation. When they went to draw water, the Holy One, blessed be He, arranged that small fish should enter their pitchers, which they drew up half full of water and half full of fish. They then set two pots on the fire, one for hot water and the other for the fish, which they carried to their husbands in the field. They washed them, anointed them, fed them, gave them to drink, and were intimate with them among the sheepfolds, as it says, "When you lie among the sheepfolds..." (Tehillim 68:14). As the reward for "when

you lie among the sheepfolds," the Israelites merited the spoils of the Egyptians.

(*Sotah* 11b)

Pharaoh's plan was to separate the Jewish family and thereby destroy *Yiddishkeit*. He knew that the basis of Torah is the Jewish family, so he sent the men to live in the fields while the women were to stay at home. The women, however, found a way around this plan. They would meet their husbands in the field to be with them in intimacy and love. They would join them in the sheepfolds, which were private and fenced in. Because of this, the whole Jewish people was rewarded with deliverance.

This Gemara, however, raises many questions. How could the entire redemption rest on the women who brought food and water to their husbands in the field? This seems to be a disproportionately huge reward for an apparently simple, albeit loving, action.

In addition, the *midrash* begins by saying that the Israelites were "delivered" from Egypt as the reward for the righteous women, but at the end of the passage we read that their reward was the spoils of Egypt — which was it, spoliation or redemption?

Another problem: The enslavement in Egypt was not a punishment for Israel, but rather it was an experience that was necessary to bring the people to holiness. When the Jewish people completed their "studies" in Egypt, they would be free to go. Why, then, are the women given credit for the redemption?

We have yet another problem. Avraham had been promised that his children would be in exile, and he had also been promised that they would be redeemed.

> God said to Avram, "Know with surety that your children shall be strangers in a land that is not theirs, and they shall serve them. They shall afflict them for four hundred years.

Also against that nation whom they shall serve will I pronounce judgment; and afterwards they shall come out with great acquisition."

(Bereishis 15:13–14)

God Himself had promised to redeem the Jewish people, so why are the women given the credit? Furthermore, God promised the children of Israel that they would come out of Egypt with great acquisition, yet the *midrash* credits the women for this achievement. This is very puzzling. What did those women do that was so unique? What did the women give to the men that they would not have had otherwise?

Finally, when the children of Israel left Egypt, they took much booty (see Shemos 12:35–36). They were headed for the Sinai Desert, for the revelation of God's Torah. What need did they have of gold and silver? Surely they were not enslaved for 210 years in order to be enriched with material goods. Surely this acquisition represents something far more important.

In Jerusalem of old, as in the shtetl of Europe, when a little boy would reach the age of three, his father would come home from shul after the morning prayers and wrap the young boy in his tallis. Covering the boy from head to foot, the father would carry him through the streets of Jerusalem to the cheder. At the cheder, the father would sit the boy on a bench in front of a table with a *chumash* and a bit of honey on it. The father would then unwrap the tallis, and the first thing the child would see of the world outside of his mother's home was the Torah. He would taste the honey and know that the Torah is sweet.

The message to the child was *As you leave your mother's home, which is a world of spirituality, love, and Torah, I don't want you to see the outside world. I don't want you to see what goes on in the streets, in the stores, or in the businesses. I'm bringing you to a place of spirituality, the cheder, so that you know that the Torah is sweet.* In other words, the child should not look at the physical;

he should continue to look to the spiritual.

Going down to Egypt meant the exact opposite. The job of the Jewish people was to go down into the physical world, a world of materialism, the capital of promiscuity. See it, taste it, feel it, sink into it — even get stuck in it — so that when they emerged from it, they would have a deep understanding of the physical world. The job of the matriarchs and patriarchs of the Jewish people, as well as our job today, was to take the physical world around us and elevate it to spirituality. This work is called *chibur*, connection.

Everything created in this physical world is created to serve God. "Everything [God created] He created for His honor" (*Kesubos* 8a). There is nothing intrinsically negative in the physical world; it is all meant to be a vehicle with which we serve God. But a person has the free will to elevate it or to use it to degrade himself. A person can make kiddush over a cup of wine and drink it as a way of connecting to God, thereby sanctifying God's name, or he can gulp the wine down to "get high."

The lesson that the Jews needed to learn in Egypt was that the physical world must be understood and appreciated as a vehicle for connecting to the spiritual. This is the function of a mitzvah — for example, when a person takes a *lulav* and *esrog*, physical instruments, and shakes them, he is transforming those physical objects into instruments for holiness and spirituality. This is the job of the Jewish people.

Egypt was the place of complete physicality, of terrible environmental influence. It was steeped in idol worship and in promiscuity. God commanded the Jewish people to sacrifice the paschal lamb, which was the object of Egyptian idol worship. The Jews were commanded to eat it until nothing remained (Shemos 12:10). If any was left, it was to be burned. The message is clear: Nothing in the physical world is bad; nothing is unusable for the service of God. Even something connected to idol worship could be used, in its entirety, for service of God.

What determines whether the physical world is positive or negative? How we use it, what we do with it, and what our intention is. An object used in a proper way, but with wrong intentions, isn't holy. The same object used with a proper intention is elevated. This was the message the women gave to the men, and this was the message that the Jewish people needed to take with them out of Egypt.

Pharaoh's decree to separate husband and wife was designed to destroy the Jewish people by depriving them of a physical home. The women, however, refused to accept this decree. They decided that if they could not have a physical home with four walls around it, they would create a home in the field. They would prepare food and drink and bring it out to the field, recreating the environment of a home. They would use the physical world and the physical relationship to create spirituality, love, and intimacy. God Himself helped them — when the women drew water from the Nile to bathe their husbands, God sent fish with which to feed them as well. The women would cook the fish, warm the water, and bring Godliness to their homes in the sheepfolds. In so doing, the women kept up the morale of their husbands, but more than that, they taught them what the physical world is really about and how it must be used to serve God.

When the Sages used the sexual relationship between husband and wife as a metaphor for holiness, they did so because it is very powerful imagery. The physical relationship can be brought to an animalistic, degrading level, but it is also possible to use that relationship for holiness. In marriage, intimacy brings *Shechinah* into the home, uniting the *yud* and the *hei*. Using love and kindness, the righteous women in Egypt not only recreated the Jewish home in the fields, but they empowered the men, as well, preparing them to receive the Torah.

The first mitzvah the Jews were told to perform after receiving the Torah was the building of the Mishkan, the Tabernacle. The gold and silver taken from Egypt as spoils were used to create a spiritual and holy sanctuary. Thus, the Tabernacle became the representation of the lessons learned in the sheepfolds — elevate the physical to serve God.

Significantly, one of the vessels of the Mishkan, the laver, was made of mirrors donated exclusively by the women.

> [Betzalel] made the laver of copper, and the frame of it of copper, out of the mirrors of the women assembling, who assembled at the entrance of the appointed tent.
>
> (Shemos 38:8)

> The Israelite women possessed mirrors of copper which they used to look into when they adorned themselves. Even these they did not hesitate to bring as a contribution to the Tabernacle. Moshe was about to reject them since they were made to pander to their vanity, but the Holy One, blessed be He, said to him, "Accept them! These are dearer to Me than all the other contributions because through them the women reared those huge hosts in Egypt!"
>
> When their husbands were tired because of the crushing labor, [the women] used to bring them food and drink and induce them to eat. Then they would take the mirrors, and each gazed at herself in her mirror together with her husband, saying endearingly to him, "See, I am handsomer than you!" Thus they awakened their husbands' affection and subsequently became the mothers of many children, as it says, "I awakened thy love under the apple tree" (Shir HaShirim 8:5), referring to the fields where the men worked. This is what it refers to when it states, "the mirrors of the women assembling." [These words can be translated as "the mirrors of the women who reared the hosts."] It was for this reason that the laver was made of them.
>
> (*Rashi*, Shemos 38:8)

The laver was placed near the entrance of the Tabernacle,

the place that connected the outside world to the inner sanctum. The *kohanim* (priests) used the laver to wash their hands and feet, thus purifying themselves for the service of God.

God told Moshe that the mirrors were dearer to Him than anything else, because through their use the women propagated the family in Egypt; they created children with those mirrors. Why did Moshe need to be told to accept the mirrors? Because Moshe didn't understand their importance. Significantly, for Moshe, language was difficult.

> Moshe replied to God, "Please, my Lord, I am not a man of words, not since yesterday, nor since the day before yesterday, nor since You first spoke to Your servant, for I am heavy of mouth and heavy of speech."
>
> (Shemos 4:10)

Moshe lived in the world of the spiritual; he walked in Heaven among the angels. He spoke to God, but he lacked the words, the language, required to connect the spiritual to the physical. This was the one thing Moshe could not do (Aharon filled this role for him). The women, on the other hand, knew how to connect the physical and spiritual through their copper mirrors and through speaking to their husbands. They transformed ordinary, mundane, material substances into tools for serving God.

God's warm acceptance of the women's mirrors was a validation of their integrity and purity of purpose. When the *kohanim* went from the outside to the inside of the Tabernacle, they washed with water from the laver in preparation for connecting to God. The laver was made from the mirrors of the women, because they, too, connected the "outside," the physical, to the "inside," the spiritual.

What was the women's role in redeeming the people from Egypt? They created homes in the fields, using the physical to create spiritual homes. The spoils of Egypt were not just the gold and silver, but the knowledge of how to use them to serve God. The reward of redemption from Egypt and the spoils of Egypt were actually the same thing. The Jewish people could not leave Egypt until they understood that Torah involves using the physical to connect to the spiritual. They were redeemed once they knew how to use the spoils of Egypt for spiritual purposes, and it was the women who enabled the men to do this.

The Spies

"Send men for you and they will tour the land of Canaan, which I [God] am giving to the people of Israel."
(Bemidbar 13:2)

God had promised the Land of Israel to the Jewish people, and when the time to take possession of it approached, the people desired to know more about this land, to spy it out. God gave permission, but when the spies returned, only two of the twelve men sent came back with a positive and enthusiastic opinion about Israel. The rest gave a negative report filled with gossip and innuendoes. The men of that generation believed the negative report and, as a result, they refused to enter the land. God punished them with forty years of wandering in the desert, and only two spies, Kalev and Yehoshua, were allowed to enter the Land of Israel. Since the time that the spies were sent, the Jewish people have been suffering from the consequences of their negative report.

The Kli Yakar notes that God instructed Moshe, "Send men *for you.*" This indicates that Moshe's choice of spies was less than ideal.

> Our Rabbis said (*Yalkut Shimoni, Pinchas* 773:27) that the men [the spies] hated the land, [as they] said, "Let's choose a leader and return to Egypt" (Bemidbar 14:4). The women [the five daughters of Tzelafchad] loved the land, [as they]

said, "Give us a portion [in the land]" (ibid. 27:4). Therefore, the Holy One, blessed be He, said, "In My opinion, since I can see the future, it would be better to send women who love the land [to spy it out], for they will not speak derogatorily about it. But you think [the men] are upright and you think they love the land, so send men." This is the meaning of "Send for you": in your opinion, men, but in My opinion, it would be better to send women.

(Kli Yakar, Bemidbar 13:2)

The contrast between the love of the land expressed by the five daughters of Tzelafchad and the disregard for the land expressed by the spies is noted in a number of commentaries. The five daughters of Tzelafchad displayed a tremendous desire and yearning for the land. Their father had died in the desert, leaving no sons. According to the law, the Land of Israel was passed down from father to son, but since the daughters of Tzelafchad had no brothers, they asked Moshe that they inherit the land of their father. God told Moshe that the daughters spoke properly, and the land should be given to them.

None of the Jewish women participated in the sin of the spies; none of them believed the negative report, and all of the women eventually entered Israel in the days of Yehoshua. The women had a natural and intense love of the land, as demonstrated by the request of the daughters of Tzelafchad.

The Torah requires the people of Israel to live in this physical world and elevate it to spirituality. The women of Israel understood that working the land — plowing, planting, and reaping — was the manner in which holiness could be extracted from physical activities. Why did the women succeed in demonstrating their love for Israel while the men failed? The men saw that the desert was the place where God's Presence was continually revealed in the form of the manna, the clouds of glory, and other heavenly manifestations. They were not ready to leave the desert, the spiritual oasis, because they did not understand that although the desert provided the ideal conditions for learning how to attain spirituality, this was not the goal, but only the training ground for life in Israel and for observance of Torah in general. The women, on the other hand, knew that the Land of Israel was particularly suited for the mission of the Jewish people — to live in the physical world and achieve holiness. Therefore, not one of them believed the report of the spies. They were rewarded for this with entry into the land they so appreciated.

Ten Measures of Speech

The Haggadah describes four sons who come to the seder table. Three of them ask questions, but one son doesn't know how to ask anything. The Haggadah instructs, "*At p'sach lo* — You [feminine] open it up for him." The Chasam Sofer explains that the Haggadah is addressing the mother. The mother, as the communicator, is the one who opens up worlds for her children. It is she who can teach the child how to ask a question, using her own speech to bridge worlds.

Speech, like all aspects of the physical world, is intrinsically neither positive or negative. When misused, it can create dissension and disharmony. But it can also be used to elevate material existence and to create a channel for bringing knowledge of God into the world.

Ten measures of speech came down to the world, and nine of them were taken by women. Why? Because women need the power of speech to bridge the physical and the spiritual. Speech is the tool for bringing intellectual and spiritual ideas into a physical world. Sarah was a greater communicator than Avraham, and she set the example which was taken up by her righteous descendants in Egypt. The Jewish women exiled in Egypt, in turn, used speech to succor their husbands, and they combined this speech with their ability to transform mundane and ordinary items into vehicles for spirituality.

When it was time for the Jewish people to work with the most definite and obvious form of physicality, the earth of the Land of Israel, the spies used speech to convince their brethren to spurn this challenge. Not one woman accepted the spies' report. Instead, they used speech to express their desire for and love of the land, grasping that the job of a Jew is to synthesize the spiritual and physical worlds, in service of God.

May we learn to use speech in its proper way, by choosing our words carefully to express holy and elevated thoughts, while avoiding negative speech and gossip. In this way, we will continue to do the job God has specified for us, begun so many centuries ago by our righteous mothers.

Rivkah: Prophecy and Voice

The formation of the Jewish people was not an easy process. Our first two patriarchs, Avraham and Yitzchak, had sons who did not live up to the high standards required to inherit the mantle of leadership — Yishmael and Eisav. It could not have been easy to deny one child and give to the other, and the Torah describes Avraham's struggle with Sarah's demand to expell Yishmael from their home.

Interestingly, Yitzchak, who also had a "problem child," did not have a similar struggle. Yitzchak had no confrontation with his wife, Rivkah. When Yitzchak prepared to bless Eisav, Rivkah proceeded with plans of her own. Without consulting her husband, Rivkah arranged for Yaakov to take the blessing that Yitzchak intended for Eisav. It was all arranged behind Yitzchak's back, leaving us wondering, Why?

> Rivkah conceived. The children struggled within her, and she said, "If so, why am I thus?"
> She went to inquire of God. God said to her, "Two nations are in your womb; two regimes from your insides shall be separated. The might shall pass from one regime to the other, and the elder shall serve the younger."
> (Bereishis 25:21–23)

Rivkah: Prophecy and Voice • 185

During her pregnancy, the matriarch Rivkah experienced great pain. Knowing that something was wrong, she went to the house of study, which was the academy of Sheim and Eiver (Noach's son and great-grandson), to seek an explanation. Through prophecy she was told she was carrying twins and that these siblings would always struggle with each other.

Rashi explains that "from your insides shall be separated" means the two were already going their separate ways, even within the womb. They would become two nations, one of which would go to evil and one of which would go to purity. Their relationship would be one of invariable, eternal conflict; they would constantly spar with each other. Rashi explains that these two nations, Eisav and Yaakov, would not be equal in strength: When one nation would rise to supremacy, the other would fall, always in relation to each other. Thus when Eisav would be strong, Yaakov would be weak; and when Yaakov would be strong, Eisav would be weak. Yaakov is, of course, the Jewish nation, and Eisav is Rome, or western civilization.

Rivkah never told her husband, Yitzchak, about this prophecy. When the twins were born, Eisav came forth first, and then came Yaakov. Rivkah and Yitzchak raised their children and watched them mature — Yaakov becoming a man who "dwells in tents" (Rashi interprets this as one who learns Torah) and Eisav becoming a man of the field — and in all that time, the secret of Rivkah's prophecy was hers alone.

This story raises some questions. First, it is difficult to understand the predestined nature of Yaakov's and Eisav's lives, given human free will. How does *hashgachah peratis* (God's interaction with this world) correlate with human free will? Furthermore, Rivkah's secrecy fascinates. Not in all the years of raising their children did she tell Yitzchak of the prophecy she had heard — not even when the aging Yitzchak decided to bless his sons and pass on the mantle of spiritual leadership. Why?

Yitzchak's Blessing

When Yitzchak had become old and his eyes dimmed from seeing, he summoned Eisav, his older *son*, and said to him, "My *son*."

He said to him, "Here I am."

He said, "See, now, I have aged; I do not know the day of my death. Sharpen, if you please, your gear, your sword and your bow, and go out to the field and hunt game for me. Then make me delicacies such as I love and bring them to me and I will eat, so that my soul may bless you before I die."

Rivkah was listening as Yitzchak spoke to Eisav, his *son*; and Eisav went to the field to hunt game to bring. Rivkah said to Yaakov, her *son*, saying, "Behold I heard your *father* speaking to your *brother*, Eisav, saying, 'Bring me some game and make me delicacies to eat, and I will bless you in the presence of God before my death.' So now, my *son*, listen to my voice, to that which I command you. Go to the flock and fetch two choice young goat kids for me, and I will make delicacies for your *father*, as he loves. Then bring it to your *father* and he shall eat, so that he may bless you before his death."

Yaakov replied to Rivkah, his *mother*, "But my *brother* Eisav is a hairy man, and I am a smooth-skinned man. Perhaps my *father* will feel me and I shall be as a mocker in his eyes; I will thus bring upon myself a curse, rather than a blessing."

But his *mother* said to him, "Your curse will be on me, my *son*; only listen to my voice and go fetch them for me."

So he went, fetched, and brought [venison] to his *mother*, and his *mother* made delicacies as his *father* loved. Rivkah then took her elder *son* Eisav's clean garments, which were with her in the house, and clothed Yaakov, her younger *son*. She covered his arms and his smooth-skinned neck with the skins of the goat-kids. She placed the delicacies and the bread which she had made into the hand of her *son* Yaakov.

He came to his *father* and said, "*Father.*"

He said, "Here I am. Who are you, my *son*?"

Yaakov said to his *father*, "It is I; Eisav your firstborn. I have done as you told me. Rise up, please, sit and eat of my game that your soul may bless me."

Yitzchak said to his *son*, "How is it that you were so quick to find [game], my *son*?"

He said, "Because the Lord, your God, arranged it for me."

Yitzchak said to Yaakov, "Come close, if you please, so I can feel you, my *son*. Are you, indeed, my *son* Eisav or not?"

So Yaakov drew close to Yitzchak, his *father*, who felt him and said, "The voice is Yaakov's voice, but the hands are Eisav's hands." But he did not recognize him because his hands were hairy like the hands of Eisav, his *brother*, so he blessed him. He said, "You are, indeed, my *son* Eisav!"

He said, "I am."

He said, "Serve me and let me eat of my *son*'s game that my soul may bless you." So he served him and he ate, and he brought him wine and he drank.

Then his father, Yitzchak, said to him, "Come close, if you please, and kiss me, my *son*."

So he drew close and kissed him. He smelled the fragrance of his garments and blessed him. He said, "See, the fragrance of my *son* is like the fragrance of a field which the Lord had blessed. And may God give you of the dew of the heavens and of the fatness of the earth, and abundant grain and wine. Peoples will serve you and regimes will prostrate themselves to you. Be a lord to your kinsmen, and your *mother's sons* will prostrate themselves to you. Cursed be they who curse you, and blessed be they who bless you."

(Bereishis 27:1–29)

Notice how often the words *son, father, mother,* and *brother* are used. The word *son* is repeated nineteen times in these verses. The word *father* is mentioned nine times, the word *mother* is mentioned five times, and the word *brother* is used three times. This language creates a deep impression — the story of Yitzchak's blessing is very much a family affair and concerns the conflict over who will be the spiritual heir of the Jewish people.

When Rivkah spoke of her son, she was always referring to Yaakov. When Yitzchak spoke of his son, however, he was always referring to Eisav. There is one exception: When Rivkah took the garments of her older son, Eisav, and gave them to her younger son, Yaakov, she referred to both men as her sons.

Rivkah then took her elder son Eisav's clean garments, which were with her in the house, and clothed Yaakov, her younger son.

(Ibid., 15)

This verse evokes our memory of Rivkah's prophecy that "the elder shall serve the younger" (Bereishis 25:23). Thus, the only time Rivkah referred to Eisav as her son was in relation to Yaakov, her younger son.

Rivkah's Voice

The language of the Torah indicates a confrontation between Yitzchak and Rivkah. Would their son Eisav be the heir or would their son Yaakov be the heir? However, the Torah does not record that Yitzchak ever had a discussion or an argument about this matter.

Earlier, the Torah explicitly stated that Yaakov would be the heir. God Himself told Rivkah that "the elder shall serve the younger." It was therefore clear to Rivkah that Yaakov, the younger, would inherit. This situation was not about two parents, each with a different favored son, disputing over who should inherit. Rivkah's behavior was not based on her personal preference. Why didn't she simply say to Yitzchak, "Forget about Eisav; God told me in prophecy that He wants Yaakov to succeed you"?

Twice Rivkah told her son Yaakov to listen to her voice. When she directed Yaakov to disguise himself as Eisav, she said, "So now, my son, listen to my voice, to that which I command you" (ibid., 8). And, in her instructions of how to prepare for the blessing, she stated, "Your curse will be on me, my son; only listen to my voice and go fetch them for me" (ibid., 13).

In contrast to Rivkah's "voice," Yitzchak spoke words: "Rivkah was listening as Yitzchak *spoke* to Eisav, his son; and Eisav went to the field to hunt game to bring. Rivkah said to Yaakov, her son, saying, 'Behold I heard your father *speaking* to your brother, Eisav...' " (ibid., 5–6).

Rivkah has a voice, in Hebrew *kol*, and Yitzchak speaks words, in Hebrew *devarim*. What is the difference between Rivkah's "voice" and Yitzchak's "words"?

Free Will

In order to understand the questions posed, we must understand two fundamental concepts: *hashgachah peratis* — God's will and His control of the world — and human free will. How can human free will operate if God controls everything that happens? How could God have already decided that "the elder would serve the younger" before the twins were born? Doesn't this interfere with the free will of both Yaakov and Eisav?

One view on this subject was expressed by Rabbi Moshe Chaim Lutzatto, the Ramchal:

> It is necessary to know that even man's deeds are not all the result of his free will. While this is true of most of his actions, there are some that result from a Divine decree.... Such decrees take place in the same manner as other natural phenomena....
>
> (*Derech Hashem* I 5:4)

When God created the world, He willed that a person's life would be determined by a combination of his free will to choose and a completely fair system of reward and punishment. If a person chooses to do good, he will be rewarded by God for his good deeds; if a person chooses to do evil, he will be punished by God for those bad deeds. In order to grant human beings this freedom, God subjugated His will, His *hashgachah peratis*, to man's will. This is an extremely staggering concept: God withdraws from His control over the world to allow a human being free will (*Derech Hashem* II 8:1–2).

To clarify this concept: God is in charge of everything that happens in the entire universe, and God can do whatever He wants at any time to any person. Yet His will is to allow human beings the freedom to make their own decisions.

God is never subjugated to the rule of any being unless He desires to be. God is never limited by human beings (or anything else), for although He grants to human beings the freedom to make decisions, if a person decides to do something that God does not want to happen, it won't happen. Whenever God desires and decrees it best to override the rules that He set up, He can do so. In so doing, He will impose His will on us and His world.

What actually happens in this world depends on what God deems best at any given moment. Therefore, there are times when human beings are given complete free will to decide what actions to take, and there are times when God says, "I'm going to decide. I will impose My will in this situation. You will do as I say." We, however, are never totally sure which is which; we cannot know if the events that happen to us result from our own power over our lives, or if we are being directed by God.

Nevertheless, we can be certain of one thing: We have complete and total free will as far as deciding whether to do good or evil. We may decide to do a mitzvah, but God may decide otherwise. We may decide to do an *aveirah* (transgression), but God may decide not to let it happen. But the freedom of intention is always in our hands, and we are rewarded or punished accordingly.

This means that we live in two realities at the same time. On one level of reality, we believe that we have free will to affect our destinies through our behavior. Reward and punishment will follow according to our deeds, our thoughts, and our decisions, so we are aware that our behavior entails consequences. We live with the belief that we are actually making all the relevant decisions concerning what we do in this world, and that all of our efforts in this world are manifested and affect our lives both in this world and in the next world (Ramchal, *Ma'amar HaIkarim: B'Hashgachah*).

The second level of reality is that God directs and determines our existence based on His wisdom, His superiority, and His authority. It is therefore possible that our free will — our efforts and our deeds — will not affect our lives in this world. God runs the world with a design, and we are restrained to the degree required by God's plan (*Derech Hashem* II 3). Whether or not our efforts and deeds are fruitful, we are accountable for the decisions we make and the efforts we make.

We live with the knowledge that "everything is in the hands of Heaven, except for the fear of Heaven" (*Berachos* 33b). The only thing we truly control all of the time, without question, is how much we fear Heaven. We can decide to do good or to sin, but whether God allows us to actually act on that decision is beyond our control.

Rivkah's Prophecy

It would seem from Rivkah's prophecy that a Divine plan, incomprehensible to us, was in effect. That Divine plan was that Eisav play a certain role in this world and Yaakov play a different role in this world. It is clear that both Eisav and Yaakov were given free will to do good or evil, because part of Rivkah's prophecy was that when one would rise the other would fall; that is, their position would depend on their behavior and their free will, and God would reward accordingly. Nevertheless, it was equally clear that they were predetermined as adversaries, that the older would serve the younger, that each would be a great nation, and that these nations would constantly spar with each other. Rivkah was told of this plan, but Yitzchak remained in the dark. Therefore, when Rivkah planned for Yaakov to usurp Eisav's blessing, she was, in effect, carrying out the Divine plan, and she acted in the mode of accepting God's will and *hashgachah peratis*.

Rivkah's clarity of vision and the resulting confrontation with her husband, albeit indirect, brings to mind another mother in Israel, Sarah. When Sarah saw Yishmael, the son of Avraham and Hagar, the Egyptian woman, mocking, she told Avraham to banish the mother and son, because Yishmael would not inherit with her son, Yitzchak. There is a striking similarity in the Torah's language:

> Sarah saw the *son* of Hagar, the Egyptian woman who had borne a *son* to Avraham, mocking. She said to Avraham, "Chase away this woman, this maidservant, and her *son*, because the child of this maidservant will not inherit with my *son*, with Yitzchak."
>
> This thing was very bad in Avraham's eyes concerning

his *son*. And so God said to Avraham, "It should not be bad in your eyes concerning the boy or concerning this maidservant. Everything that Sarah says, you should listen to her *voice*, because Yitzchak will be your inheritor. [But] I will also make the *son* of this handmaiden a nation because he is your seed."

(Bereishis 21:9–13)

This conflict between Sarah and Avraham is also about which son will inherit. In both cases, the mothers, Sarah and Rivkah, had a more lucid perception of the proper action to be taken. In both cases, God confirmed and validated the view of the woman. The word *son* in Sarah's story was used frequently, as it was in the story of Yitzchak's blessing, indicating that Avraham believed his older son should inherit with the younger. In both cases, the mothers referred to only one boy as "son." Sarah called Yitzchak "my son," and she called Yishmael "the son of the handmaiden," and not Avraham's son. Avraham, however, saw Yishmael as his son. God confirmed Sarah's perception when He said He would make "the son of this handmaiden" into a nation. Similarly, Rivkah called only Yaakov her son because God had already told her that "the elder will serve the younger." In both cases, the mothers had a clearer vision than the fathers.

Another striking similarity is the Torah's use of the word *voice* in regard to both women. Rashi explains that when God told Avraham about Sarah, "Listen to her voice," this was the voice of prophecy, and Avraham was secondary in prophecy to Sarah. The words of the Torah are very precise; if Sarah had been merely expressing her opinion, God would have said, "Listen to her words." God instead used the word *voice* to indicate that Sarah had contact with the Divine and she had clear knowledge of His will (*Sifsei Chachamim*). In the area of educating children, Sarah had more information than Avraham. This is the most striking similarity between Sarah's story and Rivkah's story.

When Rivkah said to Yaakov, "Listen to my voice," she was not saying, "Listen to me." Instead, she was saying, "I have a voice, prophecy. Listen to my prophecy."

We can now understand the verse "Rivkah was listening as Yitzchak spoke to Eisav, his son." The Ohr HaChaim explains that Rivkah was not eavesdropping, with her ear to the door. Rather, she "heard" through prophecy that this was Yitzchak's plan, and she understood what she had to do.

The clarity of the matriarchs was specific to their children. In both stories, the father had an understanding of the child that differed from the mother's, and the mothers had more clarity, through prophecy. This is because God gives prophecy to the one who can activate it.

Mussar and Torah

People generally think that prophecy is like fortune-telling, knowing what the future will bear. This is only a partial meaning of prophecy. An additional, and essential, component of prophecy is that the prophet is being told to act on his vision. An illustration of this is the story of Yosef. Yosef dreamed that the stars, the sun, and the moon bowed down to him, and he interpreted this dream to mean that his brothers, his father, and his stepmother would literally bow down to him. When Yosef became viceroy in Egypt, he activated this prophecy: He set up a situation so that his brothers and parents came down to Egypt and indeed bowed to him (*Ramban*, Bereishis 42:9). Yosef understood that if God gave him this prophecy, he was being told to make it happen. When Sarah and Rivkah were given prophecy about their children, they too understood that they had to activate the prophecy and make it happen.

The book of Mishlei says: "Listen, my son, to the *mussar* [moral instruction] of your father, and do not forsake the Torah [teaching] of your mother" (Mishlei 1:8). We learn here that there is a difference between the instruction of one's father and the teaching of one's mother. Rav Chaim Goldvicht taught that the instruction of the father is intellectual knowledge, the information and tradition of the Torah in its entirety, whereas the teaching of the mother is the primary value system that is intuitively given to a child by his mother. The father's system is about objective information. The mother's system teaches the child to know in his heart what is right.

Mishlei is teaching us, said Rav Goldvicht, that although we move from our mother's home, the place of an intuitive value system, to the school, the intellectual education system, we should never abandon the intuitive for the intellectual. The primary teaching of our mother should not be superseded by the instruction of our father, because the intuitive value system is the foundation upon which the intellectual system is based. For this reason, one of the first things we say in the daily prayers is "The beginning of wisdom is the fear of God" (Tehillim 111:10). Wisdom is intellectual; fear of God is intuitive. A person builds this wisdom upon his fear of God, on the moral, straight character he internalizes in himself.

How does the mother transmit this intuitive knowledge? She speaks to the child in such a way that the child can absorb her words. The Sages teach that mothers receive reward for "transporting their children to the house of Torah learning" (*Berachos* 17a). This doesn't mean that a mother only needs to get in her car and drive the kids to school to take a share in their Torah learning. Rather, the Gemara means that it is the mother who transports the children emotionally so that they will love Torah learning. She makes it part of their primary value system. She does this by "seducing them with words" (*Kiddushin* 31a), through love and through understanding each child.

The basis for this transmission is to "educate the child according to his way" (Mishlei 22:6). Understanding the nature of each child, the mother knows that one needs stricter guidance, one needs a hug, one needs a bribe. The mother must know how each child is different and draw each child to Torah according to his personality.

The mother's teaching is very different from the intellectual transmission of the father, the *mussar*, because the intellectual transmission is objective and informational. "This is what you do, this is what you don't do. This is what we believe, this is what we don't believe." The instruction of the father's *mussar* requires less knowledge of the inner workings of the child, because it is pure and unfiltered.

Rivkah was the primary giver of intuitive knowledge. It was therefore necessary for her to understand the nature of each of her children so that she could relate to them accordingly. Her prophecy was given to her in the very beginning, while the children were still in utero, because she was the one who would be required to fulfill and activate it. Eisav would be Eisav and Yaakov would be Yaakov, and it was she who would create the primary foundation on which each son would build his life. It was her job to bring about each son's destiny, working with his possibilities and limitations.

Rivkah and Yitzchak

Although Rivkah had to know the inner workings of her two children, was it necessary for Yitzchak to remain blind to his children's natures? Could not Rivkah, in the many years of their marriage, have shared the prophecy with her husband? Why did God conceal His plans from Yitzchak? To understand the answer to these questions, we must review an earlier part of the story, the initial encounter of Rivkah and Yitzchak.

> [Rivkah's family] called Rivkah and said to her, "Will you go with this man [to marry Yitzchak]?"
>
> She said, "I will go." ... Then Rivkah arose with her maidens. They mounted the camels and followed the

man. The servant took Rivkah and went.

Yitzchak came from having gone to Be'er Lachai Ro'i, for he dwelt in the south country. Yitzchak went out to supplicate in the field toward evening and he raised his eyes and saw camels approaching.

Rivkah raised her eyes and saw Yitzchak. She inclined while upon the camel. She said to the servant, "Who is that man walking in the field toward us?"

The servant said, "He is my master [Yitzchak]."

She then took the veil and covered herself.

(Bereishis 24:65)

Avraham sent his servant, Eliezer, to find a wife for his son, Yitzchak, from Avraham's kindred. Eliezer went to Aram Naharayim, where Avraham's relatives lived and met Rivkah, who "had been born to Besuel, the son of Milkah, the wife of Nachor, brother of Avraham" (Bereishis 24:15). Seeing that Rivkah was an exceedingly kind and righteous person, Eliezer arranged to bring her back to Canaan to marry Yitzchak.

As they approached her future husband's home, Rivkah saw Yitzchak praying in the field. Yitzchak's dominating characteristic was his awe and reverence of God. He had achieved the ultimate in self-control, self-negation, and introspection. He prayed in this mode, standing in the position of servant of God, aware always of God's greatness. Rivkah was overwhelmed by the awesomeness of Yitzchak's presence.

The Netziv writes:

> [Rivkah covered herself with a veil] out of overwhelming awe and modesty because she understood that she was unworthy to be his wife. From then on, awe was imbedded in her heart. Her relationship with Yitzchak wasn't like Sarah's with Avraham or Rachel's with Yaakov. For when [Sarah and Rachel] had some complaint against [their husbands], they were not embarrassed to speak frankly to

them. This was not so with Rivkah. All of this [the story of their first meeting] is the means of introducing the story that will come in *parashas Toldos* when Yitzchak and Rivkah had different opinions, at the time of the blessing of Yaakov.... All of this was caused by the Holy One, blessed be He, so that the blessings would come to Yaakov in this fashion.... All of this was Divine intervention. Rivkah met Yitzchak in this hour [of his *minchah* prayer] and was shocked by him, so in the end, it would come out according to the will of God.

(Ha'Amek Davar, Bereishis 24:58–65)

Rivkah grew up in a place populated by idol-worshippers, cheaters, and adulterers. Her encounter with someone who radiated purity and holiness caused her to feel that he was beyond her. From this moment on, Rivkah was always a little bit afraid of Yitzchak, in awe of him. Consequently, her relationship with him was based on an overriding respect, and she was loathe to contradict him directly.

Sarah expressed her feelings about Yishmael bluntly and directly. She said, "Chase away this...maidservant and her son" (Bereishis 21:10). Two generations later, Rachel was unable to have children and said to Yaakov, "Give me children — otherwise I will die!" (Bereishis 30:1). Like Sarah, Rachel was blunt and direct, holding nothing back. Rivkah, on the other hand, never confronted Yitzchak directly. When she saw that Yitzchak didn't know that Yaakov was to be his spiritual successor, she didn't say, "Yitzchak, you're mistaken. Let me tell you about the prophecy I heard." She handled the situation in a roundabout manner. From the moment of their first encounter, Rivkah did what she had to do, without direct expression of her wishes.

The Netziv tells us that God wanted this to be Rivkah's relationship with Yitzchak. Why? Because God wanted Yitzchak's blessing to come to Yaakov in an indirect manner. Had Rivkah been more like Sarah or Rachel, this couldn't have happened.

Rivkah's act of removing her veil and covering herself was symbolic of her relationship with Yitzchak. She was always somewhat veiled around him. She never tried to overcome her first impression of Yitzchak, nor was she supposed to. Although Rivkah's relationship with Yitzchak was one of great respect and love, of a common goal for the building of a nation, communication between them was indirect and nonconfrontational.

The Role of the Father

As we discussed earlier, Rivkah's role as the mother was to discern the nature of each of her children and to guide them accordingly. She was given her prophecy so that she could understand and nurture their individual talents, strengths, and abilities. She also had the task of actualizing the prophecy itself.

Meanwhile, what about Yitzchak? Yitzchak learned Torah from his father, Avraham, and taught it to his children. Yitzchak was the transmitter of Torah, the link between the past and future generations. In order for Yitzchak to teach Torah, he had to believe in the potential of his students, his two sons. He had to believe in the total free will of each one of them in order to faithfully give over the Torah in its pure, objective, unfiltered form and in order to allow them the full choice to perform mitzvos or commit transgressions. Knowledge and intimate understanding of the predestined roles of Yaakov and Eisav might have hindered his ability to transmit.

Perhaps if Yitzchak knew who Eisav was, he would never have bothered transmitting Torah to him. Eisav, then, would have had less capability to intelligently choose between good and evil, for he would have had less information. However, since Yitzchak transmitted Torah equally to Eisav and Yaakov, Eisav's Torah learning gave him the potential to choose right from wrong. Perhaps it was inherently difficult for him to choose to do right, but not impossible. Since he had the opportunity to learn pure, true Torah from the righteous Yitzchak, he had every possibility of deciding to do good.

Avraham and Yitzchak had to transmit *mussar*, instruction and unfiltered Torah, while "blind" to the nature of their children. This blindness (which was literal blindness in Yitzchak's case) allowed them to focus on the goal of building their nation and continuing their tradition, and not on the individual child. They transmitted Torah with total faith that there would be a good outcome. They had to make every effort to do this, all the while knowing that the destiny of their sons was ultimately dependent upon their own free will and the plan of God.

The patriarchs were focused on giving their sons Torah so that these sons could carry on the tradition in the world at large. They saw their sons as part of a greater whole, as part of the People of Israel. They had total faith in the potential of each son, seeing their roles as fathers with a broad view.

Sarah and Rivkah, having clarity of God's plan in this world for their sons and of *hashgachah peratis*, operated differently. They were given intimate knowledge of God's will through their prophecy, through their voices, and they used that knowledge to make practical, functional decisions. The mothers focused on each child's individuality and on each child's unique abilities.

The mothers and fathers were each given the vision they needed in order to fulfill their roles in the best possible way. Today, studies are being conducted on the roles of fathers and mothers, and because divorce is rampant, social scientists research the effect of growing up in a one-parent family. One such study concluded that the mother gives a child a good feeling about who he is as an individual, and the father gives the child a good feeling of who he is vis-à-vis the outside world. The mother builds the child's self-esteem. The father, on the other hand, motivates the child to succeed in the world at large. A child needs both kinds of parenting to reach his maximum potential.

The basic value system given to the child by his mother is

built on the intuitive understanding of his individuality. The intellectual value system transmitted primarily by the father gives the child a vision of himself as part of a greater whole — that is, as part of *klal Yisrael*. We stand before God in both modes, as individuals and as part of a whole.

Jewish law, the halachah, reflects the different roles of father and mother. We are taught, "Honor your father and your mother" (Shemos 20:12) and "Every man, his mother and his father shall he respect" (Vayikra 19:3). The reversal of "father" and "mother" in the two verses reflects the idea that a child feels differently toward his father than he does toward his mother because of their different roles. It is more natural for a child to respect and fear his father, who motivates him to bigger goals, and to honor and love his mother, who nurtures his individuality, but he is obligated to honor and respect both. Respect and honor reflect the different roles of each parent (*Kiddushin* 31a).

What's in a Name?

We no longer have the type of prophecy that was given to our ancestors. No longer are we told, "This child will be like this" or "That child will be like that." The Arizal teaches that we do not remain totally clueless, however; when parents give a name to their child, there's *ruach hakodesh* (Divine inspiration) in the name. Obviously, this doesn't mean that the day before a child is named, the parents hear voices. It means that when a parent has an idea — *this is the name I'd like to give my child* — that idea was put into his head by God, because the name given to the new baby reflects his essence. The Arizal's statement implies that from the very beginning, the parent has a sense of the child, his potential, his personality, his essence.

This is reflected in the Torah, where parents often state the reason for a name they have given. For instance, when Chavah gave birth to her first son, the Torah says, "[Chavah] gave birth to Kayin, and she said, 'I acquired [*kanisi*] a man with God'" (Bereishis 4:1). Sometimes there's a difference of opinion between the parents over what to name their child. When Binyamin was born, Rachel named him Ben-oni — "son of my affliction," while Yaakov named him Binyamin — "son of my right hand, my strength" (ibid. 35:18). Yaakov was right and so the name Binyamin was the name he carried for the rest of his life. Sometimes God names the child. For example, He gave the names for Yitzchak (ibid. 17:19) and Yishmael (ibid. 16:11). A child's name includes the essence of the child; it's the intuitive, the knowing of who each child is.

When the Torah tells us who named the child, it is important information. Any understanding that we have of a child, be it his name or any other understanding, comes with the help of God, much as it came through prophecy to Rivkah. Women have more intuitive understanding (*binah*) than men do. This extra measure of perception is their help from God, and it enables them to understand the inner workings of the child in order to guide him properly.

The Bottom Line

While we all know our children, we are also blind to certain aspects of them. The blindness that our parents had for us and the blindness that we have for our own children is, in fact, a good thing.

The children of psychiatrists often feel that their parents read their minds. This is jolting for a child, frightening and even painful. Of course, no one can read another's mind, but the fear of being emotionally naked is a painful one, even paralyzing. In other words, it's good to understand our children, but being "blind" is also important because it allows the child more free will. In addition, this blindness reminds us that we are not in total control of our children's lives. Our blindness teaches us that we're not ultimately in charge of our child's destiny; God is. Our children have free will, just as we do. Yet God determines what will ultimately happen according to His plan.

Our goals remain the same as those of Rivkah and Yitzchak, all these thousands of years later. We must transmit an intuitive value system as well as an intellectual one. We must be in touch with the individuality of each child, his capabilities and limitations. We must give him a sense of his importance as an individual as well as a sense of his place within the Jewish people. It's a big job, and we might feel overwhelmed if we forget that we have a partner in this: God. God has the clear vision, the endless knowledge, the perfect wisdom, and it is He who ultimately determines a person's destiny. So in addition to the day-to-day work of raising a child, we have another resource — prayer.

We must pray for the help of God in raising our children. A very beautiful prayer of this nature was composed by the Chazon Ish, and many people include it in their daily *Shemoneh Esrei* prayer:

> May it be Your will, my God and God of my fathers, that You have mercy on my son [*name*], son of [*mother's name*], and turn his heart to love and to fear Your name and to immerse himself in Your holy Torah. May You remove from him every obstacle that prevents him from immersing himself in Your holy Torah and prepare for him all the circumstances that will bring him to Your holy Torah, because You listen to the prayer of Your people Israel. Blessed are You, God, who hears prayer.

We ask God for guidance and wisdom. We ask Him to safeguard our children and help them to grow up to be Torah Jews. God is our partner in raising our children and in understanding them. Although we are sometimes blind, He sees everything. In His wisdom and kindness, He will help us see what we should see, and He will blind us to that which we shouldn't see.

Man of Exile, Woman of Return

We have been in a long and difficult exile for almost two thousand years. Yet, despite this harsh punishment and despite the fact that the Jewish people are uniquely a people of exile, we are sure of God's love for us, and we have confidence in His promise for a final redemption. What, then, is the exile for? Is exile simply a punishment, or does it have meaning, purpose, and an end goal? Why is exile specific to the Jewish people? And what can we do to hasten the redemption? The Torah reveals the secrets of exile and return in the story of Yaakov and Rachel.

After living in Egypt for seventeen years, Yaakov knew that his death was approaching, and he spoke of it on three occasions.

> [The nation of] Yisrael dwelled in the land of Egypt, in the land of Goshen, and they took possession of it. They increased and multiplied exceedingly. Yaakov lived in the land of Egypt for seventeen years, and the days of Yaakov's life were 147 years.
>
> The time drew near for Yisrael [Yaakov] to die, so he called his son Yosef and said to him, "If I have now found

favor in your eyes, please put your hand under my thigh and deal kindly and truly with me. Do not bury me in Egypt. When I will die you shall carry me out of Egypt and bury me in [my father's] burying place."

[Yosef] said, "I will do as you have said."

He said, "Swear to me."

He swore to him, and Yisrael bowed himself upon the bed's head.

(Bereishis 47:27–31)

Yaakov wanted to be buried with his ancestors in the Cave of Machpeilah and asked his son Yosef to swear that he would guarantee this final request. Afterwards, Yosef had a second audience with his father. In this audience, Yaakov spoke of Yosef's two sons, Menasheh and Efrayim, and of two incidents from his past.

It came to pass after these things that Yosef was told, "Behold, your father is sick." [He went to his father] and he took with him his two sons, Menasheh and Efrayim.

Yaakov was told, "Behold, your son Yosef is coming to you." Yisrael strengthened himself, and sat upon the bed.

Yaakov said to Yosef, "God Almighty appeared to me at Luz, in the land of Canaan, and blessed me. He said to me: 'Behold, I will make you fruitful and multiply you, I will make of you a multitude of people, and I will give this land to your offspring after you for an everlasting possession.'

"And now your two sons, Efrayim and Menasheh, who were born to you in the land of Egypt before I came to Egypt, are mine; as Reuven and Shimon, they shall be mine. And your offspring which will be born after them shall be yours, called after the name of their brothers in their inheritance. As for me, when I came from Padan, Rachel died by me in the land of Canaan on the way, when there was yet but a little way to come to Efras. I buried her there on the way to Efras, that is, Beis Lechem."

(Ibid. 48:1–7)

Then, in a final meeting with all of his sons, Yaakov again spoke of his desire to be buried in the Cave of Machpeilah.

Then [Yaakov] instructed [his sons], "I shall soon die. Bury me with my fathers in the cave that is in the field of Efron the Hittite, in the cave that is in the field of Machpeilah, which faces Mamrei, in the land of Canaan, which Avraham bought with the field from Efron the Hittite as a burial estate. There they buried Avraham and Sarah, his wife; there they buried Yitzchak and Rivkah, his wife; and there I buried Leah. The purchase of the field and the cave within it was from the sons of Cheis."

When Yaakov finished instructing his sons, he drew his feet onto the bed, expired, and was gathered to his people.

(Ibid. 49:29–33)

First Yaakov asked his son Yosef to take his body out of Egypt and bury him in Chevron. Yosef swore that he would do as his father wished. At the second meeting between Yaakov and Yosef, Yaakov recalled the death of Yosef's mother, Rachel. Then, when Yaakov was about to die, he gathered all of his sons together, blessed them, and gave specific instructions, once again, that he was to be buried in the Cave of Machpeilah, in the land of Canaan.

Rashi explains that the second meeting between Yaakov and Yosef also concerned Yaakov's burial.

[Yaakov was telling Yosef,] "[Please fulfill my request] although I trouble you to take me for burial into the land of Canaan and I did not do this for your mother [i.e., I did not take the trouble to bury her anywhere other than the place where she died, which was by the roadside].... I know that in your heart you feel some resentment against me. Know, however, that I buried her there by the command of God, so that she might help her children when Nevuzaradan would take them into captivity. When they pass along that road, Rachel comes forth by her tomb, weeping and beseeching mercy for them, as it says, 'A voice is heard on high — wailing, bitterly weeping. Rachel weeps for her children; she refuses to be consoled for her children, for they are gone' (Yirmiyahu 31:14). The Holy One, blessed be He, replies to her, 'There is a reward for your accomplishment...for your children will return to their border' (ibid., 15)."

(*Rashi*, Bereishis 48:7)

In other words, Yaakov wanted to reassure Yosef that he had a good reason for burying Rachel on the road to Efras, rather than in the Cave of Machpeilah. God Himself wanted Rachel to be buried there, because the Jews would pass this place when they were taken into exile, and they would also pass Rachel's grave when they returned home.

On the surface, all of this seems simple enough, yet several questions remain:

1. Yaakov first gave instructions to Yosef who, as viceroy of Egypt, had the power to have his father buried in the Cave of Machpeilah, and then Yaakov later repeated these instructions to all of his sons. Why did Yaakov feel it necessary to repeat the message to the whole family? Why did he have two separate audiences with Yosef? And why not mention the burial of Rachel during the first audience, when he asked Yosef to promise to bury him in Chevron? Wouldn't it make sense for Yaakov to set Yosef's mind at ease when making his original request?

2. Why did Yaakov explain Rachel's burial specifically after he discussed Yosef's sons, Efrayim and Menasheh? Is there a connection between Efrayim and Menasheh being equal-status tribes and Rachel being buried on the road to Efras?
3. Why did Yaakov bring up his vision that happened in Luz many years ago? Why is this vision mentioned in conjunction with Efrayim and Menasheh?
4. Finally, why does Yirmiyahu HaNavi tell us clearly that it is Rachel who cries for her children? Don't we have many patriarchs, matriarchs, and prophets who cry for us? Where is everybody else?

The Actions of the Fathers

The actions of the fathers are a sign for the children.

(*Sotah* 34a)

This teaching of our Rabbis is not symbolic. It means that when we want to understand current events, future history, and past history, we can find everything we need to know in the Tanach. Everything written in the Tanach about our patriarchs and matriarchs applies to all historical situations that the Jewish people have found or will find themselves in. Therefore, the Tanach is read not only as a history book, a *mussar* (ethical) book, or a book of laws; it is read as an explanation of and insight into current events, just as a newspaper is read.

The life of Yaakov is the prototype of the state of Jewish exile. After Yaakov received Yitzchak's blessing, he was forced to leave Eretz Yisrael because Eisav wanted to kill him. Yitzchak instructed him to go to Lavan, his mother's brother, and find a wife. The twenty years Yaakov spent in Lavan's home were extremely difficult ones for him. Lavan was a very evil person, and he betrayed Yaakov again and again. During this period of time,

Yaakov suffered intensely but without complaint.

In this exile, Yaakov worked and married, and he had many children. He also developed personally in this exile. Whereas his grandfather, Avraham, developed a relationship with God in the mode of *chesed* (kindness), and his father, Yitzchak, developed a relationship with God in the mode of *gevurah* (discipline and awe of God), Yaakov developed his own quality of serving God. This was the quality of *emes* (truth), a balance between *chesed* and *gevurah*. It was in this exile that Yaakov became his own man. He learned how to live a life of Truth, of Torah, in a world of falsehood and deceit. He dealt with imperfect and even evil behavior without caving in, giving up, or compromising his relationship with God. In other words, exile was beneficial for Yaakov in many ways. He married four wives, had eleven children, and developed the ability to stand firmly in Truth in a place where nobody else could have done it.

Exile

Finally, after twenty difficult years with Lavan, Yaakov returned to Israel, hoping to dwell there permanently.

> Yaakov settled [*vayeishev*] in the land of his father's sojournings, in the land of Canaan.
>
> (Bereishis 37:1)

Vayeishev means to dwell permanently. Yaakov was tired. Many years earlier he had fled from his brother Eisav, and he had spent fourteen years learning in the academy of Sheim and Eiver. Afterwards, he spent twenty years with Lavan, where he toiled day and night and where he was forced to be on guard against Lavan's treachery at all times. Then, God told him to return to Eretz Yisrael, and he withstood the dangerous return home, risking Eisav's wrath. After leaving Eisav, his beloved wife Rachel died on the road, and his mother also died while he had been away. At this point, Yaakov wanted to rest; he wanted a peaceful life for his final years in this world.

> Yaakov desired to dwell in peace, [but] the troubles of Yosef sprang upon him. The righteous desire to dwell in peace; but the Holy One, blessed be He, said, "It is not sufficient for the righteous that which is prepared for them in the world to come, but they seek to dwell in peace [also] in this world!"
>
> (*Rashi*, Bereishis 37:1)

The lesson here is that a Jew is never finished; the job is never done. Yaakov desired to experience peace and comfort, but Yosef was taken from him. Yaakov desired to dwell permanently in Israel, but God brought a famine to the land, and Yaakov was forced to leave. After thirty-five years of living in Israel, most of that time spent grieving for Yosef, Yaakov found himself back in exile.

Seventeen years later, as his life in this world drew to a close, Yaakov had an urgent need to make certain that he would buried in his homeland. Why was he afraid that his sons would fail to do this?

> [The nation] Yisrael settled [*vayeishev*] in the land of Egypt, in the land of Goshen, and they took possession of [*vayei'achzu*] it. They increased and multiplied exceedingly.
>
> (Bereishis 47:27)

There are two key words in this verse: *vayeishev*, which means to dwell permanently, and *vayei'achzu*, which means they acquired property and took possession of it. There are two different Hebrew words used in the Torah for living in a place: *yoshev*, from the same root as *vayeishev*, indicating permanent dwelling; and *gar*, which indicates temporary dwelling. The verse indicates that the children of Israel thought themselves to be permanent dwellers in the land of Egypt. Therefore, they grabbed hold of it, so to speak. From their point of view, Egypt became their possession (*Kli Yakar*). They thought, *We're here! We've arrived! We're settled; this is our land.*

This worried Yaakov. When he called for Yosef the first time, his message was "Yosef, Egypt is not our land. Israel is our land. I want to be buried in Israel, our land. You must promise to do this for me."

This apprehension did not suddenly enter Yaakov's mind on his deathbed. It actually predated the journey to Egypt.

> [God] said [to Yaakov], "I am the mighty God, the God of your father. Do not be afraid to go down into Egypt, for there I will make you a great nation. I will go down with you into Egypt, and I Myself will also bring you up again...."
>
> (Bereishis 46:3-4)

As Yaakov prepared to journey down to Egypt to see his son Yosef after the long years of separation, God appeared to him and told him not to be afraid. From this we understand that Yaakov was afraid — why would God tell him not to worry unless he was worried?

Yaakov was afraid that if he went down to Egypt he wouldn't come back. If he went down, the days of bondage promised to Avraham would begin (*Chizkuni*). He was afraid that the Jewish people would cease to be a distinct nation (*Ha'Amek Davar*). Yaakov, who had experienced and survived the exile with Lavan, knew personally how difficult it is to be a stranger in a strange land, remaining distinct and different from everyone else. He knew how hard it is to stand firmly in truth in a world of deceit. God told Yaakov, "Do not be afraid...I will make of you a great nation," in order to assure him that his people would maintain their Jewish identity and they would not be absorbed into the Egyptian people. God also promised, "I will go down with you into Egypt," because Yaakov had been afraid that the Divine Presence wouldn't be with them in exile. God's assurance was that this exile would not be the end of the Jewish people, nor would they remain forever in Egypt, because He, God, would accompany them home.

Yaakov was clearly afraid of exile, yet exile had been good for him. Exile can lead to creativity and productivity. When things are going well for a person, he isn't forced to stretch his limits. But when life is difficult and laden with anxiety, when a person experiences insecurity and worry, when he feels backed up against the wall, he has to find a way out, and he finds his most creative self. This is true on a national level as well as on a personal level.

As an example, during the Israeli War of Independence, the Jews were attacked by the Arabs. The Jews were vastly outnumbered, ill-equipped, and scarcely had weapons. So they fought with every means at their disposal — the soldiers would throw seltzer bottles out of airplane windows, and the carbon dioxide released created a noise that sounded like a bomb. Another such "weapon," used in Tzefat, was the *davidkah*, which was little more than a noisemaker. When it was fired, the enemies thought a massive bomb attack was taking place, and they fled. Having no choice, the Israeli "army" was forced to be creative and imaginative.

Exile and troubles cause a person to stretch himself to the limits of his imagination and courage, to bring forth his inner self. Exile is a place for personal and national development. Nevertheless, our goal is to remember always that we are in a temporary situation and to remember and maintain our deep desire to return home. Yaakov understood that there was a reason for exile, and there are advantages in it, but he didn't want to be trapped in it. For this reason, he made his son Yosef swear not once, but twice, that he would be buried in Israel.

Yaakov's Vision

During Yaakov's second audience with Yosef, he recalled the time God spoke to him at Luz. During that vision, God promised that the Jews would be a great people and have an everlasting inheritance in the Land of Israel. Yaakov recounted the episode almost word-for-word, but he made two minor changes.

Whenever the Torah repeats a story with minor changes, those changes are very significant. In the original version, the Torah reports:

> God said to him, "I am God Almighty. Be fruitful and multiply. A nation and a congregation of nations shall descend from you, and kings shall issue from your loins. The land that I gave to Avraham and to Yitzchak, I will give to you, and to your offspring after you I will give the land."
>
> (Bereishis 35:11–12)

Many years later, on his deathbed, Yaakov relates:

> "God Almighty appeared to me at Luz, in the land of Canaan, and blessed me. He said to me: 'Behold, I will make you fruitful and multiply you, I will make of you a multitude of people, and I will give this land to your offspring after you for an everlasting possession.'"
>
> (Ibid. 48:3–4)

Yaakov deliberately left out God's message that "kings shall issue from your loins," because he didn't want Yosef to think that the vision had already been fulfilled through him. Although Yosef was a viceroy in Egypt, the kings promised by God were the kings of Israel, the kings who would rule the Jewish people in their own land.

The other change, very significant, is that Yaakov added two words when he described the land: it was to be an "everlasting possession." In Hebrew, the words are *"achuzas olam."* The meaning of *"achuzas"* is the same as *"vayei'achzu"* — "to take possession of" or "take hold of." Yaakov meant, "This Egypt is not your possession; it does not belong to you. The real inheritance, the real possession, is the Land of Israel." Although God never spoke those words, Yaakov added them to reinforce the fact that Egypt might have been pleasant at that moment, but the truth was that their life in Egypt was an exile.

Efrayim and Menasheh

Why did Yaakov recall his vision at Luz specifically before he spoke of Yosef's sons, Efrayim and Menasheh? Efrayim and Menasheh were the first children of the twelve tribes to be born in exile. Yaakov wanted to make it clear to Yosef that the Land of Israel belonged to those children every bit as much as it belonged to the Jewish children who were born in the Land of Israel.

The discussion about Efrayim and Menasheh is sandwiched between "I will give this land to your offspring after you for an everlasting possession" and "Rachel died by me in the land of Canaan on the way." Said Yaakov: "Efrayim and Menasheh are my children just as Binyamin and Yosef are my children, and they are Rachel's children as well. These two boys, born in exile, are equal in status to those children born in Israel. And just as Rachel waits for the return of those sent into exile, she waits for the return of those born in exile." The Diaspora is not home (even if we are born there) — only the Land of Israel is our everlasting possession. Rachel is buried on the way to our true and only home, in order to welcome all of the Jewish people when we return.

Déjà Vu

The Rabbis tell us, over and over again, that just as Yaakov's life is a prototype of exile, the exile in Egypt is a prototype for our present exile. If a Jew wants to understand the present exile, he should study the life of Yaakov and the exile and enslavement in Egypt. He will learn that exile is difficult, bitter, full of suffering, lonely. But it's also creative, full of growth, and induces productivity. Although it's a world of suffering and separation, there is always that end goal, that goal of return.

> Yaakov's descent into Egypt alludes to our present exile at the hand of...Rome, for it was Yaakov's sons themselves, who, by the sale of their brother Yosef, caused their descent. Yaakov, moreover, went there on account of the famine, thinking to find relief with his son in [Pharaoh's] house...for Pharaoh loved Yosef and considered him a son. It was their hope to ascend from there as soon as the famine would cease in the land of Canaan, as they said, "To sojourn in the land we have come, for your servants have no pasture for their flocks, for the famine is heavy in the land of Canaan" (Bereishis 47:4). But then they did not come up. Instead, the exile was prolonged, and Yaakov died there. His bones ascended from [Egypt] accompanied by all the elders and courtiers of Pharaoh, who instituted severe lamentation for him.
>
> Our relationship with our brothers Rome and Edom is similar. We have caused ourselves to fall into their clutches, as [the Jews of the period] made a covenant with the Romans, and Agrippa II, the last king during the Second Temple, fled to them for help. It was due to famine that Jerusalem was captured by the Romans, and the exile has been exceedingly long for us. Its end, unlike the other exiles, is unknown. We are in it as the dead, who say, "Our bones are dried up, we are completely cut off." But in the end they will bring us up from all the nations as an offering to the Eternal, and they will feel deep sorrow as they behold our glory, and we will see the vengeance of the Eternal, may He raise us, that we may live in His presence.
> (*Ramban*, Bereishis 47:28)

Ramban refers to the historical events that followed our victory over the Greeks (at the time of the Chanukah miracle). Yehudah the Maccabbee, the son of Mattisyahu the Hasmonean, proposed an alliance with Rome in order to safeguard the Jewish independence from Greece. This proposal was greeted with enthusiasm by Rome, a Jewish delegation was honored by the Roman Senate, and an alliance was concluded. Many years later, King Agrippa II asked the Jews' "ally," Rome, for aid to squash a rebellion at home in Israel. The end result of this "alliance" was the destruction of the Temple by the Romans and the exile and enslavement of thousands of Jews. Says the Ramban, just as Yaakov ended up in Egypt because his children made "alliances" to get rid of Yosef, so, too, did the Jews in the days of the Second Temple bring exile upon themselves by making "alliances" they should not have made. Their only alliance should have been with God, and no one else should have been trusted.

When the Jews first came to Egypt, they never dreamed they would be there for 210 years, that they would settle, take possession of the land, and perceive Egypt as their home. Just as the exile in Egypt seemed endless, says the Ramban, so, too, does our present exile seem endless. We are like dead people, with our bones dried up, not remembering, not believing that the exile is a means and not an end, that redemption is at hand. In the end, however, just as Yaakov's bones were accompanied to his final burial place by the servants of Pharaoh, we will be returned to our land, all of us, as a *minchah* offering to God.

Yaakov was the victim of two exiles, one in the house of Lavan and one in Egypt. Yet during both exiles, Yaakov never forgot where he was, in a place of exile, and he was at all times aware that the end goal was to return home.

Rachel

As the First Temple burned, the Jews were being driven to Babylon in chains, thirsty, hungry, and degraded. It looked like the end of national existence. A very moving *midrash* in *Pesikta d'Eichah Rabbasi* describes a great tumult taking place in Heaven as one after the other of the patriarchs appears before God to plead for mercy for the Jews.

> Avraham began to speak before God. "Lord of the Universe, when I was one hundred years old You gave me a son. When he achieved understanding and was a youth of thirty-seven, You said to me, 'Bring him up before Me as an offering.' I was brutal toward him and showed him no compassion, but bound him myself. Will You not remember this for me, and will You not have compassion over my sons?"
>
> Yitzchak said: "Lord of the Universe, when my father said to me, 'God will see for Himself a sheep for an offering, my son' (Bereishis 22:8) I did not resist Your words and was willingly bound on the altar. I stretched forth my throat under the knife. Will You not remember this for me, and will You have no compassion over my sons?"
>
> Yaakov said: "Lord of the Universe, did I not stay in the house of Lavan twenty years? And when I came out of his house, the iniquitous Eisav came upon me and wanted to kill my sons. I offered my life for them. And now they have been handed over to their enemies like sheep to slaughter, after I raised them like little birds and suffered over them the anguish of raising children. Will You not remember this for me and have compassion over my sons?"
>
> Moshe said: "Lord of the Universe, was I not a loyal shepherd for Israel for forty years? Did I not run before them like a horse, in the wilderness? When the time came for them to enter the land, You decreed that my bones

were to fall in the wilderness. And now that they have gone into exile, You have sent me to lament and weep over them?"...

At that hour Moshe said to Yirmiyahu, "Go before me, and I will go to [*klal Yisrael*] and see [the enemy] who is putting his hand on them."

Yirmiyahu said to him, "It is not possible to walk on the road because of the slain."

Said he, "Nevertheless!"

Moshe went with Yirmiyahu before him, till they reached the rivers of Babylon. [The Jews there] saw Moshe and said to one another, "The son of Amram has come from his grave to redeem us from the hands of our enemies."

A *bas kol* [a voice from Heaven] said, "It is a decree from Me!"

Immediately Moshe said to them, "My sons, to bring you back is impossible, for the decree has already been issued." At that hour they raised their voices in great weeping, till their cries ascended on high. Of this it was said, "By the rivers of Babylon there we sat, we also wept..." (Tehillim 137:1).

At that hour, our mother Rachel threw herself before the Holy One, blessed be He, and said, "Master of the Universe, it is revealed to You that Yaakov loved me with an extra measure of love, and that he worked for my father for seven years to marry me. When...the time came for me to marry my husband, my father contrived to replace me with my sister.... I was not jealous of my sister, nor did I expose her to shame. And if I, a creature of flesh and blood, formed of dust and ashes, was not jealous of one who caused me pain, why were You, merciful and eternal King, jealous of idols, in which there is no reality, and why have You exiled my children?"

Immediately, the mercy of the Holy One, blessed be He, was aroused, and He said, "For your sake, Rachel, I will return Israel to their place." And so it is written: "Thus said Hashem, 'A voice is heard on high — wailing, bitterly weeping. Rachel weeps for her children; she refuses to be comforted for her children, for they are gone. Thus said Hashem: 'Restrain your voice from weeping and your eyes from tears; for there is reward for your accomplishment... and they will return from the enemy's land. There is hope for your future,' says Hashem, 'and your children will return to their border' " (Yirmiyahu 31:14–16).

(Pesikta d'Eichah Rabbasi 23)

Why was God's mercy aroused only for Rachel? Wouldn't it make more sense that God's mercy would be aroused for the patriarchs? The Jews being exiled were all the children of the patriarchs, but not all were Rachel's children. Some were from the tribe of Rachel's son Binyamin, but the majority was from the tribes of Levi and Yehudah, descendants of Leah. (The rest of the tribes, the ten "lost tribes," had already been exiled to Assyria.) Nevertheless, Rachel cried for the Jewish people as if they all were her children, and she refused to be comforted.

When God did not accept the arguments of Avraham, Yitzchak, Yaakov, Moshe, and Yirmiyahu, those *tzaddikim* walked away. Why? Because they knew that a certain amount of punishment is good for us. There is an atonement in it. We sin, God sends punishment, and the people learn to correct their transgressions. We Jews have always accepted punishment with the knowledge that God is fair and just and does only what is good for us. What was different about Rachel?

For Rachel, the fact that punishment is good for us was not enough. For Rachel, there was no comfort to be found in her children's immeasurable suffering because she wanted more than atonement. She wanted greatness for the Jewish people. For all she had sacrificed, for all she had suffered, she wanted more than survival; she wanted her children to be great, distinct, and upright.

Rachel, like all the matriarchs, was a prophetess, and she perceived that God wanted the Jewish people to be built up through more than one mother. Therefore, she willingly gave her sister to Yaakov on her own wedding night (although that decision was painful), and she willingly shared the future children of Israel with three other wives. When it seemed that this sacrifice was for nothing ("they are gone"), she argued with God. Her contention was that since she, a mere human, was able to accept the world as is, and make the necessary sacrifices, why wouldn't He accept her children as they were, including their failings? They were, after all, born into the world that He created.

The verse says that Rachel cried for her children because *einenu*, literally "he is gone" — in the singular. Rachel saw all the children of Israel — no matter which mother they come from — as one single nation. This nation is the Jewish people, the nation set up by Rachel.

Although Leah had six children, Bilhah had two children, and Zilpah had two children, all this was due to Rachel. If not for Rachel's generosity and kindness, Leah would not have married Yaakov. Rachel could have refused to let her father substitute Leah for herself under the *chuppah*, but she did not want Leah to be embarrassed. If not for Rachel's sacrifice and sensitivity, the Jewish people would have been totally different. There would have been no tribe of Yehudah and no tribe of Levi. All Jews would be biological children of Rachel. But Rachel suffered her sacrifices willingly, without jealousy, and also continually. When Rachel suffered the pain of infertility and there was no answer to her prayers, she gave her maidservant, Bilhah, to Yaakov so that more children could be born to Israel.

It is clear that Rachel never had a personal agenda; her whole life was devoted to building the Jewish people. She was the one who gave up the most, and she was the one who cried the most. And she refused to be comforted when her children fell into national disaster and calamity.

Unity

The Gur Aryeh (the Maharal) explains that Rachel understood and accepted that this world is built on fragmentation (*pirud*) (on Bereishis 47:7). We live in a world that looks like a broken mirror. Nothing fits. We see jagged fragments, not a whole picture. Yet fragmentation and dichotomy is there for a reason: So that we can unify the world, so that we can put the pieces back together and create a unified whole.

Unity does not mean that everyone should be exactly the same. Unity (*achdus*) means bringing many fragmented pieces together, making of them one thing. Unity cannot be created unless we begin with disunity, *pirud*. For example, one piece of paper is one. Twelve pieces of paper stapled together is unity. Twelve different tribes with twelve different personalities and different needs and different ways of serving God is good, when those tribes are brought together to form one nation.

Without disunity, there is no such thing as unity. What we see in this life is the disunity aspect, the *pirud*, and it's like looking into a broken mirror. The world seems to make no sense to us. Good people suffer, children die, evil exists. The world is fragmented. Yet behind the scenes is God. God sends both good and "bad." We need to understand that when God sends us things that feel bad they are really good.

Every day we cover our eyes and say "*Shema Yisrael, Hashem Elokeinu, Hashem echad* — Hear O Israel, the Lord is our God, the Lord is One." We cover our eyes because intellectually we know God is One, but we don't see it. It doesn't look like it. The total unity and oneness of God cannot be grasped in this world. Intellectually, we understand that "bad" is good and that it all comes from One, from God. Yet in truth, we remain in the dark, unable to see unity, the "One."

At the end of *Aleinu* we say, "On that day God will be One and His name will be One" (Zecharyah 14:9). The Gemara asks on this verse,

> Is He not One now? Said Rabbi Acha bar Chanina, "The future world is not like this world. In this world, for good tidings one says, 'He is good, and He does good,' while for evil tidings he says, 'Blessed be the true Judge.' In the future world it shall be only 'He is good and He does good."
>
> (*Pesachim* 50a)

Of course, God is One now, but it doesn't look like it. When we experience something we perceive as good, we say the *berachah* "*hatov vehameitiv* — God is good and does good." When we experience something we perceive as bad, we say "*baruch Dayan HaEmes* — blessed is the True Judge." This is a reflection of our perception. When we bless God as the True Judge, it is a reflection of the way we synthesize the pain of misfortune or loss with our trust in God. It is an acknowledgment that although something harsh feels bad and hurts, we accept God's judgment, however difficult. In other words, this *berachah* expresses our reaction to the "external wrapper," which looks and feels bad to us. We know that in the next world, we will be able to look back at the past and understand that everything that ever happened in this world was good. We'll see the internal meaning of our suffering, and we'll understand that it was truly for our own good, that God is One, and that all that emanates from Him is good, even the "bad." "On that day God will be One and His name will be One."

Mother of Return

Just as Yaakov is the prototype for exile, Rachel is the prototype of our redemption (*geulah*). Rachel was the person who understood the most that we live in a fragmented world that makes no sense. It didn't make sense that a righteous person like Leah should be embarrassed. It didn't make sense that Rachel should be kept away from her beloved Yaakov. It didn't make sense that Rachel, who gave away her place to her sister, without jealousy, should have no children.

But, of course, it all makes sense. *Hashem echad* — God is One. Rachel was able to live with her sacrifices because she understood that although the world looks fragmented, it all emanates from One, from God. Out of the fragmentation, one can build unity. The children of Israel would be born from four different wives, and Leah would be the partner of Yaakov in the hidden world, in the world to come, while Rachel would be the partner of Yaakov only in the lower world. Leah would become the mother of the kingdom of Yehudah, and Rachel would become the mother of the kingdom of Israel, and there would be disunity. Why? So that we, the Jewish people, could build and unify. Built into our national makeup are differences — we are twelve tribes, each with a different personality; we are Ashkenazim and Sefardim; we are *misnagdim* and chassidim. There are all kinds of Jews — built in — and all of us, together, are to create harmony from our differences, just as an artist takes the different hues on his palette and creates a beautiful painting.

Rachel understood this purpose and this potential, so she accepted her part in the process and she was able to give Yaakov to Leah from a deep sense of love — love for the unborn children, love for the Jewish people, love for the future. Yet when her children were led into exile, in chains and in pain, she cried. Was all that she had suffered for nothing? She refused to accept that, and she argued with God — "God, You built the world in such a way that it's fragmented. You created a divided world. Are You surprised that we can't get everything right in Your world? Are You so surprised that in this world of Yours, where it's so difficult to see Your Oneness, we go off the right path, we make mistakes, and we even worship idols?" Rachel's argument was that it was natural for the Jewish people to sin, so God should forgive them for what was natural. God should have compassion and mercy on His people, who fail because of their inability to see Him. It was a powerful argument, and God responded to it (*Gur Aryeh*).

> Rabbi Yitzchak interprets that Rachel was the essence [*ikar*] of [Yaakov's] home. "And Rachel was barren [*akarah*]" [read as] "the essence".... Rabbi Shimon ben Yochai [said], "Everything was dependent on Rachel. Therefore, Israel is called by her name, [as it says,] 'Rachel cries for her children' (Yirmiyahu 31:14). And not only that, Israel is called by her son's name, [as it says,] 'Perhaps Hashem will have pity on the remnant of Yosef' (Amos 5:15)."
>
> (*Bereishis Rabbah* 71:2)

Rachel is called the "*akeres habayis*" — she is the essence of Yaakov's home. She is the *beis Yaakov*; she is his home and our home. A home is a place that includes and unites all within it. Rachel, the essence of the Jewish home, unites us because she sees us as one family, one unit, despite our differences. Not only at the inception of the Jewish people as a nation, but in the final redemption as well.

The Gur Aryeh reveals a deeper meaning to this *midrash*. When Rachel is called *akeres habayis*, this means that all of the Jewish people exist because of her. The Jewish people are also called "*knesses Yisrael*," the gathering of Israel. This hints to the final redemption, when Rachel's children will be gathered home to be reunited with God.

The fragmentation of the exile contains within it the potential for tremendous unity. Rachel was buried on the road because her partner in this world is not in Chevron, where the other matriarchs and patriarchs are buried. Rachel's partner is *knesses Yisrael*, the Jewish people, so she was buried on the road where they would go into exile and come home from exile (*Gur Aryeh*).

The road represents a transition point. Traveling on the road means we are not there yet, but we are on the way. We are on the way into exile which is productive and creative, yet painful and fragmented. And we are also on our way back from exile, to a place of harmony and unity. Rachel is waiting on the road, waiting for us to come home, because she accepts the gap between these two places — exile and redemption — and she longs for the integration. Rachel understands that redemption is the potential born of that longing.

Man of Exile, Woman of Return

Why was Yaakov was so concerned about burial in the Land of Israel that he needed to be promised twice that he would be buried there? The second time, Yaakov was speaking about something different — he was speaking about the future, about Efrayim and Menasheh, about the children who would be born in exile. "Remember, when you are in the next exile," said Yaakov, "you are still my children, my centerpoint." He declared that Efrayim and Menasheh were his own children so that every one of us born in exile, forever afterwards, would remember that we, too, belong to Yaakov; we are all the children of Israel. More than that, Yaakov reminded Yosef that Rachel waits on the road for Efrayim and Menasheh and for all the children born in exile to return home. Yaakov reminded Yosef that our partner, Rachel, is "there" — waiting for the long exile to end, and for her children to return.

Yaakov connected his vision in Luz with Efrayim and Menasheh because we must never think that the condition of exile, disruption, and dichotomy is the end point. We must understand that even when it's good, it's creative, and it develops our individuality, it is never the goal and it's not the end. The end is coming home. Yaakov reminded Yosef, Efrayim, and Menasheh, that our everlasting inheritance is found not there, but in Israel.

Both Yaakov and Rachel understood that exile was a place of growth and creativity, and both wanted to use exile to build the Jewish people. But they always knew that the world of exile is merely the means to the end. Yaakov, the man of exile, made his children promise that he would be returned to his home, to Israel. Rachel, the woman of redemption, is waiting on the road. She's waiting for her children, every one of us, to unite as one people, to unite with God, and to return to our land.

Menasheh and Efrayim, the first Jewish children born in the exile, represent the potential to forge a dichotomy into harmony. We, too, live in a world of disunity and fragmentation, a world that makes no sense. But we learn from our ancestors that we can build something from this. Although we don't yet see the Oneness of God, we can learn to see His Oneness — and thereby to bring His Holy Unity into evidence, into expression. When we train ourselves to see that God is behind the scenes at every single moment of existence and we learn to forge the dichotomy into harmony, our job will be done, we can come home, and Rachel will weep no more.

Building the Future

Leah and Rachel: Inside and Out

(Based on a *shiur* by HaRav Chaim Goldvicht,
Asufos Maarchos, vol. I.)

One of the most fascinating narratives in the Torah is the story of Yaakov's marriage to two sisters, Rachel and Leah. This story is beautiful even at a simple level, but there is a deeper meaning to this episode which can be gleaned from the Midrash and commentaries. When we delve into the narrative, we find multiple story lines, each of which is like a piece of a puzzle. Fitting the pieces together, a unified and cohesive picture is formed.

Two Sons

> The boys grew up and Eisav became one who knows hunting, a man of the field, and Yaakov was a man abiding in tents. Yitzchak loved Eisav, for venison was in his mouth; but Rivkah loved Yaakov.
>
> (Bereishis 25:27–28)

The twin brothers, Eisav and Yaakov, were different in temperament, personality, and focus. Eisav, the elder brother, was a hunter; whereas Yaakov, the younger brother, was a man whose focus was on Torah learning, as Rashi explains. Eisav served his father game prepared from the hunt, and his father loved him. When Yitzchak decided to give the elder son, Eisav, the blessing of leadership of the Jewish people, Rivkah, loving the younger son, took steps to prevent it. She understood that Eisav was a false personality, and that the blessing had to be given to Yaakov.

> Rivkah said to Yaakov, her son, saying, "Behold I heard your father speaking to your brother, Eisav, saying: 'Bring me some game and make me delicacies to eat, and I will bless you in the presence of God before my death.' So now, my son, heed my voice, to that which I command you. Go to the flock and fetch two choice young goat kids for me, and I will make delicacies for your father, as he loves. Then bring it to your father and he shall eat, so that he may bless you before his death."
>
> Yaakov replied to Rivkah, his mother, "But my brother Eisav is a hairy man, and I am a smooth-skinned man. Perhaps my father will feel me and I shall be as a mocker in his eyes; I will thus bring upon myself a curse rather than a blessing."
>
> But his mother said to him, "Your curse will be on me, my son; only listen to my voice and go fetch them for me."
>
> So he went, fetched, and brought [venison] to his mother, and his mother made delicacies as his father loved. Rivkah then took her older son Eisav's clean garments, which were with her in the house, and clothed Yaakov, her younger son. She covered his arms and his smooth-skinned neck with the skins of the goat kids. She placed the delicacies and the bread which she had made into the hand of her son Yaakov....
>
> Yitzchak said to Yaakov, "Come close, if you please, so I can feel you, my son. Are you, indeed, my son Eisav or not?"

So Yaakov drew close to Yitzchak, his father, who felt him and said, "The voice is Yaakov's voice, but the hands are Eisav's hands." But he did not recognize him because his hands were hairy like the hands of Eisav, his brother, so he blessed him.

He said, "You are, indeed, my son Eisav!"

He said, "I am."

(Ibid. 27:6–24)

In her instructions to Yaakov, Rivkah was specific as to what had to be prepared. She told him to fetch "two choice young goat kids" which she would prepare as food for Yitzchak. The goats would also provide a "cover" for Yaakov's smooth skin.

Two Goats

Rivkah's instructions are puzzling. Why did she need two goats for Yitzchak's meal? How much can one person eat?

The Midrash explains that Yaakov's new role as leader was similar to the role of a shepherd herding his flock. In her instructions to take two goats, Rivkah was actually telling him to begin the process of building the nation:

> "Go and advance the nation that is compared to a flock, [as it says,] 'You are my flock, the flock of my pasture' (Yechezkel 34:31).... Good for you and good for your children: good for you, because through them you will take the blessings; good for your children, because through them they will be forgiven, as it is written, 'For on this day He will forgive you' (Vayikra 16:30)."
>
> (*Yalkut Shimoni, Bereishis* 114:27)

When Rivkah asked her son to take two goats from the flock, she was alluding to a future ceremony in the Temple.

From the assembly of the children of Israel [Aharon] shall

take two he-goats for a sin-offering....

(Vayikra 16:5)

During the days of the Temple, one of the central services on Yom Kippur was the sacrifice of two identical goats. Through a lottery, one goat was designated "for God," and the other goat was to be "for Azazel." The *kohen gadol* (high priest) would take the goat for God, put his hand on the goat's head, and confess the sins of the Jewish people. This goat was sacrificed as an atonement for their sins (Vayikra 16:20–22). The second goat, "for Azazel," was led out of Jerusalem and down to the valley of Gehinnom, toward the desert. When they arrived at the wilderness of Judea, this goat was turned around, so its landing mechanism wouldn't work, and pushed off a cliff. This goat atoned for the sins of Israel as a nation.

The two goats that Yaakov took and his mother prepared, then, did not solely concern Yitzchak's supper that day. The two goats concerned the Jewish people and atonement; they were connected with Yom Kippur and the Temple. Clearly, the Midrash is stating that what Yaakov did was bigger than what it appeared to be. Not only was he preparing to receive the blessing of leadership, but he was also setting the stage for the future of his people.

Two Sisters

Leah's eyes were tender, while Rachel was beautiful of form and beautiful of appearance.

(Bereishis 29:17)

Rivkah had a brother, Lavan, who was an evil person. Lavan had two daughters, and each one was destined to marry one of Rivkah's sons. In describing the physical appearance of these young women, the Torah also discloses their qualities. The external, beautiful appearance of Rachel reflects her inner soul, her inner beauty. Why, however, would the Torah speak disparagingly of Rachel's sister Leah, a mother of Israel, by describing her as a person with tender eyes? Since the language of the Torah is always very sensitive, this description is difficult to understand.

Actually, the text does not describe an unsightly physical blemish. The Torah is speaking about something far deeper:

> [The condition of Leah's eyes] was no disgrace to her but a credit, for at the crossroads she heard people saying, "Rivkah has two sons, [and] Lavan has two daughters. The elder [son should be married] to the elder [daughter], and the younger [son should be married] to the younger [daughter]."
>
> Leah sat at the crossroads [and asked], "How does the elder one conduct himself?"
>
> [She was told,] "He is a wicked man, a highway robber."
>
> "How does the younger man conduct himself?"
>
> "A quiet man dwelling in tents."
>
> And she wept until her eyelashes dropped.
>
> *(Bava Basra* 123a)

Leah's eyes were tender from crying about her destiny to marry an evil person. Talk of her marriage to Eisav was not idle gossip, it was indeed her destiny — the elder for the elder, the younger for the younger. Thus, the Torah's description of her tender eyes was in praise of her abhorrence of evil.

> Yaakov loved Rachel, so he said [to Lavan], "I will work for you seven years for Rachel your younger daughter."
>
> Lavan said, "It is better that I give her to you than that I give her to another man; remain with me."
>
> So Yaakov worked seven years for Rachel, and they seemed to him a few days because of his love for her. [Then] Yaakov said to Lavan, "Deliver my wife for my term is fulfilled, and I will marry her."
>
> (Bereishis 29:18–21)

As the wedding night approached, Rachel and Yaakov suspected that Lavan would substitute Leah for Rachel. The custom in those days was that the younger daughter would not marry before the older one. The bride wore a thick veil, and no one could see who was underneath it. It would be easy for Lavan to switch brides. Yaakov therefore created a code, words which he and Rachel would exchange under the *chuppah*, so that if there was a switch, he would know it and stop the marriage proceedings.

On the wedding night, Lavan indeed made the switch. However, Rachel had pity on her sister. She imagined her sister's humiliation should Yaakov refuse to continue with the wedding. The whole town would see what had happened and Leah would be shamed. Therefore, Rachel revealed the code to her sister, and the marriage between Leah and Yaakov took place. The couple proceeded to the bridal chamber, and Lavan made sure no candles were there to light the room. Yaakov, therefore, was unaware of the deception until the next morning. What was his reaction?

> All that night he called her "Rachel" and she answered him. In the morning [he saw that] she was Leah. He said to her, "What?! Cheater and daughter of a cheater! Didn't I call you 'Rachel' at night and didn't you answer me?"
>
> She said to him, "Is there a barber who has no apprentice? Wasn't it the same when your father called you 'Eisav' and you answered him?"
>
> (*Bereishis Rabbah* 70:7)

Implicit in this *midrash* is an accusation that Yaakov lied to his father. Therefore, measure for measure, he was lied to. God always pays us back measure for measure; we get what we give.

Nevertheless, this Midrash is difficult to understand. Superficially, it appears that Yaakov, a man of truth, and Leah, a woman of magnificent character, engaged in a very nasty conversation, in tones of anger and acrimony, after the wedding night no less. This, of course, is not possible, so we must look more deeply into the *midrash* to understand what took place.

Two Variations of One Dream

Rachel married Yaakov, too, and she had two children with him. The firstborn son, Yosef, was sold by his brothers into slavery. Yosef went down to Egypt and became the viceroy to Pharaoh. But before this, when Yosef was a young lad, still at home with his brothers, he had a dream.

> Yosef dreamed a dream which he told to his brothers, and they hated him even more. He said to them, "Hear, if you please, this dream which I dreamed — we were binding sheaves in the middle of the field, when my sheaf arose and also remained standing. Then your sheaves gathered around and bowed down to my sheaf."
>
> His brothers said to him, "Would you then reign over us? Would you then dominate us?" And they hated him even more — because of his dreams and because of his talk.
>
> (Bereishis 37:6–8)

Although Yosef made no attempt to interpret his dream to his brothers, they intuitively grasped its meaning: Yosef would rule over them.

The Midrash expands this dream and explains the source of Yosef's domination.

> [Yosef said to his brothers,] "You were gathering in fruit and I was gathering in fruit, yet yours rotted while mine stood sound; thus, 'my sheaf arose and also remained standing....' And what stood me in good stead? My mother's silence [during her sister's marriage (*Rashi*)]."
>
> (*Bereishis Rabbah* 84:10)

According to the Midrash, the sheaves in the dream were fruit, and they were not standing in the middle of the field, but being gathered in from the field. Not only that, the fruit gathered by the brothers decayed, whereas Yosef's fruit remained fresh. Why does the Midrash change wheat into fruit, and why did Yosef's fruit retain its freshness while his brothers' fruit decayed? In addition, how does the silence of Rachel lead to Yosef's dominion over his brothers? The key to understanding these questions comes with the examination of a basic Jewish principle: There are two ways in which we serve God, internally and externally.

Two Modes of Service

The Jewish people serve God in two ways. We shall call these modes of service "internal service" and "external service."

"Internal service" is a direct interfacing with holiness. The goal of this type of activity is to achieve spirituality, and the person engaged in this type of service does something that is, in itself, spiritual. For example, the goal of prayer is to connect with God, and the action of prayer is itself the connection. It is an act that looks spiritual and is spiritual. A person learning Torah appears to be doing something religious, and, indeed, he *is* doing something religious.

On the other hand, a person involved in "external service" appears to be doing a physical action, but in truth he is also doing something spiritual. He is not engaged in an overtly holy activity, but his actions are governed by religious motivation. For instance, an accountant might appear to be dealing solely with his accounts. It doesn't look holy. But if all of his actions reflect his desire to serve God — that is, if he is honest, considerate, and conscientious, then he is acting as a servant of God. A shoe repairman who is scrupulous in his repair work is doing holy service of God. A parent who changes diapers is doing an act of

Leah and Rachel: Inside and Out • 237

lovingkindness. The act may not look holy, but it is indeed an indirect interplay with holiness.

God requires both types of service: external and internal. Some mitzvos focus on one and some on the other, but all mitzvos ultimately lead to a holy life and all mitzvos are part of Divine service. When the work is external service, it might not appear to be so holy. Nevertheless, an adherence to God's laws in the external world counts as much as laws concerning prayer or tefillin.

Yitzchak was aware that the Jewish people would be diverse and that the Torah would require both external and internal service of God. Most Jews would serve God in both ways, but there would have to be "specialists" in both areas. It would be necessary for some Jews to sit in yeshivah all day long and learn, so that they could keep their brethren focused on the center of Jewish life, the Torah. There would be other people who would go out and work in the outside world, and their honesty and integrity would create a *kiddush Hashem*, an elevation and sanctification of God's name. This was expressed most obviously in the relationship between the tribes of Zevulun and Yissachar — the tribe of Zevulun worked full time, the tribe of Yissachar learned Torah full time, and the two tribes shared their wealth, physical and spiritual.

Yitzchak viewed Eisav as the potential leader of the external world and Yaakov as the potential leader of the internal world. Yaakov, who dwelled in the tents, would be in charge of the spirituality, of being focused on God, and of learning Torah. Eisav, the hunter, would be the integrated Jew who manages to stay focused on God while involved in the outside world, doing secular work. The two would work hand in hand. Yaakov's focus on Torah would help keep Eisav "straight," reminding him constantly of what his real goal was; and Eisav's involvement with the material concerns of the outside world would extract the sparks of holiness from the physical world, elevating them in the service of God (*Sefas Emes, Toldos* 5655).

This was Yitzchak's goal in blessing Eisav — to give him a blessing of leadership for the "external service." He believed Eisav worthy and suited to this role because of Eisav's demeanor when serving him.

> Rabbi Shimon ben Gamliel said, "I served my father all my life, but not one-hundredth as well as Eisav served Yitzchak. I served my father in dirty clothes and went out on the road in clean clothes. But Eisav, when serving his father, wore clothes of royalty."
>
> (*Bereishis Rabbah* 65:16)

Clothing, although physical and external, is very important. Clothing expresses a person's view of himself, and therefore every person dresses according to his persona, the part he believes he plays in the world. If he thinks he is lowly, he wears shabby clothing. If he thinks his value as a human being rests with his physical body, he wears scanty clothes. If he perceives himself as a child of the King of Kings, then he wears royal clothing, that is, garments that are clean, respectable, and modest. He wears his finest garments in honor of Shabbos. During the days of the Temple, the *kohanim* (priests) wore special clothing to perform the service in the Temple. In short, although clothing is part of the external world, it is an expression of a person's internal view of himself; it is an external symbol of the person's internal essence.

Eisav honored his father, and he expressed this honor when he served his father by wearing royal clothes. Yitzchak therefore thought his son was holy. However, clothing can only be a symbol of a person's essence if the external honestly reflects the internal. Eisav dressed himself in a holy way, but his dress did not match his internal self. It is possible to put on a yarmulke and dress as a religious person without being honest or righteous or religious. When someone does this, he is not integrated and he is dishonest.

Yitzchak saw Eisav for what he purported to be, and so he was blind to Eisav's shortcomings. Since it appeared to Yitzchak that Eisav could be the leader of the external service of God, he prepared a blessing for him.

Two Blessings

Yitzchak understood that since there would be two types of work to be done by the Jewish people, two types of blessings were required. One blessing was designed specifically for Eisav and his job, and the other blessing was designed specifically for Yaakov and his job. Each son would receive the appropriate blessing and each would be a leader.

> "May God give you of the dew of the heavens and of the fatness of the earth, and abundant grain and wine."
>
> (Bereishis 27:28)

This blessing, about physicality, is the blessing that was meant for Eisav. This is the blessing for leadership in the physical world, which enables the Jew to elevate the physical aspect of the world and make it spiritual. Yitzchak thought this role would be Eisav's.

After Yitzchak discovered that he had given Eisav's blessing to Yaakov he called Yaakov to him and blessed him again, saying,

> "May God bless you, make you fruitful and make you numerous, and may you be a congregation of peoples. May He grant the blessing of Avraham to you and to your offspring with you, that you may possess the land of your sojourns which God gave to Avraham."
>
> (Ibid. 28:1-4)

This is the spiritual blessing. This is the blessing Yitzchak always intended to give to Yaakov, since Yaakov was to be the leader of the spiritual world. Yitzchak had prepared two blessings because he believed that Eisav and Yaakov would be partners, and each would be blessed with the appropriate strengths required to get the job done.

Rivkah, however, saw through Eisav's external behavior; she understood that although he dressed the part, the external did not accurately reflect the internal. Rivkah therefore made the decision to instruct Yaakov to "take" Eisav's blessing as well as his own. She wanted to combine both kinds of leadership in him. Yaakov would be the single leader of the Jewish people, and he would provide guidance for both the internal and external service.

Therefore, Rivkah asked him to prepare two goats. Why two goats? One was for the blessing Yaakov was taking in Eisav's stead, the other for his own blessing. Two goats were needed because there are two kinds of Jews: the Jew who serves God "inside the Temple," that is, the Jew who does internal service; and the Jew who serves God "outside the Temple," that is, the Jew who does God's work in the external world. These two goats symbolize the same ideas that goats of the Yom Kippur service symbolize. One of the goats would be sacrificed inside the Temple. The other goat would be taken out of the Temple and pushed over a cliff. These two goats would atone for the sins of the entire people of Israel.

Rivkah also gave Yaakov Eisav's clothing to wear. Since clothes are the external expression of an internal status, when Yaakov wore Eisav's clothing, he "wore" his leadership role, as well.

Two Partners, Two Partnerships

Eisav and Yaakov needed partners to help them fulfill their missions. When a person wants to form a partnership, he needs a partner who will contribute strengths other than those he already possesses. Since Eisav's strength was to be in the material, external world, he would need a partner who specialized in spiritual, internal strength. Yaakov, on the other hand, who was to be the leader of spiritual, internal service, needed a partner whose strength was in the physical, external world. Since he would be focused inwardly, he needed a partner who could help him maneuver in the outside world.

Rachel is described as a very beautiful woman externally. In other words, she was the partner in the outside world to Yaakov's inside world. She would be his partner in developing spiritual leadership. Leah, on the other hand, is portrayed as having tender eyes; her beauty was inside. She would be Eisav's partner in developing external leadership. He would contribute expertise in dealing outside, and she would provide the spiritual, internal underpinnings necessary to do the outside job properly — that is, without forgetting God.

This is what was intended, but it didn't work out that way because Eisav did not develop into a man capable of leading the Jewish people. Instead, he sought idol worship.

This explains why Leah sat at the crossroads crying. She was aware that her destiny was to marry Eisav. That was fine with her; she was thrilled to be his partner in the building of the external world, in elevating the physical to the spiritual. But when she heard that Eisav was a wicked robber and he did every abomination against God, she realized that there could be no partnership with him. So she cried over her destiny to marry such a person. Her tears brought her to a state that her eyelashes fell out, and her eyes were constantly tender. True, no one could force her to marry the wicked Eisav, but what would she do? How would she be involved in the creation of the Jewish people with no partner?

Yaakov, however, took the blessing for the external job, and he was also given the spiritual blessing. (Yitzchak did not withhold Yaakov's spiritual blessing in retaliation for his having taken the external blessing. Eisav himself admitted to Yitzchak that he had already given over his leadership privilege to

Yaakov; see Bereishis 27:36.) He then left his home, because Eisav wanted to kill him and, in addition, because he needed to find a wife, a partner.

When Yaakov met Rachel for the first time, he immediately fell in love with her because he recognized that she was his destined partner. She would help him do the spiritual work, the work of connecting to God. Yaakov loved Rachel because he realized that the outcome of their building would be eternal. It was the love of eternity, the love of partnership, the love of setting up spirituality as the core of the Jewish people.

When Yaakov took his brother's blessing in addition to his own, he took over Eisav's position as leader of the external service as well. As a result, he unknowingly inherited Eisav's partner, Leah, as his helpmate (*Sefas Emes, Vayeitzei* 5647). Therefore, though there would be only one leader for both internal and external service, there would be two partners, Rachel and Leah. We might think that, according to the previous plan, Rachel would be Yaakov's "internal service" partner, and Leah would be his "external service" partner, but the dynamics of the situation were dramatically altered.

Two Wives

The Jewish people have two jobs, but only one is permanent. When Adam and Chavah sinned, good and evil became intertwined. In this physical world, therefore, it's not always easy to figure out what is good and what is evil. "Filters" are needed — people of God who are trained to recognize good from evil. These people are the Jewish people, and the job of the Jew in the external world is to identify the holiness found in the physical world and use it for spirituality. By definition, then, the external work will not have permanence. It will last as long as good and evil are intertwined in the physical world, but not forever. Eventually, the world will change and its spiritual core will be dominant. The revelation of Mashiach will return us to a Gan Eden situation, where the spiritual content of the physical world will be obvious. At that time, the external work will no longer be necessary.

Even now, when we have both internal and external work to do, we have to develop the internal aspect of ourselves first. The internal service is the permanent and essential core. A Jew can't function properly unless he first knows what is holy and what is not. It isn't good enough to put on the right clothes — without a strong foundation, there will be no integration of character and the person will fail. Each individual requires proper internal development in order to enter the external world with the appropriate tools. First he learns Torah. Afterwards, when he understands good and evil and has a strong sense of *derech eretz* (proper behavior), he can go outside into the world and use his knowledge. Knowing what holiness looks like, having integrated holiness into his character, the Jew is prepared to filter the holiness in his physical environment and to separate the good from the evil. The internal work must take priority in our development as Jews, because it is the foundation of Torah existence in the external work.

Internal service of God lasts eternally, and, therefore, being Yaakov's partner for the internal work meant being his partner into eternity. This was to be Rachel's role, but when Lavan switched the brides, making Leah Yaakov's wife first, the roles were switched. Leah became Yaakov's partner for the primary service, the spiritual, internal service of God that must be developed first. Rachel was left with the secondary position and became Yaakov's partner in the external world.

At this point, we can begin to have a glimmer of understanding about the greatness of our mother Rachel. When Rachel gave over those signs, allowing Yaakov to marry Leah first, she gave to Leah the role of partner to Yaakov in the internal service of God. Allowing Leah to stand in her place under the *chuppah*, she gave over the partnership of eternity. Leah is buried with Yaakov in the Cave of Machpeilah. Leah is Yaakov's partner in the next world. Leah is Yaakov's partner in the time of Mashiach. Rachel gave it all away so that her sister wouldn't be shamed.

> All that night he called her "Rachel" and she answered him. In the morning [he saw that] she was Leah. He said to her, "What?! Cheater and daughter of a cheater! Didn't I call you 'Rachel' at night and didn't you answer me?"
>
> She said to him, "Is there a barber who has no apprentice? Wasn't it the same when your father called you 'Eisav' and you answered him?"
>
> (*Bereishis Rabbah* 70:7)

This seemingly coarse discussion between Yaakov and Leah can now be understood. Leah's words contain an inner meaning. When Yaakov called her "cheater and daughter of a cheater," he was telling her that she belonged to Eisav, to a different spiritual framework, and that by marrying him she had "cheated" the place where she belonged. Leah answered that by taking Eisav's blessings, he had changed the spiritual situation.

We learn from the episode of the stolen blessings that there are spiritual pathways that cannot be taken without some kind of detour. Just as Tamar couldn't bring about the seed of Mashiach without tricking Yehudah, Rivkah needed to fool Yitzchak in order that the blessings be given to the appropriate son. Leah followed a similar detour in her marriage to Yaakov.

Therefore, Leah's reply to Yaakov, "Is there a barber who has no apprentice?" meant that she had followed his own path, the path that allowed him to inherit the leadership of external service. He set the example; his action laid the groundwork for her own. He did what he needed to do, and so did Leah, his apprentice. Just as Rivkah understood that Yaakov had to be both external and internal leader, and just as Tamar realized that her union with a member of Yehudah's family was necessary to bring forth the seed of Mashiach, so too did Leah know that it was incumbent upon her to participate in the formation of the Jewish people. In taking Eisav's role, Yaakov took Eisav's partner as well (*Sefas Emes, Vayeitzei* 5647).

When Leah took Rachel's place under the *chuppah*, this had an impact on the destiny of future generations. The "signs" given to her by Rachel overturned the spiritual framework. When Leah took Rachel's place she took, as well, her role of external partner to the internal service. When Rachel gave her the "signs," she gave Leah the tools necessary for this job.

Two Legacies

When discussing Yosef's dream, the Midrash refers to the wheat as fruit, because fruit decays while wheat does not. In Yosef's dream, the brothers' fruit was gathered in but decayed, whereas his fruit was gathered in and did not decay. The "gathering in" represents bringing holiness (*kedushah*) from the outside world to the inner, holy realm. The fruit of Yosef stayed fresh because he had the tools that are required to "use" the external world, and he was therefore able to gather sparks of holiness from it. The brothers were not experts in this realm. They would not have succeeded in maintaining holiness in Egypt as Yosef did. And why is that? Yosef explained, "Because of my mother's silence." He meant, "Because when my mother was silent that night, the night of your mother's wedding, she rearranged your spiritual destiny and mine. As Rachel's son, I became the leader of the external world, whereas you, Leah's sons, took the role of the internal world."

> "The name of the elder [*gedolah*] was Leah" (Bereishis 29:16). [She was] greater [*gedolah*] in her gifts, eternal priesthood and eternal kingship, as it is written, "But Yehudah will remain forever..." (Yoel 4:20); and it is

written, "This is My resting place forever" (Tehillim 132:14).

"And the name of the younger [*ketanah*] was Rachel" (Bereishis 29:16). [She was] lesser [*ketanah*] in her gifts: [the rulership of] Yosef was temporary, [the rulership of] Shaul was temporary, and [the Mishkan in] Shilo was temporary. "He rejected the tabernacle of Yosef and did not choose the tribe of Efrayim" (Tehillim 78:67).

(Bereishis Rabbah 70:15)

The Jewish people has two kings: Yosef and Yehudah. Yosef was the son of Rachel, and Yehudah was the son of Leah. Yehudah, through his descendant King David, is the king forever; Yosef is a king for a temporary period of time. Yosef was king in Egypt, the external world, the world of the physical. In this world, Yosef acted righteously, elevating himself despite the difficult obstacles he encountered daily. Within this world, he acted in a Godly manner. When Potifar's wife attempted to seduce him, he maintained his righteousness. When interacting in the king's court, he maintained the dignity and honesty incumbent on the leader of external service. He resisted taking credit for his triumph and assigned all of his success to God. Nevertheless, Yosef was a temporal king, an allusion to the temporary physical world in which we live.

Yehudah, the son of Leah, on the other hand, is the ancestor of King David. All future kings descend from the house of David, even until the time of Mashiach, who will also be a descendant of David. Yehudah and David are the leaders of the spiritual, internal service, the service that will last forever. "And Yehudah will remain forever."

There were two tabernacles. The temporary tabernacle, the Mishkan, was set up in Shilo, in the portion of the tribe of Yosef. The other tabernacle, the Beis HaMikdash, was built in Jerusalem, the portion of the tribe of Yehudah. Although it was twice destroyed, it will be rebuilt once more, and it will then last forever. "This is My resting place forever."

The first Jewish king was King Shaul, who descended from Rachel's second son, Binyamin. Shaul's kingship was a necessary precursor to David's, but it was never meant to last forever. God took the kingship away from King Shaul and gave it to the house of David, permanently.

Rachel's gifts are smaller and temporary. Leah's gifts are extensive — that is, long lasting, permanent.

One Nation

Although there are two services of God in this world, external and internal, there is one nation and every Jew supports that nation. Some Jews spend all of their time specializing in the internal world, learning in yeshivos, teaching Torah, serving in rabbinical positions; some Jews spend most of their time doing external work, as professionals, businessmen, farmers, laborers. We need each other. The center of our lives is the internal, and it is from this center that we expand to the outside world, remembering that Torah remains the core. Thanks to the spiritual strength given to us by our patriarchs and matriarchs, we have been able to serve God in all of these areas for thousands of years.

We anxiously await the time when Mashiach will be revealed to us. Until that time we continue to function as servants of God in the manner of Yosef and Yehudah. In the future, there will be two Mashiachs. Mashiach ben Yosef, a descendant of Rachel, will come first. He will fight a great battle, but his leadership will be temporary. After Mashiach ben Yosef, Mashiach ben David, the permanent Mashiach, will come. As a descendant of Yehudah, a child of the internal world, he will bring a permanent state of spirituality to the Jewish people, to all of us, as one nation.

May this occur speedily in our days.

In the Merit of the Righteous Women

(Based on the book *Zechus Nashim Tzidkanios* by HaRav Ben Zion Rabinovitz, the Biale Rebbe)

Recalling our righteous matriarchs often brings to mind their prayers and their tears. We learn that even today we can follow their example and use their spiritual strength to develop a relationship with God and to serve Him with wholehearted faith. However, we may ask, is the function of those prayers and tears solely a matter of fortifying our faith and developing a closer relationship with God, or do the words and the tears of our mothers have a deeper implication as well?

The First Exile

When the children of Israel were walking into exile in chains, after having witnessed the destruction of the First Temple, our righteous ancestors stood before God, in Heaven, to beseech Him for clemency and for the continuity of the Jewish people.

Avraham began to speak before God. "Lord of the Universe, when I was one hundred years old You gave me a son; when he achieved understanding, and was a youth of thirty-seven You said to me, 'Bring him up before Me as an offering.' I was brutal toward him and showed him no compassion, but bound him myself. Will You not remember this for me, and will You not have compassion over my sons?"

Yitzchak said: "Lord of the Universe, when my father said to me, 'God will see for Himself a sheep for an offering, my son' (Bereishis 22:8), I did not resist Your words and was willingly bound on the altar. I stretched forth my throat under the knife. Will You not remember this for me, and will You have no compassion over my sons?"

Yaakov said: "Lord of the Universe, did I not stay in the house of Lavan twenty years? And when I came out of his house, the iniquitous Eisav came upon me and wanted to kill my sons. I offered my life for them. And now they have been handed over to their enemies like sheep to slaughter, after I raised them like little birds and suffered over them the anguish of raising children. Will You not remember this for me and have compassion over my sons?"

Moshe said: "Lord of the Universe, was I not a loyal shepherd for Israel forty years? Did I not run before them like a horse, in the wilderness? When the time came for them to enter the land, You decreed that my bones were to fall in the wilderness. And now that they have gone into exile, You have sent me to lament and weep over them?"...

At that hour Moshe said to Yirmiyahu: "Go before me, and I will go to [*klal Yisrael*] and see [the enemy] who is putting his hand on them."

Yirmiyahu said to him, "It is not possible to walk on the road because of the slain."

Said he, "Nevertheless!"

Moshe went with Yirmiyahu before him, till they reached the rivers of Babylon. [The Jews there] saw Moshe and said to one another, "The son of Amram has come from his grave to redeem us from the hands of our enemies."

A *bas kol* [a voice from Heaven] said, "It is a decree from Me!"

Immediately Moshe said to them, "My sons, to bring you back is impossible, for the decree has already been issued." At that hour they raised their voices in great weeping, till their cries ascended on high. Of this it was said, "By the rivers of Babylon there we sat, we also wept..." (Tehillim 137:1).

At that hour our mother Rachel threw herself before the Holy One, blessed be He, and said, "Master of the Universe, it is revealed to You that Your servant Yaakov loved me an extra measure of love, and that he worked for my father for seven years to marry me. When those seven years were completed and the time came for me to marry my husband, my father contrived to replace me with my sister. It was very hard for me, because the plot was known to me and I disclosed it to my husband. I gave him a sign whereby he could distinguish between me and my sister, so that my father should not be able to make the substitution.

"After that I relented, suppressed my desire, and had pity on my sister so she should not be exposed to shame. In the evening they substituted my sister for me, and I delivered to my sister all the signs which I had arranged with my husband, so that he should think that she was Rachel....

"I was not jealous of my sister, nor did I expose her to shame. And if I, a creature of flesh and blood, formed of dust and ashes, was not jealous of one who caused me pain, why were You, merciful and eternal King, jealous of idols in which there is no reality, and why have You exiled my children? They were slain by the sword, and their enemies did to them as they wished!"

Immediately, the mercy of the Holy One, blessed be He, was aroused, and He said, "For your sake, Rachel, I will return Israel to their place." And so it is written: "Thus said Hashem, 'A voice is heard on high — wailing, bitterly weeping. Rachel weeps for her children; she refuses to be comforted for her children, for they are gone.' Thus said Hashem: 'Restrain your voice from weeping, and your eyes from tears; and there is reward for your accomplishment...and they will return from the enemy's land. There is hope for your future,' says Hashem; 'and your children will return to their border' " (Yirmiyahu 31:14–16).

(Pesikta d'Eichah Rabbasi 23)

Although each of the patriarchs begged for mercy, and although Moshe and Yirmiyahu pleaded with God, He remained silent and did not answer them. It was as if God had turned a deaf ear to their prayers, and nothing they said could convince Him to change His decree. Only when Rachel spoke her piece did God agree to return the Jewish people to their place of glory, to their place in the Land of Israel.

The Egyptian Exile

Nine hundred years before the Babylonian exile, the Jewish people had been exiled in Egypt, where they were enslaved, oppressed, and degraded. One of the cruelest actions against the Jewish people was the royal decree that all male Jewish babies were to be murdered. Despite Pharaoh's order to throw Jewish babies into the Nile River, our mothers continued to give birth to babies. One such woman, Yocheved, attempted to save her child's life:

> [Yocheved] saw that [Moshe] was good and she hid him for three months. [When] she could no longer conceal him, she took for him a wicker basket and smeared it with clay and pitch, placed the child into it, and placed it among the reeds at the bank of the river. His sister [Miriam] stationed herself at a distance to know what would be done with him.
>
> Pharaoh's daughter went down to bathe by the river, and her maidens walked along the river. She saw the basket among the reeds, and she sent her maidservant and took it. She opened it and saw him, the child, and behold the youth was crying. She took pity on him and said, "This is one of the Hebrew boys."
>
> His sister said to Pharaoh's daughter, "Shall I go and summon for you a wet nurse from the Hebrew women, who will nurse the boy for you?"
>
> Pharaoh's daughter said, "Go."
>
> The girl went and called the boy's mother.
>
> (Shemos 2:2–8)

Moshe cried in his basket as his sister watched from afar. The Torah tell us nothing about the mother's anguish, nothing of her emotional state as she waited at home for news. But the *Zohar* does:

> The child's mother was crying. This is what is written: "A voice is heard on high. It is the sound of bitter weeping, Rachel is crying for her children" (Yirmiyahu 31:14). He cries, and the mother of the child cries.... What is written about the future? "They will come with tears and pleading" (Yirmiyahu 31:8). What is the meaning of "And they will come with tears"? In the merit of the tears of the child's mother — that is, Rachel — they will come and be gathered in from exile.
>
> (*Zohar, Shemos* 12:2)

When Miriam returns home to Yocheved, she finds her mother crying bitter tears, disconsolate over the separation from her child. In a dream-like sequence, a transformation takes place. The mother is no longer Yocheved, but becomes Rachel. The baby is no longer Moshe, but becomes the Jewish people. The mother and the baby are crying, and the mother's tears are about the child's exile. The mother is crying and pleading with God to bring her child home. In the merit of these tears, the child, the Jewish people, will be returned from exile.

What is the connection between these mothers and these children? Why are the tears of one mother equated with the tears of the other?

Bris Imahos

It is well known that God made a covenant (*bris*) with our fathers, but it is less well known that He also made a covenant with our mothers.

> [God said,] "Then I will remember My covenant with [*es*] Yaakov, and also My covenant with [*es*] Yitzchak, and also My covenant with [*es*] Avraham I will remember; and the land I will remember" (Vayikra 26:42). This only tells us about the fathers; how do we know [that God will also remember] the mothers? The Talmud tells us [we learn it from] *es* — the *esim* refer to the mothers.
>
> (*Vayikra Rabbah* 36:4)

In addition to the covenant of the patriarchs and the covenant of the matriarchs, we have an additional connection with our ancestors: the merit of the patriarchs (*zechus avos*) and the merit of the matriarchs (*zechus imahos*).

> "The voice of my Beloved is coming suddenly to redeem me, as if leaping over mountains, skipping over hills" (Shir HaShirim 2:8). "As if leaping over mountains" — this is

the merit of our forefathers. "Skipping over hills" — this is the merit of our foremothers.

(*Rosh HaShanah* 11:2)

The Beloved is God, who comes to save the Jewish people from their troubles. How does He come? Over the mountains, through the hills — the Gemara teaches that this means He comes through the merits of our patriarchs and matriarchs.

The Jewish people could not exist without the merits of the fathers, not even for a short time, and certainly not for thousands of years. When God wanted to destroy the Jewish people, He told Moshe that He would kill the entire nation and start again from Moshe. But Moshe argued, "If the people of Israel cannot stand on three legs, the legs of their three patriarchs, how are they to stand on only one?" Just as a chair needs three legs and can't stand on one, so, too, do we stand on the three legs of our patriarchs, Avraham, Yitzchak, and Yaakov (*Berachos* 32a).

Nevertheless, we are told in the Gemara that the merit of the fathers has ended — all of the merits of Avraham, Yitzchak, and Yaakov have been used up (*Shabbos* 55a). There is a discussion about when the merit of our fathers ended — during the time of the prophet Hoshea, the time of King Chazael of Aram, the time of the prophet Eliyahu, or the time of King Chizkiyahu. *Tosafos* posits that our patriarchs' merits do continue, but only for the righteous. For most of us, however, the bottom line seems to be that the merit of the fathers no longer exists. If we are left with no legs to stand on, no merit, how do we survive?

If the merit of the fathers no longer stands for us (because we don't deserve it), the merit of the mothers remains. These merits will never be used up, and, therefore, they stand at the center of our salvation. Every time the Jewish people needed salvation, there has been a Jewish woman or women who brought about redemption.

It is well known that we were redeemed from the Egyptian exile in the merit of the righteous women. In the two other holidays that commemorate redemption from exile, Purim and Chanukah, women also served as God's messengers in the redemptive process: Queen Esther, who risked her life to save the Jewish people in Shushan, is the center of the Purim salvation; and Yehudis at the time of the Chanukah story acted courageously and killed the enemy general (*Sefer HaMakkabim*). Because of the participation of righteous women in these three miraculous redemptions, women are commanded to keep all of the mitzvos of the holidays of Pesach, Purim, and Chanukah (although they are time-bound positive mitzvos from which women are usually exempt), "since they were involved in that miracle" (*Pesachim* 108a, *Megillah* 4a, *Shabbos* 23a). Just as all past redemptions came through the hands of the women, so, too, all future redemptions from exile will be brought about by the women. This is because the merits of the matriarchs remain forever.

What is the difference between the merit of the fathers and the merit of the mothers? What did the women do to deserve such special merit? Why is the merit of the matriarchs permanent and unconditional, whereas the merit of the patriarchs is not?

Chuldah

We can understand and answer these questions by comparing the prophetess Chuldah to her contemporary, Yirmiyahu. Both prophesied the destruction of the Temple and the exile from Israel. Yirmiyahu was by far the greater prophet, and yet we find that when King Yoshiyahu needed to understand the meaning of a particular situation, he sent his men to talk to Chuldah, instead of Yirmiyahu.

> Chilkiyah the Kohen, Achikam, Achbor, Shafan, and Asayah went to Chuldah the prophetess, the wife of Shalum — the son of Tikvah the son of Charchas — the

keeper of the [royal] garments. She dwelled in Yerushalayim, in the study house, and they spoke to her [presenting the question]. She said to them, "Thus said Hashem, God of Israel: 'Behold, I am bringing evil upon this place and upon its inhabitants — all the words of the Scroll that the king of Yehudah read — because they have forsaken Me and burned offerings to the gods of others, in order to anger Me with all their handiwork. My wrath has been incited against this place, and it will not be extinguished.' "

(Melachim II 22:14–17)

Why did King Yoshiyahu send his men to Chuldah? What did he hope to accomplish by consulting a (lesser) prophetess?

How could Yoshiyahu pass over Yirmiyahu and send [his men] to [Chuldah]? The members of the school of Rabbi Shila explained, "Because women are tender-hearted."

(*Megillah* 14a)

Because women are compassionate, Yoshiyahu hoped to get a more merciful prophecy from Chuldah than from Yirmiyahu. When Yirmiyahu prophesied the destruction of the Temple, his prophecy, of course, was a message from God and he was only the conduit through which God related future events. This is true, as well, of Chuldah. Could Chuldah deliver a different prophesy, a different message? She had no power to change the truth! Can a prophecy be changed because the prophet herself is merciful?

The Maggid of Mezeritch explains that although prophets could never change the prophecy, each prophet had his own way of speaking, his own "tune." This tune of the prophet was the emphasis of the prophecy, and it would vary according to how the prophet "sang" his words. Chuldah sang her prophecy in the tone of mercy; her prophecy reflected the mercy of a mother. Although Chuldah spoke of future destruction, her words were said in the tone of mercy, a "tune" which could arouse God to mercy. We learn from this that sometimes a prophecy of strict justice can be changed into one of compassion, if the bearer of the message delivers it with mercy.

"Rachel is crying for her children" is a tune. "The mother and the child cry" is a tune that brings the Jewish people back from exile to the original status of beloved. When a prophetess speaks with mercy and when a mother cries for her child, the mercy of God is awakened. Rachel cried for the continuity of the Jewish people of Israel, and through her tears — that is, as a response to her "tune" — she changed God's anger to mercy and compassion. This tune of mercy functions even in the darkest exile and even when the merit of the patriarchs runs out. It functions during the times when we degrade ourselves, not behaving as Jews should.

The tune of mercy functions not because the child deserves kindness, but because the mother loves the child, solely because he is her child. This quality of mercy functions even when we, the Jewish people, don't deserve it. It functions because we are God's children and He loves us. Although our sins cause God to be angry at us, He will forgive us and He will never abandon us, just as a mother would never abandon her child, regardless of his shortcomings.

How can the tears of our mothers arouse God's love for us? Why should God deal with us with patience, compassion, and mercy? Haven't we been given enough chances already?

> [Moshe] said to [Yehoshua] before all of Israel, "Be strong and of good courage. This nation that I am giving over to you are still…young children. Do not be strict with them for what they do, as it says, 'For Yisrael is a youth and I love him, and from Egypt I called to My sons' (Hoshea 11:1)." When they stood by the sea, they were rebelling, as it says, "And they rebelled by the sea at Yam Suf" (Tehillim 106:7). The angels said [to God at that time], "They are

rebelling and angering You, and You are quiet?" [God] answered them, "They are youths, and one is not exacting with youths. Just like a baby comes out dirty from his mother's womb, and they wash him, so, too, Yisrael. 'I will wash your blood off of you, I will anoint you with oil, I will clothe you in embroidered garments, and I will put leather shoes on your feet' (Yechezkel 16:9–11)."

(Yalkut Shimoni, Hoshea 1127)

Moshe, in passing the mantle of leadership to Yehoshua, told him to be gentle with the Jewish people, for they are children. Though the Jews rebelled at the crossing of the Yam Suf, God told the angels that the Jewish people are lads, and one mustn't be so strict with children. God speaks to us as a mother to her infant: "You, My children, are like newborn babies, covered with the blood from the womb, but I will wash you off, and I'll love you because you are Mine."

All the babies in a nursery look alike. But each mother thinks her baby is the cutest and the sweetest and the best, for no other reason than that baby is her child. She carried him, she had labor pains for him, and she gave birth to him. Although he comes out red and dirty, with a misshapen head, the mother thinks he's beautiful. She loves her child deeply, with kindness, compassion, and joy. When her child is in pain or in danger, she cries for him, because she has mercy on him. That's the tune of the matriarch; that's Rachel crying on the road and Yocheved crying for Moshe. And that's the difference in prophecy between Chuldah and Yirmiyahu.

There were *keruvim* (cherubs) on top of the holy ark, *keruvim* with the faces of children. They reminded God that we are his children, and He should have mercy on us.

Windows and Lattices

> The voice of my Beloved is coming suddenly to redeem me, as if leaping over mountains, skipping over hills. In His swiftness to redeem me, my Beloved is like a gazelle or a young hart. I thought I would be forever alone, but behold He was standing behind our wall, observing through the windows, peering through the lattices.
>
> (Shir HaShirim 2:8–9)

This metaphorical image describes how God hurriedly leaps and skips to redeem the Jews (*Rashi*). Though we despair of salvation, thinking we are alone, He is watching us through the windows, through the lattices.

> "Observing through the windows" — this is the merit of our fathers; "peering through the lattices" — this is the merit of our mothers. It teaches us that just like there is a difference between one window and another, so too, there is a difference between the merit of our forefathers and foremothers.
>
> (*Pesikta Rabbasi, Parashas HaChodesh* 15)

It would appear that the merit of the fathers is greater because it comes to us through a window, whereas the merit of the mothers seeps in through the tiny holes of the lattices. The merit of the fathers is "big" and public; everyone sees it, clear and bright. The merit of the mothers, on the other hand, filters through small spaces. It is humble and hidden; we might or might not notice it. But the merit of the fathers is present only when Israel is worthy. When we are lowly, when we aren't worthy of the public merit, the merit of the mothers continues to come to us through the cracks. The tears of the mothers arouse God's mercy and compassion. And so, although it appears that the merit of the fathers is greater, the merit of the mother is actually greater because it functions even when we don't deserve it.

Rachel's Tears

The tears of Rachel are the tears of the mercy of the mothers. As the Jewish people went into exile, Rachel cried. She cried as a mother who loves her child not because of what he did, but because of who he is. And because of her mercy and tears, God responded and promised a return. His anger was turned to mercy, strict judgment was turned to kindness — even after the harshest decree, even after the exile had begun. The Jews were marching in chains to Babylonia, marching in pain and despair. Avraham, Yitzchak, Yaakov, Moshe, and Yirmiyahu each stood before the Throne of God to beseech Him for mercy. But only when Rachel began to cry and beg for compassion did God promise that her children would be returned to their borders. They would be returned to their status of the beloved of God. The enemies of Israel would never triumph over the spirituality of the mothers.

God knew that we would have to be exiled, and He knew that the merit of the fathers would not be enough to sustain us in exile. What was required were the tears of a Jewish mother, the mercy of the mother who loves her child no matter what he has done, no matter how much he has failed, and no matter how far he has strayed. This mercy, these tears, would sustain us even in the darkest exile. When there would be no light pouring through the window, there would always be a small, humble glimpse of light, shining steadily through the cracks. Rachel was buried on the road for her merit is constant, even as the Jewish people fall to their nadir.

Why Rachel, and not Sarah or Rivkah or Leah? Rachel is the one who gave the signs to her sister, as we saw in the first *midrash*. Giving those signs was an act of tremendous self-sacrifice, beyond anything that the other matriarchs and patriarchs did. The quality of Rachel's sacrifice on the day of her wedding was unprecedented.

The self-sacrifice of the patriarchs was always for the purpose of bringing God's glory into the world. The ability to self-negate, to put God's agenda first, was given to us as an inheritance from our patriarchs, and we have this power to this day. Avraham was willing to jump into the fiery furnace of Nimrod as a testimony to his faith in God. Yitzchak was prepared to die at the *akeidah* (binding at the altar) because he, too, believed. But Rachel's sacrifice was different. When she gave over the signs to her sister, she didn't do it to reveal the glory of God; she did it so that her sister would not be shamed. Rachel's sacrifice did not bring her the satisfaction of demonstrating her deeply held convictions; it was not the public, courageous act of a great heroine. Rachel was focused on someone else's situation, on the pain and humiliation her sister would feel were she to be exposed under the *chuppah*.

But even greater than her sacrifice was the fact that when the whole thing was over, she was silent. She never said a word. She never complained, even to God. She asked God for nothing in return. She could have said at the time that she had fertility problems, "Dear God, I gave my husband to my sister, and now I remain barren. Where is my reward?" But she didn't. Rachel never said a word about what she had done for Leah because she gave all of her merit to her children, to Israel. That is the mercy of a mother: "It's not for me, it's for the children. I want nothing for myself, save it for them."

So when Israel went into exile, Rachel could stand before God and He responded to her prayer, measure-for-measure. As she put aside her feelings to save her sister, so God would put aside His "feelings" of anger and save the Jewish people. Instead of asking for a reward, Rachel allocated her merits to her children. God, who never withholds reward, promised that He would also allocate her merits to her children. Rachel's merits have no limit, because she did not limit her sacrifice by requesting a reward, either material or spiritual.

Rachel also did something else that brought great merit to her children. Avraham entered the fiery furnace, but he survived. Yitzchak offered his life at the *akeidah*, but it was not taken. Yaakov suffered the intense pain of raising children and was willing to die to protect them, but he lived a long life. But Rachel died giving birth to Binyamin when she was only thirty-six years old — she literally gave her life for her child. And when a person gives his life for something holy, that thing has permanence. Our survival in exile and our eternal existence were guaranteed by Rachel giving her life to bring us into the world.

The Redemption from Egypt

Rachel is the essence of the mother in Israel throughout all of the exile. She exemplifies the ability of all Jewish women to build their homes and their families even when the Jewish people are suffering, even when it is difficult. The incredible strength of every mother in Israel is rooted in the self-sacrifice of Rachel.

And so, it was in the merit of the righteous women that we were redeemed from Egypt. We can't imagine what it was like to live in Egypt under Pharaoh's rule, where a woman giving birth didn't know if her baby would live. At best, the children would be raised as slaves, and, at worst, they would be thrown into the river or bricked up in the pyramids. Nevertheless, our mothers gave birth. They had pure faith, and this wholehearted belief in God is what saved us in our exile.

We have had many persecutions during our current bitter exile. Those Jews whose belief was wholehearted were the ones who refused to convert, despite the threat of the sword. As the Chassid Yavetz HaSefardi, one of the survivors of the Spanish expulsion, testified, the ones willing to die rather than convert were the simple folk and the women. These Jews held their faith more than the scholars or the philosophers. They were the ones who believed totally. They were the ones who kept Torah alive.

In the Merit of the Mothers

Another mother of Israel, Devorah the prophetess, carried Rachel's essence with her into battle. Although she asked the general Barak to lead the war, he worried that without her merit they wouldn't win. So Devorah went with him into the battlefield, and they routed the enemy. Afterwards, Devorah sang a song of victory:

> The inhabitants of the village ceased, they ceased in Yisrael. Until I, Devorah, arose, I arose, a mother in Yisrael.
> (Shoftim 5:7)

The Jewish people were not saved by a general or by the soldiers, but by motherhood. The motherhood that saves us in exile also saves us from our enemies in war.

The power of the tears of the mothers of Israel is beyond our comprehension. The cry of a Jewish mother is so powerful that it can even save a soul from Gehinnom. When Chanah gave birth to her child, she praised God, "The Lord makes poor and makes rich. He brings low and raises up" (Shmuel I 2:7). We learn from this that the people who went down to Gehinnom with Korach were brought up through the prayers of Chanah (*Sanhedrin* 108a). Her prayer had the power to raise people who had sunk so low that one might think they were spiritually doomed.

When the Temple was destroyed, the gates of prayer were closed, and all looked hopeless. However, the gates of tears remained open (*Berachos* 26b). Sometimes we feel as though our tears haven't helped. Have we not cried buckets of tears throughout the centuries of exile and persecution without being redeemed? But the truth is that our tears, the tears of the mothers of Israel, the tears of Rachel, do penetrate Heaven. How do we know? Because we're still here. We're still around despite our failings and despite our sins.

> Thus Rachel died, and was buried on the road to Efras, which is Beis Lechem. Yaakov set up a monument over her grave; it is the monument of Rachel's grave *until today.*
>
> (Bereishis 35:19–20)

During these long centuries, foreign rulers have come and gone in the Holy Land. It is wondrous that even in times when Jews were not permitted by the ruling authorities of Israel to daven in Chevron, at the tomb of the patriarchs, we were usually permitted to go to Kever Rachel, the tomb of Rachel. To be guaranteed access to our patriarchs' tomb, we must deserve it. We receive from the merits of our fathers only when we earn them. But the merits of the mothers stand even when we don't deserve them, so throughout almost all periods of Jewish history we have been able to pray at the tomb of Rachel. Whether we pray there for a personal redemption or for a national one, the tears of our mother Rachel are merits on our behalf.

The Biale Rebbe's Prayer

Every year, on 11 Cheshvan, Rachel's *yahrtzeit*, thousands of Jews pour into Beis Lechem to worship at her grave. There they recite Tehillim, cry in personal anguish, and pray for an end to the calamities that continue to befall the Jewish people. The Biale Rebbe's prayer on the occasion of Rachel's *yahrtzeit* expresses our fervent desire that the tears of our mothers should awaken the mercy of God in times of national distress or in times of personal trouble.

> In these days of pain, we come to beg for mercy for the children of Yaakov. For although we have returned from the land of the enemy, and the children have returned to their borders, blood still flows in the land like water, and the trouble of Israel reaches to the Heavens. We plead to Rachel: Intercede for all of Israel, stand before the throne

of God and awaken the mercy of Hashem for Israel, as the prophet said, "A voice is heard on high — wailing, bitterly weeping. Rachel weeps for her children." May redemption come for the Jewish people, as a whole and as individuals. Awaken the mercy of the mother, the quality of mercy for the Jewish people. Beseech and plead before the Holy Throne that He will have mercy on us and redeem us from our troubles, that He will bring salvation to the nation and to its individuals, that we will merit to see the revelation of the *Shechinah* and the redemption from this exile. May the Mashiach come in mercy and kindness quickly, in our days.

    Amen and Amen.

In memory of my beloved husband
Rabbi Dr. Joseph Babad, *zt"l,*
and in honor of my niece
Rebbetzin Holly Pavlov
Mrs. Esther Babad

In loving memory of our son and brother
עמיתי שמחה בן יהודה ע"ה
Allan "Big Al" Goldsmith

He was the personification of living in spite of challenges

Of overcoming obstacles

Of finding joy where others might succumb to pain

He was inspired

And taught wherever he went, through his example and deeds

He was driven to wring from every moment of life its greatest satisfaction

And brought *simchah* to all who knew him

May his memory be a blessing to us and to all *klal Yisrael*

Who may sojourn in Your tent?

Who may dwell on Your holy mountain?

One who walks in perfect innocence

And does what is right

And speaks the truth from his heart.   *(Psalms 15)*

His parents, William and Joan Goldsmith,
And siblings, Wendy and Daniel Goldsmith

The She'arim Alumnae Dedication Page

As Rebbetzin Pavlov's students, we are grateful for all she has given to us over the years. May she continue in her pursuit of helping Jewish women grow through Torah, until 120!

Reuven and Michelle Abedon; Carolyn B. Abrams in memory of my *bubbie* Miriam Reiser; Leora Adam in memory of Aryeh Leib (Leonard) Fine; Jennifer and Jerome Albom in memory of Carole Ruth Bransky; Chava (Garfinkel) and David Axelrod; Suzanne and Elliot Balaban in memory of Suzanne's Uncle Mick Margo; Jackie and Yonaton Behar in memory of David Behar; Andy Belitzky in memory of Malka Wolf; Avi and Arlene (Bergman) Ben Zev; Joan Berger in memory of Pauline Weissman Boxbaum; Rabbi Joshua and Michal Berman in tribute to our *shadchanit* and teacher Holly Pavlov; Devorah Bloom; Yisroel and Devorah Blumberg; Gabi, Shelley, and Meir Bookatz in honor of Bella Bookatz; Yaakov and Hadas Boxer; Hazel and David Brief in memory of Hazel's mother, Sylvia Kassel; Joanna and Jeremy Bruce; Linda and Dov Chaitowitz לעילוי נשמת מאיר דוד בן שלמה אליעזר ואברהם שלום בן שניאור זלמן; Peninah Cohen in memory of my father Binyamin Ze'ev; Miriam Crosbie in honor of Joshua and Sarah Crosbie; Tzvia Davis in honor of Robert and Shelly

Davis; Denise de Vriend in loving memory of my kind, gentle and devoted grandfather Louis Hoed ז״ל; Netta Yocheved de Vriend in memory of my parents Jacques Sjouwerman ז״ל and Cato de Vries ז״ל; Michael, Golda, Chaim Aryeh, and Aharon Yaakov Doniger; Chava and Dovid Dumas in memory of Raizel *bas* Tova and Bat-Sheva *bas* Devorah; Debbie Eisenstein; Etay and Malka Eitan in memory of Moshe *ben* Yehoshua David; Daniella Feldman in memory of Yehuda Leib *ben* Ludwig and Chanan *ben* Mordechai; Rivka and Avi Fine in memory of Hillel *ben* Yosef and Miriam *bas* Yehuda HaLevi; Heidi Friedman; Yerachmiel and Layah Friedman; Elisa and Eric Fuld; Alexis Gaffin in memory of my mother, Miriam Esther *bas* Aharon Halevi; Emanuel and Pam Gentilcore in honor of our parents; Lauren Ginns in memory of Eva Lundy; Anna Gold; Leslie Gold in memory of my mother, Raizel *bat* Yosef and Faige; Tracy Goldenson in memory of my grandparents David and Roslyn Goldenson; Batsheva and Yaakov Goldman in memory of Henrietta Glaser; Jennifer (Lott) and Naftali Goldsmith in honor of our parents, Jerry and Ellen Lott and Lawrence and Stephanie Goldsmith; Wendy/Chava Goldsmith; Geraldine and Sidney Goldstein; Beth, Daniel, and Zecharya Shmuel, Yehoshua Dovid, Naomi Devora, and Moshe Leib Gordon; Devorah Talia and Noson Gordon in memory of Hanna Mendel; Chava and Jay Gottlieb in memory of our parents, Lester Eisner, Ruth and Louis Gottlieb; Frances and Gabriel Gozland; Jill (Kunzman) and Shmuel Greene; Laura Greene in honor of my parents; Laura and Daniel Greer in honor of Amy Greer; Sara Groffman in memory of Yitzchak Dovid *ben* Shmuel Yosef; BatSheva Haber; Jenni and Moshe Handel in memory of Martin Rothfield; Susan Harris in memory of my grandmother Molly Resnick; Samara Hendrickson in memory of Abe and Selma Krames and

Yolan Baumgarten; Alison Herman; Marci and Jeff Herman in memory of Richard Herman and Lewis Herman; Jacqueline Herring in memory of Yona Libah *bas* Faige and Leibel; Denise (Greenstein) and Joshua Herschberg; Yisrael and Yael Hershberg in memory of our grandmothers הענא בת מרים ופעסא בת חנה; Ruth Hirsch; Julie and Chaim Hoch; Marcia and Alan Hochster in memory of Marcia's father William Rich; Tzvi and Muriel Honickman in memory of our parents Moshe Dovid and Yitta Chaya Schaffer, Moshe Ephraim and Chaya Honickman; Naomi Intract in memory of Miriam Lewis (Miriam *bat* Esther Pearl); Debbie Isaacman; Leah Kaess in memory of my great-grandmother Leah Schneider; Andrea, Jonathan, Miriam, and Bayla Kamens; Mimi and Steve Kamilar; Janet Kaplan in honor of Arnold and Ayalah Kaplan; Rachel and Bennett Kaplan; Nurit and Shmuel Katz; Dr. Louis and Rita Katz in honor of our parents Molly and Harold Andelman's sixtieth wedding anniversary; Sonja Kent in memory of Jeffrey M. Weston (Yaacov *ben* Mordechai); Tovah Kersner in memory of my parents; Sharon and Chanoch Kleinerman in memory of Leila Avrin; Robert and Susan Koltai; Rachel Korn in memory of my grandfather ר׳ יצחק בן ר׳ אשר אנשיל הכהן; Rivkah Kravitz in memory of Jacob Kravitz; Lauren Lapinsky in memory of Paye Lurie; Chana and Yisroel Mordechai Lebow; Kalman and Marti (Davida) Leebhoff; Shoshana Sora (Holstein) Lev in memory of my grandfather Dr. Harry A. Becker (Aaron *ben* Daniel); Kimberly A. Levine; Michoel and Sara Levy; Yehudit (Kaye) and Chaim Levy in honor of our families; Annabel Lewitton in memory of my grandmother Risha *bat* Ester; Panina (Medow) and Jacob Licht in memory of Panina's *bubbie* Francis Feldman; Sheryl S. Lipton; AnnBeth Litt; Liora Lurie in memory of Cynthia Lurie; Malka Magen in honor of my grandmothers, Fay and Sarah; Yocheved

Malkin in memory of my grandmother, Hannah Goldstein; Jodi Maltzman in memory of my grandmother, Yocheved (Ethel) Maltzman; Rifki Mann in memory of זיסל בת לייב; Ilana Manspeizer; Adina Maxfield; Ron-Ami and Miriam Meir in memory of Joseph Meyers; Elissa (Chava) Menasse in memory of David Bruce Wolff; Naomi and Jeremy Meyer; Leslie and Mitch Morrison in memory of Ruben and Helen Morrison; Lisa Novogrodsky in memory of David Shain; Asher Messod and Yoneet (Goldszlager) Ohayon in memory of Yoneet's grandfather Mordechai *ben* Simcha; Dov and Karen Pear in honor of Tobi Rodin; Stefanie L. Pearson; Melissa (Waldman) and Mordechai Peller; Laurence and Shelley Peretz in honor of Gil and Gail Peretz and Bernie and Salome Barnett; Marisa Pickar in memory of my grandmother Malkie/Florence Markenson; Elisheva (Lisa Gorelick-Gray) Rabinowitz in memory of my mother, Hentsha *bas* Melech; Vanessa Radom in memory of Rachel Zysman and Raizel Farkas; Paula and Dan Rand in memory of our grandmothers; Miriam Rebibo and the Rebibo family; Rochel Reichlin; Helen Rosen; Randi Rothenberg in memory of Rose Rothenberg; Miriam and David Saul in memory of George Saul; Joel and Janice Savage in memory of Sam and Ricky Savage; Karin and Michael Savitz in memory of Oscar Rubinstein; Stevie Schiff; Sharon Schuldiner; Bracha and Shalom Schwarz; Michelle Segall in memory of Barbara Barish; Aleta and Barry Shiff; Jennie and Yochanan Silverman in memory of Dr. Bernd Silver; Sara (Siegel) Simon; Bonnie Singer; Devorah and Yaakov Singer; Baruch and Chana Sirota; Yona Skiddell; Anne J. Sperling; Julie Starr in memory of Esther Weisbrod; Miriam Steinberg in memory of my parents Jack and Libby Steinberg; Yochana Stone זכר אחי חיים ואריה בני דורטי; Pam and Gary Swickley in memory of Eleanor and Gus

Swickley; Pam Thompson in memory of Kari and Jeremy Thompson; Sara Wendy Uren; Yael Waxman; Bobby and Julie Weinmann in honor of Shoshana; Jenny Weisberg in honor of my daughters Hadas Eliana and Hallel Rivka; David and Ellen Weiss; Fonda and Yitzchak Weiss; Joanna Wiseman; Aura Wolfe; Gina Wunsch; Yitzchak and Aviva Kushner Yoselis in memory of Gitel Kushner; Michelle Zelin in memory of אימי ומורתי ציפורה בת רייזל, Cheryl Zelin.

Pam and Ben Hindes

The Levitch Family, in honor of our sons Daniel and Ariel

Dr. and Mrs. Marc Lowen in memory of Marie Levinson Herbst

Sylvia Moss

The Phaff Family

Mrs. Nita Quint

In loving memory of Milton and Ida Ruskin

In loving memory of David Wasserman